Prison Rape

Prison Rape

AN AMERICAN INSTITUTION?

Michael Singer

 PRAEGER

AN IMPRINT OF ABC-CLIO, LLC
Santa Barbara, California • Denver, Colorado • Oxford, England

Library of Congress Cataloging-in-Publication Data

Singer, Michael, 1942–
  Prison rape : an American institution? / Michael Singer.
    pages cm.
  Includes bibliographical references and index.
  ISBN 978-1-4408-0271-3 (hardcopy: alk. paper) — ISBN 978-1-4408-0272-0 (ebook)
1. Rape—United States. 2. Prisoners—Legal status, laws, etc.—United States.
3. Prisoners—Sexual behavior—United States. 4. Sex crimes—United States.
5. Prison violence—United States. I. Title.
  KF9329.S56 2013
  365'.6—dc23   2012042479

ISBN: 978-1-4408-0271-3
EISBN: 978-1-4408-0272-0

17 16 15 14 13   1 2 3 4 5

This book is also available on the World Wide Web as an eBook.
Visit www.abc-clio.com for details.

Praeger
An Imprint of ABC-CLIO, LLC

ABC-CLIO, LLC
130 Cremona Drive, P.O. Box 1911
Santa Barbara, California 93116-1911

This book is printed on acid-free paper ∞

Manufactured in the United States of America

Contents

IV. The Prison Rape Elimination Act

Acknowledgments

My chief debt of gratitude is to the many courageous survivors of prison rape in America who have been willing to speak out about their suffering. I have also benefited from conversations with a range of individuals who are working tirelessly and devotedly to combat sexual and other abuses in the American incarceration system.

Courtney W. Howland was a constant support throughout the stressful process of researching and writing this book. She also gave her time generously to reading drafts of the text and provided crucially important critical comments and constructive input that have substantially influenced the book.

Valentina Tursini, as acquisitions editor at Praeger, inspired the development of this book from its initial concept. It would not exist without her understanding and guidance. Beth Ptalis has been an admirably responsive, encouraging, and patient editor throughout.

I also thank the Dickson Poon School of Law of King's College London for providing me for the past thirteen years with the great privilege of a stimulating and supportive scholarly environment.

Michael Singer

Introduction

A federal prosecutor did not want to go through the lengthy legal process to bring to trial a number of men who were fugitives from justice, so he gave them an incentive to turn themselves in right away. In an interview on a public radio program he explained the consequences they would face if they insisted on waiting out the legal process. He told them: "You're going to be the boyfriend of a very bad man" when we eventually get you into prison. As a court of justice later recognized, the federal prosecutor meant that each of them would be forced to share a cell with a stronger inmate with a reputation as a sexual predator and would inevitably be anally raped or otherwise sexually abused.[1]

It was unusual for a prosecutor to publicly broadcast the threat of sexual abuse, but the practice that his threat revealed is quite common. Prosecutors, both federal and state, routinely use threats of sexual abuse to strike advantageous deals with defendants. They do so regardless of the fact that sexual abuse of any kind is a criminal offense. They are able to do so because sexual abuse of every kind is rife throughout the American incarceration system. Large numbers of male inmates are sexually abused by stronger inmates—with many cases involving repeated gang rapes—as well as by corrections officers. Large numbers of female inmates are also sexually abused; most of the abusers are male corrections officers, who now comprise the great majority of corrections officers in women's prisons and jails.

The prosecutor gave his broadcast interview in 1997. Sexual abuse had by then been rife throughout the American incarceration system for so many years that it could be fairly described as institutionalized into the system of punishment. The federal legislature—Congress—appropriately described sexual abuse as *epidemic* throughout the American incarceration system. The most recent data show that this remains the case today.

This situation is incompatible with America's claim to be a civilized society subject to the rule of law. Congress recognized this in 2003 when it enacted, by unanimous vote in both houses, a statute aimed at putting an end to the institution of prison rape. This is the Prison Rape Elimination Act (PREA). Although this statute has so far had relatively little overall effect on the level of sexual abuse in incarceration nationwide, there is some ground today for hoping that sexual abuse may eventually cease to be an institution of the American system of incarceration.

The ground for hope is that after years of delay the federal Department of Justice has finally, in 2012, promulgated national standards under the statute that are expressly aimed at combating all forms of sexual abuse throughout the incarceration system. However, the statute makes compliance with these standards largely voluntary. Because of this, the standards will not be implemented across the country unless there are deep cultural changes in the incarceration system, the justice system, and American society as a whole. If these cultural changes do not take place, prison rape will remain established as an American institution, to the continuing shame of American society.

Part I of this book assesses the extent of sexual abuse in incarceration. It begins with an overview of the complex and extensive American system of incarceration and supervision, comprising prisons, jails, juvenile detention, lockups, community corrections of various forms, and a range of other facilities. It continues with a survey of the studies that, starting from the 1960s, led to growing social awareness of pervasive sexual abuse throughout this system. These studies were carried out by academic researchers and human rights organizations and dealt with sexual abuse of both female and male inmates.

The main sources of information on sexual abuse in incarceration are now the several series of reports produced by the Bureau of Justice Statistics (BJS) of the Department of Justice under the authority of PREA and also the Regulatory Impact Assessment (RIA) produced by the Department of Justice in 2012 along with the national standards. Part I continues with a review of these publications. They cover jails and juvenile facilities as well as prisons. By guaranteeing confidentiality to inmates they deal effectively with the problems of obtaining reliable information on this sensitive subject.

An important aspect of the BJS reports and the RIA is the development of uniform definitions and classifications of abusive sexual acts. These publications are also careful to distinguish sexual abuse from consensual sexual activity between inmates, which is not the concern of this book. However, all sexual activity between staff and inmates is illegal and treated as sexual abuse.

The RIA finds that in a single year at least one hundred and fifty thousand individuals suffer some form of sexual abuse in adult prisons and jails and in juvenile detention facilities. This is a very conservative estimate, and the RIA also gives the more probable estimate that the number is actually over two hundred thousand. This does not include those who are abused in lockups, community corrections, and other facilities.

Part I concludes with a review of recent developments. Some incarceration facilities have succeeded in virtually eliminating sexual abuse of their inmates. Their experience shows the need for strong, consistent leadership implementing cultural change throughout the facility. But many correctional authorities have made no changes at all, and sexual abuse remains rife in their facilities. As a recent negative development, a number of these authorities rely on a small, deeply flawed academic study to simply deny that sexual abuse is prevalent. Unfortunately, the overall level of sexual abuse in incarceration across America has remained virtually unchanged through the decade since enactment of PREA.

Part II assesses the cost of sexual abuse in incarceration. It begins with often-harrowing accounts of the suffering of victims. Many are severely injured and infected with disease, resulting in long-term physical suffering and incapacity. Many are psychologically wounded, resulting in long-term mental damage and incapacity. The suffering is intensified by the generally inadequate medical treatment provided to inmates. In addition, victims are frequently denied any protection from further sexual abuse. When protection is available, it is often in the form of isolation in separate housing, which effectively amounts to a further punishment.

This part of the book next presents the RIA assessment of the dollar cost to American society of sexual abuse in incarceration. It includes medical and mental health costs as well as monetary estimates for the suffering and lost quality of life of the victims, and also for a range of other factors. Using very conservative estimates, the RIA assesses the quantifiable part of the cost of sexual abuse of adults in prisons and jails and of juveniles in juvenile facilities. This Department of Justice estimate is that in any one year the cost certainly amounts to at least $26 billion and may well be as much as $50 billion, or even more.

This assessment does not cover a range of costs on society as a whole that cannot be readily expressed in monetary terms. These include the spread of sexually transmitted disease from former inmates who were infected through sexual abuse. They also include increased crime resulting from the social alienation of sexually abused former inmates.

Finally, part II considers the moral cost to American society. It is not clear how far the commitment in PREA and the national standards promulgated under PREA to combat sexual abuse in incarceration will be fulfilled. In addition, the justice system and the general society exploit the existence of systemic sexual abuse in incarceration in reprehensible ways. Correctional authorities at times directly and intentionally employ sexual abuse to control inmates. Prosecutors use the threat of sexual abuse in incarceration to induce defendants to surrender a range of their legal rights and privileges. Sexual abuse in incarceration, particularly anal rape of male inmates, is a staple topic of American popular culture that is often portrayed as entertainment.

These are systemic moral wrongs. They diminish the moral stature of American society as a whole because they are committed in the name of our society and because our society is responsible for them. American society is morally responsible for the safety of those that it incarcerates but has so far failed to meet its responsibilities.

We take pride in the accomplishments of American society, even if we are not in any way personally involved in those accomplishments. But the counterpart of pride is shame. Accordingly, moral honesty demands that we acknowledge our shame in the existence of systemic sexual abuse in the incarceration system and the exploitation of that sexual abuse. This shame is a moral cost on all of us and on our society as a whole.

Part III surveys the currently available methods for combating sexual abuse in incarceration through the courts. In a few cases, judges have been willing to impose a reduced sentence on particularly vulnerable convicted defendants. But this can only be a minor palliative for a small number of individuals. It does not effectively combat the continuing, pervasive sexual abuse throughout the incarceration system.

Sexual abuse of any person is a criminal offense, so it ought to be possible to combat sexual abuse in incarceration in the same way as other criminal offenses: by prosecuting the offenders. And indeed sexually abusive corrections officers are now being effectively prosecuted in various parts of the country. But in much of America, correctional authorities and state prosecutors continue to treat sexual abuse by corrections officers lightly, refusing to prosecute or imposing penalties too low to act as a deterrent. Also, it is very rare for an inmate to be prosecuted for sexual abuse of another inmate. Overall, criminal prosecution does not yet amount to effective action against prevalent sexual abuse in incarceration.

Sexual abuse of any person is also a civil wrong (a tort), so it ought to be possible to combat sexual abuse in incarceration in the same way as other civil wrongs: by the victims bringing civil actions against the perpetrators or against correctional authorities that permitted the abuse to take place. There have in fact been some substantial settlements and awards for sexual abuse by corrections officers, but they are relatively rare and have so far amounted overall to little more than token action against the nationwide problem of pervasive sexual abuse in incarceration. Also, it is virtually unknown for an inmate to succeed in a civil lawsuit regarding sexual abuse by another inmate.

This part of the book continues with the complex topic of federal lawsuits that inmates can bring to invoke constitutional protections against sexually abusive corrections officers. There are substantial barriers. A federal statute requires that inmates first exhaust administrative remedies; this includes any grievance procedures that the correctional authorities have instituted. Many correctional authorities have taken advantage of this by instituting highly complex grievance systems that inmates are often unable to cope with. In addition, there are constitutional barriers that bar lawsuits directly against state or federal correctional authorities. There are also judicially created barriers that limit lawsuits against local correctional authorities and against individual state and local corrections officers.

An inmate who successfully negotiates all these barriers must then establish that his substantive constitutional rights have been violated. But the courts have interpreted the constitutional provisions protecting inmates so narrowly that inmates can rarely establish liability for sexual abuse higher in the corrections hierarchy than an individual low-ranking officer. As a result, federal constitutional lawsuits do not yet amount to effective action against prevalent sexual abuse in incarceration.

This part of the book concludes with a brief discussion of the Civil Rights of Institutionalized Persons Act, a federal statute aimed at protecting inmates from the most serious and harmful unconstitutional practices of correctional authorities. This statute authorizes the attorney general to investigate violations and bring a lawsuit if necessary. But the number of investigations is far too low to make any substantial overall contribution to the reduction of sexual abuse in the American incarceration system.

Part IV is devoted to PREA. It begins with a detailed explanation of the provisions of this statute and continues with a review of the process that culminated in the Department of Justice issuing the final PREA national standards in 2012. One provision of PREA established the National Prison Rape Elimination Commission (NPREC) as a body tasked with undertaking a comprehensive study of sexual abuse in the American incarceration system, taking into account its penological, physical, mental, medical, social, and economic impacts. In 2009, the NPREC issued a thorough report with its own recommendations for national standards.

The terms of PREA then required the Department of Justice to promulgate national standards, taking the NPREC recommendations into account but ultimately exercising its own independent judgment. The Department of Justice commissioned a private firm to undertake a cost analysis for implementing the NPREC-recommended national standards and, later, a cost analysis for implementing the Department of Justice's own proposed standards.

The cost analyses were of particular concern because PREA requires that the national standards must not impose substantial additional costs compared to current correctional authority expenditures. Also, the Department of Justice took into account that although PREA requires the federal prison system to comply with the national standards, it leaves compliance voluntary for state and local incarceration facilities. State prison systems that do not comply may lose a small amount of federal prison funding, but local incarceration facilities pay no penalty at all for noncompliance.

Accordingly, the Department of Justice was concerned to keep costs at a level giving correctional authorities the best possible incentive to comply with the national standards. Because of this, its final national standards rejected some of the NPREC recommendations and curtailed some others.

The Department of Justice assesses the projected annual cost of full implementation of the final national standards at about $470 million. This is about 0.6 percent of the current $80 billion annual expenditure on incarceration nationwide. The cost justification analysis for the national standards shows that they will be fully justified in monetary terms alone if they reduce the prevalence of sexual abuse by only about 1.5 percent in adult facilities and only 3 percent in juvenile facilities from the present level. It is broadly agreed that full compliance with the national standards would achieve at least this level of reduction.

In fact, the Department of Justice goes further. It reasonably claims that the national standards would, if fully implemented, succeed in reducing the prevalence of prison rape by at least 4 percent per year from current levels. Yet a reduction of this amount would obviously be far too small to substantially weaken the American institution of prison rape.

The promulgation of the PREA national standards is a substantial positive step and a ground for hope that sexual abuse in American incarceration will eventually be substantially reduced. But there are still major challenges. Cultural change is needed in many correctional authorities nationwide as well as in the courts and the general society. Support through the Department of Justice is now available for correctional authorities that seek to change their culture. But motivation for cultural change must ultimately come from within correctional authorities, and effective change depends on thorough training of corrections staff at all levels.

The book concludes that doing away with the culture of sexual abuse in the American incarceration system will require strong and enduring efforts and expenditures over a number of years. Unless there is such a continuing commitment to overcome the challenges, it remains all too possible that prison rape will shamefully survive as an American institution.

Part I

The Extent of Sexual Abuse in Incarceration

Chapter 1

Recognition of the Prevalence of Sexual Abuse

It is helpful to begin with a brief overview of the complex and extensive system of incarceration and supervision in America. The most obvious institutions in this system are *prisons* and *jails*. There is a federal prison system, and each state has its own prison system. In addition, there are thousands of local jails throughout America, operated by city and county authorities within the states. But not every state has a separate jail system. In a number of states, prisons and jails have now been integrated into a single incarceration system.[1]

In theory, the major distinction between prisons and jails is that individuals who have been convicted and sentenced to a year or more of incarceration are sent to a prison; individuals who are being held in custody before trial, or who have been convicted and sentenced to less than a year of incarceration, are held in a jail. But in practice the distinction is not so clear. In fact, nowadays extreme overcrowding in prisons has led to many long-term inmates being incarcerated in jails.[2]

Prisons and jails primarily hold adult inmates, although a number of juveniles are held in prisons and jails along with adult inmates. But most incarcerated juveniles are held in separate juvenile detention facilities at the state and local levels. It is proper to describe a juvenile held in a juvenile facility as a *resident* of the facility, but for ease of discussion this book will often simply use the more general term "inmate."

Jails are also used to hold a range of individuals who have not been convicted of any criminal offense. For example, jails receive individuals pending arraignment and hold them awaiting trial and during trial. They also temporarily detain juveniles pending transfer to juvenile authorities. In addition, jails hold a variety of individuals who have not even been accused of any criminal offense. For example, they hold individuals for protective custody and for the courts as witnesses. They also hold mentally ill persons pending their movement to appropriate health facilities.[3]

In addition to prisons and jails, there are also local *lockups*. These are facilities where individuals may be held following arrest. It is proper to describe a person held in a lockup as a *detainee* in the facility, but for ease of discussion this book will often simply use the more general term "inmate."

There is also a broad range of federal, state, and local supervision structures classified as *community corrections*. These include residential facilities such as halfway houses and treatment facilities. Individuals held in these various facilities are usually allowed to work, attend school, and otherwise engage in the outside community. It is proper to describe a person held in a residential community corrections facility as a *resident* of the facility, but for ease of discussion this book will sometimes simply use the more general term "inmate."

Within the community corrections structure there are also many forms of nonresidential supervision. These include "probation, parole, pretrial supervision, court-mandated substance abuse treatment, court diversionary programs, day-reporting centers, community service programs, probation before judgment, furloughs, electronic monitoring, and home detention. Individuals generally live in their own homes and have an even greater degree of freedom, as long as they abide by the conditions of their release agreement."[4]

Most of these various facilities are public facilities, administered directly by government. But there are also many administered by commercial enterprises under contract with federal, state, or local government. In addition, there are facilities administered by nonprofit entities under contract with government.

There are also incarceration facilities for particular populations or particular purposes. These include Native American county jails, military-operated facilities, and facilities operated by or for the Bureau of Immigration and Customs Enforcement.

Currently, the prison population is about 1.6 million and the jail population is about three-quarters of a million, giving a total of about 2.35 million. There is no estimate available for the population of lockups. Even the number of lockups across the country is not exactly known; it is conservatively estimated at 4,500. In addition, there are nearly five million adults under supervision in the community on either probation or parole.[5]

There is a continuing flow of individuals being released from incarceration and other individuals entering incarceration. This is notably true of jails, where the average detention period is estimated at approximately two days. So the number of people who spend time in incarceration is far greater than the number incarcerated at any one time. In fact, according to the Department of Justice, "the number of people who are arrested and pass through jail or a lockup each year is . . . estimated at 13.4 million."[6]

FROM AWARENESS TO ACKNOWLEDGMENT OF SEXUAL ABUSE

Experts in the field of criminal justice have long been aware that sexual abuse pervades the American incarceration system.[7] Corrections officers have also long been aware of this. Inmates—as victims, perpetrators, or onlookers—have of course known well that vast numbers of coerced sexual acts take place in incarceration facilities, regardless of what terms they use to describe such acts. But it was only recently that government officially acknowledged the pervasiveness of sexual abuse in incarceration and accepted its responsibility to eliminate it.

The federal government ultimately acknowledged this in a statute, the Prison Rape Elimination Act of 2003 (PREA). This statute recognizes that rape and other forms of sexual abuse are so prevalent in incarceration as to be "epidemic."[8] It declares as its goal the elimination of all forms of sexual abuse. The statute is fully discussed in part IV. Note that statutes such as PREA, as well as books and academic articles, often use the term "prison rape" for brevity to encompass all forms of sexual abuse in all forms of incarceration.

General awareness of the pervasiveness of sexual abuse in the American incarceration system had developed through several decades before enactment of PREA. A lawsuit brought in the late 1960s by two men who had been sexually abused by other inmates while in a Wisconsin jail demonstrates this broad awareness. The men sued the sheriff in charge of the jail in federal court, claiming that he had violated their civil rights by failing in his responsibility to secure them from assault. The plaintiffs' expert in psychiatry and penology testified "that homosexual assault is a usual and predictable problem in jail environments throughout the United States and that jailors are aware of such activities among inmates."[9]

The sheriff, as defendant in the case, actually agreed on this with the plaintiffs' expert. Yet, despite this, the plaintiffs lost their case. The sheriff pointed out that the incarceration system was overcrowded, that the facilities were unsuitable, and that there were insufficient staff—and then simply argued that in such a system pervasive sexual abuse of every kind was unavoidable. This implied that the problem was systemic and not his fault personally. The federal appellate court largely accepted the sheriff's argument.[10]

A decade later—but still more than a decade before PREA was enacted—two members of the Supreme Court acknowledged the overall situation in men's incarceration facilities:

The atrocities and inhuman conditions of prison life in America are almost unbelievable; surely they are nothing less than shocking. . . . A youthful inmate can expect to be subjected to homosexual gang rape his first night in jail, or, it has been said, even in the van on the way to jail. Weaker inmates become the property of stronger prisoners or gangs, who sell the sexual services of the victim. Prison officials either are disinterested in stopping abuse of prisoners by other prisoners or are incapable of doing so, given the limited resources society allocates to the prison system. . . . Even more appalling is the fact that guards frequently participate in the brutalization of inmates.[11]

The reference in both of these court opinions to "homosexual" forms of abuse is typical of earlier reporting on sexual abuse in incarceration, whether in court opinions or in books and articles. In many cases, the label "homosexual" seems to have been applied to the abuse without much thought, based on the plain fact that in these cases of sexual abuse of one inmate by another, the abuser and the victim were of the same sex. But a number of court opinions, books, and articles designate the abuse as "homosexual" as part of a broad view of the likely sexual propensities of the abuser or of the victim.

The designation "homosexual" is now generally recognized as unhelpful in the context of sexual abuse in incarceration. Stephen Donaldson, who was raped countless times during several years in incarceration, declared in testimony before the Massachusetts legislature:

The bandits and the jockers and daddies, I must stress, are not homosexual in any psychologically meaningful sense. They are heterosexuals on the Street and they pretty much treat the punks and queens just like they are used to treating women. That's the model they bring into the joint with them. . . . And most of the victims are straight. So, please, please, banish the phrase "homosexual rape" from your vocabulary; it's an insult to real homosexuals and simply misleads most of the people who hear it. When you're discussing sex-segregated prisons, just talking about "rape" or "sexual aggressors" is quite clear enough. The last thing we need is more confusion.[12]

Yet there may well be consensual sexual activity between inmates in incarceration. In fact, in many corrections institutions all sexual activity between inmates is a rule violation, but this is not a concern of this book. This book raises no issues whatsoever regarding any form of consensual sexual activity between inmates.

However, it is often extremely difficult to conclude that a sexual interaction between inmates is truly consensual. In the context of male incarceration, a federal trial court explains: "By the time an inmate reaches his initial classification destination [within incarceration facility housing], be it maximum, medium, or minimum, it is difficult to discern non-consensual homosexual activity, because the resistance of most non-consensual victims has been broken by that time."[13]

In particular, Donaldson explains how a vulnerable male inmate might take the "survival-driven" course of "hooking up" in a "protective pair" arrangement with "either a strong individual or a small clique or a big gang":

You become a sex slave and have to engage in continual unwanted sex acts, but you're now pretty safe from gang-rapes, robberies, stabbings, and you can actually negotiate a bit with your owner(s). That is what most victims end up doing, as much as they detest it and hate themselves for doing it; it's the only way to survive. . . . Sex for a hooked-up punk is neither assaultive nor fully consentual [sic], it just doesn't fit into our standard legal categories, including the ones enshrined in disciplinary codes.[14]

In fact, though, for the cases of sexual abuse that this book considers there is rarely any difficulty regarding lack of consent. These are cases where an inmate involved in the sexual interaction reports it as nonconsensual. Also, in the great majority of these cases coercion is all too obvious.

THE DAVIS PHILADELPHIA INVESTIGATION

Although experts, corrections officers, and inmates were aware of sexual abuse in incarceration, until relatively recently there was little attempt to assess the nature and extent of the problem. A very early attempt was a 1968 investigation by the highly respected Philadelphia attorney Alan Davis. Davis, who at the time was chief assistant district attorney of Philadelphia, supervised an investigation of sexual abuse of male inmates by other inmates in the Philadelphia system of incarceration. The Philadelphia system of incarceration is officially called the Philadelphia Prison System, but in fact it is a jail system in the usual sense: it is operated by a city rather than a state authority and largely holds individuals awaiting trial or serving relatively short sentences. However, at the time when Davis carried out his study some of the inmates of this system were serving quite long sentences.

The Davis investigation was unusual in that it was carried out by and on behalf of public authorities external to the prison system. After a criminal defense attorney informed a Philadelphia judge that two of his clients had been sexually abused—one of them anally gang-raped repeatedly—in the Philadelphia system, the judge ordered an investigation and appointed Davis to carry it out. The police commissioner also started an investigation, and these two investigations were then merged under the supervision of Davis.

The investigation focused on the inmates who had passed through the Philadelphia system in the preceding two years. These numbered about sixty thousand, and the investigation interviewed more than three thousand of them. Virtually all of those interviewed were still inmates at the time of the investigation.

At that time it was quite usual for research on sexual abuse in incarceration to be based on personal interviews with inmates. However, this method of inquiry is now widely recognized as being problematic. It is problematic because, for a range of reasons discussed later in this chapter and in chapter 2, inmates are often reluctant to disclose to researchers that they have suffered sexual abuse. As a result, research on sexual abuse in incarceration that is based on personal interviews with inmates is likely to underestimate the extent of abuse.

The Davis investigation in fact compounded this problem of likely underestimation. It did not even place full reliance on the accounts that inmates gave in interviews of the sexual abuse that they had suffered. Rather, it accepted as true only those incidents of sexual abuse that "could be documented and substantiated—through institutional records, polygraph examinations, or other corroboration."[15] If an inmate did not tell the investigators about an incident of sexual abuse he had suffered, there would obviously be no record of the incident in the investigation report. If an inmate did tell the investigators but the incident could not be substantiated, there would still be no record of it in the investigation report.

The consequence of this approach is that there was no likelihood at all that the Davis investigation would overestimate the extent of sexual abuse. On the contrary, the following summary that the report gives must be viewed as a very conservative assessment of the situation:

In brief, we found that sexual assaults in the Philadelphia prison system are epidemic. As Superintendent Hendrick and three of the wardens admitted, virtually every slightly-built young man committed by the courts is sexually approached within a day or two after his admission to prison. Many of these young men are repeatedly raped by gangs of inmates. Others, because of the threat of gang rape, seek protection by entering into a homosexual relationship with an individual tormentor. Only the tougher and more hardened young men, and those few so obviously frail that they are immediately locked up for their own protection, escape homosexual rape.[16]

The investigation found that during the two-year period in question there had been approximately 25 substantiated incidents of anal rape per thousand inmates, as well as a considerable number of incidents of forced oral sex and other forms of sexual abuse. The investigators were well aware of the issues resulting in underreporting and concluded: "these figures represent only the top of the iceberg."[17]

A significant aspect of the Davis investigation is that it acknowledged the issue of race in the context of sexual abuse in incarceration. In the Philadelphia system at that time, 80 percent of the inmates were African American. But of the documented assaults in which the races of both aggressors and victims were known, in over 70 percent of the incidents the victims were white. Black-on-white assaults made up a majority of the incidents. Davis comments that "it is safer for a member of a majority group to single out for attack a member of a minority group. . . . But it also seems true that current racial tensions and hostilities in the outside community are aggravated in a criminal population."[18]

Race remains a much-discussed issue in the context of sexual abuse in incarceration. But the extensive surveys of sexual abuse in incarceration now being carried out under the authority of the Department of Justice (see chapter 2) show that the issue is far more complex than the Davis investigation was able to ascertain. In fact, these and other surveys suggest that "after controlling for other explanatory variables (such as prior sexual abuse, sexual orientation, and criminal justice history) that contribute to prison rape, white inmates' likelihood of sexual victimization was not significantly different from that of black inmates or those of other races."[19]

THE STRUCKMAN-JOHNSON STUDIES

The issue of sexual abuse in incarceration received very little attention for a number of years following the Davis study. Writing in the mid-1990s, psychology professor Cindy Struckman-Johnson, together with other scholars, was still able to describe sexual abuse in incarceration as "a subject largely ignored by both society and scientists."[20] But this changed, and there has been a considerable amount of research and writing on the subject since then.

Several societal developments have encouraged this more recent development of research. One development regarding sexual abuse of incarcerated men was the HIV/AIDS epidemic. It became known that a relatively high proportion of inmates are infected, making anal rape and coerced oral sex potentially a yet more serious matter. In fact, this helped to dispel ignorance of the fact that men could be raped. It was still widely true in the 1990s that, as Struckman-Johnson wrote: "Many people have difficulty understanding how a heterosexual man can be forced to participate in sexual acts against his will. Consequently, they may wrongly assume that forced sex in prison is a homosexual activity, victims have in some way given their consent to participate, and the consequences of assault are not substantial."[21]

A development regarding sexual abuse of incarcerated women was the arrival of male corrections officers in women's incarceration facilities. For many years, it was routine that only women corrections officers would have close or extended contact with women inmates. But this changed following enactment of Title VII of the federal Civil Rights Act of 1964 and the Equal Employment Opportunity Act of 1972. Women's incarceration facilities could no longer straightforwardly discriminate on the basis of sex in hiring corrections officers. Men in considerable numbers quickly applied for positions in women's facilities and soon made up a substantial proportion of the corrections officers. By the early 1990s, men made up the majority of corrections officers working in women's incarceration facilities in America. In a number of facilities, men already constituted as many as three-quarters of corrections officers.[22] This development made women inmates vulnerable to all forms of sexual abuse by men, which encouraged researchers to focus on the subject.

This is the context in which Struckman-Johnson and her colleagues conducted their research. Their subject was the sexual coercion of men and women inmates in midwestern state prison systems.

It is notoriously difficult to obtain reliable information on sexual abuse in incarceration. First, it requires full cooperation on the part of the authorities in the facility, since they exercise close control over every aspect of access to inmates. Even then, an inmate who has suffered sexual abuse may be unwilling to tell researchers about it. Struckman-Johnson explains the difficulties of research in this area:

[I]t is not easy for inmates . . . to tell unknown strangers about an event as personal and traumatic as forced sex. In fact, half of the targets [that is, those who informed the researchers that they had been pressured or forced to have sexual contact] said that they had not told anyone about being sexually coerced until they took our survey. Many targeted inmates informed us in returned surveys that they were very worried about being "found out" by other inmates or prison officials. We were also told that some inmates suspected that we were prison officials masquerading as researchers.[23]

Inmates are even more reluctant to report to corrections officers that they have been sexually abused than to inform researchers or other persons of the abuse. A report from the Bureau of Justice Statistics (BJS) of the Department of Justice, discussed in chapter 2, explains: "Due to a fear of reprisal from perpetrators, a code of silence among inmates, personal embarrassment, and lack of trust in staff, victims are often reluctant to report incidents to correctional authorities."[24]

Judicial opinions have attested to the code of silence among inmates. As one federal court explains: "it is apparent that the inmates have an unwritten code of silence which results in most of the acts of violence going undetected." Another recognizes that "the evidence is absolutely clear that the inmate code exists and that it prevents the reporting of a great many episodes of actual or threatened violence." Yet another explains: "A cardinal precept of the convict culture is that no inmate should report another inmate to officials."[25]

An inmate who breaks this code of silence is labeled a "snitch," which can lead to further abuse. A federal appellate court opinion explains: "Being labeled a 'snitch' was dreaded, because it could make the inmate a target for other prisoners' attacks." Davis attested in his report on sexual abuse in the Philadelphia incarceration system: "Almost all of the victims still in prison were so terrified of retaliation by other prisoners that they were very reluctant to cooperate with us." As an official of the Oklahoma Crime Commission concluded after describing a prison gang rape, if the victim tells the guards, "his life isn't worth a nickel."[26]

There is yet another reason beyond the code of silence for an inmate rape victim to remain silent. As a federal appellate court explained, "once a prisoner has been thus victimized, word spreads throughout the prison and he becomes a special target for subsequent attacks." T.J. Parsell described the aftermath of the first time he was raped in prison: "I hoped no one would find out about it, but as I walked the yard in a daze, other inmates pointed and laughed. . . . Once an inmate has been turned out, he's considered a target wherever he goes."[27]

The code of silence applies equally to an inmate who witnesses the sexual abuse of another inmate. In a civil action for wrongful death brought against Alabama prison authorities, the magistrate found: "Gullatte witnessed the mass homosexual rape of his cell mate. At the request of the Board of Corrections investigator, Gullatte gave a statement as to the identity of the perpetrators and agreed to testify at any future disciplinary hearing against them. By so doing, Gullatte became what is known in prison jargon as a 'snitch.'" Gullatte was murdered by other inmates shortly afterward.[28]

Because of these considerations, Struckman-Johnson departed from the method that most prior research on sexual abuse in incarceration had used, which was to rely on personal interviews with inmates. As her research group noted, reliance on personal interviews "can easily result in underreporting this sensitive behavior."[29] An obvious reason for this is that within the confines of an incarceration facility, under the tight control of the authorities, it is extremely difficult to assure inmates that what they say will not be overheard, revealed, or even reported to the authorities.

The method of Struckman-Johnson was based on distributing survey forms, to be completed in writing anonymously and returned by mail. It is now standard practice to gather data on sexual abuse by surveying inmates anonymously, either through written survey forms or computer-administered questionnaires. This is the method that the BJS uses in its periodic surveys of inmates conducted under the auspices of PREA, discussed in chapter 2.

In the Struckman-Johnson study, survey forms were distributed not only to the inmate population but also to a sampling of the prison staff, in order to compare inmate and staff assessments of rates of sexual coercion. There was some divergence between the estimates made by staff and by inmates, but it was not extreme. Staff on average estimated that 15 percent of inmates had been pressured or forced to have sexual contact at some time during their incarceration; inmates on average estimated this at 19 percent. A prior study based on anonymous surveys had, quite similarly, found rates of around 14 percent. Professors Cindy Struckman-Johnson and David Struckman-Johnson carried out a further study of midwestern prisons a few years later, also based on anonymous surveys. This found rates of pressured or forced sexual contact that were on average somewhat higher, but with considerable variation from one facility to another. However, the overall rate was still within a comparable range to the earlier studies.[30]

The Struckman-Johnson studies gave a good deal of further information. This information will not be detailed here because the periodic BJS surveys now give more up-to-date information. Notably, though, the Struckman-Johnson studies gave separate information for women and men in incarceration. They also gave information regarding the number of incidents of sexual abuse that victims had suffered and regarding the kind of sexual contact involved.

THE HUMAN RIGHTS WATCH REPORTS

In the 1990s, the organization Human Rights Watch carried out research on sexual abuse in American incarceration that resulted in two extensive, groundbreaking reports. Both reports dealt only with prisons and not with jails. They also did not consider sexual abuse in other confinement facilities such as immigration and juvenile detention facilities.

The first of these Human Rights Watch reports, *All Too Familiar*, examined the sexual abuse of female inmates in state prisons. The research and the report were largely confined to abuse perpetrated by male corrections officers. Sexual abuse of female inmates by other female inmates was not considered and nor was sexual abuse of female inmates by female corrections officers.

The second report, *No Escape*, examined the sexual abuse of male inmates in state prisons. This report dealt only with abuse perpetrated by other inmates. It did not consider the sexual abuse of male inmates by corrections officers, male or female.

The *No Escape* report incorporated the findings of earlier studies on the extent of sexual abuse, including the Struckman-Johnson studies. It also explained how retaliation for reporting sexual abuse results in severe underreporting. A typical account given to Human Rights Watch was: "[T]he first time I was raped, I did the right thing. I went to an officer, told him what happened, got the rectal check, the whole works. Results? I get shipped to [another prison]. Six months later, same dude that raped me is out of seg and on the same wing as I am. I have to deal with 2 jackets now: snitch & punk." Another victim reported: "The first time [I was raped] I told on my attackers. All [the authorities] did was moved me from one facility to another. And I saw my attacker again not too long after I tolded on him. Then I paid for it. Because I tolded on him, he got even with me. So after that, I would not, did not tell again."[31]

The *No Escape* report noted that the governing correctional authorities uniformly insisted that there was virtually no sexual abuse of inmates. But it also found that the corrections officers who directly supervised inmates were aware of pervasive sexual abuse. As one example: "A corrections department internal survey of guards in a southern state (provided to Human Rights Watch on the condition that the state not be identified) found that line officers—those charged with the direct supervision of inmates—estimated that roughly one-fifth of all prisoners were being coerced into participation in inmate-on-inmate sex."[32] Beyond this, the report did not attempt to quantify the extent of sexual abuse in American incarceration.

Other aspects of the *No Escape* report are discussed in later chapters. A number of its case histories are among those discussed in chapter 4. The issues it raises regarding procedures for dealing with inmate grievances in incarceration facilities and concerning legal standards are discussed in part III.

The *All Too Familiar* report on incarceration of women also incorporated the findings of earlier studies on the extent of sexual abuse. In addition, it summarized a number of judicial decisions that had recognized pervasive sexual abuse of women inmates by corrections officers. Among these is a case brought by women incarcerated in the District of Columbia, in which the trial court found "that there was a pattern of sexual harassment of incarcerated women by male corrections staff." Regarding another case, brought by Georgia inmates, the Human Rights Watch report commented on the situation before a consent decree was finalized between the women inmates and the correctional authorities:

[O]fficers raped, sexually assaulted and sexually harassed female prisoners with little regard for legal or institutional constraints. Although Georgia criminal law formally prohibited sexual contact between prison officials and prisoners, the law was not enforced. Similarly, the departmental policies arguably barring such abuses were belied by the impunity with which prison staff, including supervisory staff, engaged in sexual relations with prisoners. Unlike most other states, however, Georgia has been forced to take meaningful steps to put a stop to these abuses.[33]

The report did not attempt to quantify the extent of sexual abuse in American incarceration, but it did focus on the underreporting of sexual abuse that results from fear of retaliation. The situation in Michigan was typical of the kind of retaliatory measures used: "Prisoners who have themselves reported sexual misconduct through the grievance or investigatory process, or those whose abuse was revealed by others, have been subjected repeatedly to room searches, pat-frisks and disciplinary tickets. . . . [H]arassment is constant and insidious for those who challenge sexual abuse. They receive misconducts for the most minute infractions of rules that are not generally enforced against anyone else."[34]

The District of Columbia case referred to in the Human Rights Watch report also noted the underreporting of sexual abuse that results from fear of retaliation. The trial court found: "By leaking private information [about complaints of sexual abuse] prison officials coerce women prisoners and staff into silence and insulate themselves from scrutiny."[35]

In addition, the *All Too Familiar* report provides a range of case histories as well as material on grievance procedures in women's prisons. It also provides an extensive analysis of the relevant legal standards. As with the *No Escape* report, these matters are discussed in later chapters.

JUST DETENTION INTERNATIONAL

The human rights organization now known as Just Detention International (JDI) was founded in 1980 under the name of People Organized to Stop the Rape of Imprisoned Persons (POSRIP). The name was soon changed to Stop Prisoner Rape, which it remained until 2008, when the organization became JDI. The organization's founder, Russell Dan Smith, had been raped in incarceration by other inmates. Donaldson was a successor in developing the organization. A later president of the organization was Tom Cahill, an air force veteran who had been arrested on charges of civil disobedience in 1968 and gang-raped by other inmates for more than twenty-four hours.[36]

From its earliest days, this organization has drawn attention to the pervasive sexual abuse in American incarceration and worked to achieve reform. It was instrumental in securing enactment of PREA, as discussed in chapter 2.

Yet JDI remains closely aware that sexual abuse in incarceration has continued despite enactment of PREA: "As the leading advocates addressing the problem of sexual violence in detention, JDI hears from prisoner rape survivors across the country on a daily basis. JDI does not solicit such correspondence, and does not conduct outreach to prisoners. Rather, survivors tend to hear about JDI through word-of-mouth and contact the organization simply because they feel they have nowhere else to turn." In calendar year 2010, JDI received unsolicited letters from 534 survivors of sexual violence in incarceration.[37]

THE CASE OF *LUCAS v WHITE*

The case of *Lucas v White* was filed and resolved in the late 1990s. It provides insight into pervasive sexual abuse of women inmates in the federal prison system and also shows how retaliation and the threat of retaliation inhibit reporting of sexual abuse.

The case was brought by women inmates of a federal prison in California against the federal Bureau of Prisons, which is an agency of the Department of Justice. The case was eventually resolved in a private settlement agreement. Under this agreement, the Bureau of Prisons was required to implement a wide range of reforms affecting every federal prison throughout America and pay the inmate plaintiffs the sum of $500,000 in damages. In addition, the federal district court awarded the plaintiffs a total of well over $600,000 in attorneys' fees and costs.[38]

It is routine with a settlement agreement that the defendant does not admit wrongdoing or even denies wrongdoing. But the government does not agree to implement reforms throughout its entire prison system and pay out over a million dollars unless it recognizes that it has engaged in wrongdoing and foresees that it may well lose the case at trial. In fact, in the case of *Lucas v White* the trial court observed that "the only evidence before the Court supports the validity of plaintiffs' claims."

Accordingly, it is wholly fair to accept the plaintiffs' allegations in this case as true.

The conduct of which the plaintiffs complained "consisted of placing women in an otherwise all-male security housing unit, opening plaintiffs' cell doors for male prisoners' access, allowing for the physical and sexual harassment of plaintiffs, allowing correctional officers and male prisoners to assault and rape plaintiffs in retaliation for previous claims of wrongdoing, and failing to properly evaluate, train, discipline, and supervise custodial personnel so as to prevent such occurrences." The retaliation against the lead plaintiff in the case was severe:

Plaintiffs repeatedly asked prison personnel to stop the above conduct and in late August 1995, Lucas made an official complaint regarding the practice of allowing male inmates into her cell in the middle of the night. Within days, her complaint became common knowledge among the male prisoners and correctional personnel; nonetheless, she was not transferred to another place of confinement. . . . On or about September 22, 1995, Lucas' cell door was opened while she was asleep and three men entered her cell, and restrained and handcuffed her from behind. She was then brutally beaten, raped, and sodomized. Her life was also threatened and she was informed that the attack was in retaliation for her complaint.

Despite this, Lucas persisted with her lawsuit. But it would take far less retaliatory action than this to silence many people. There is no doubt that many inmates who have suffered sexual abuse have been silenced by the threat or the actuality of retaliation.

Chapter 2

Assessment of the Prevalence of Sexual Abuse

Toward the end of the 1990s, the various research publications and reports discussed in chapter 1 were increasing nationwide awareness of pervasive sexual abuse in incarceration. This stimulated a movement for reform. Some states passed laws and developed policies and programs ostensibly to address the problem of sexual abuse of inmates by corrections officers. However, these have mostly not been very effective.[1]

An attempt to pass a law of this kind for the federal system failed in Congress in 1999, but the movement for reform eventually led to enactment of PREA in 2003. The Human Rights Watch reports and the work of Just Detention International (JDI) were influential in ensuring passage of the statute and also helped to ensure that the statute would have a broad reach. Many earlier attempts at reform had been confined to sexual abuse of inmates perpetrated by corrections officers, but PREA applies also to sexual abuse of inmates by other inmates (see part IV).

The move to enact PREA gained wide support across the spectrum of American political opinion. Liberal and conservative institutions alike supported the act, as did a range of faith-based organizations. No organization actively opposed it. In both houses of Congress the bill was introduced by Democrat and Republican cosponsors, and it passed in both houses without a single dissenting vote.[2]

THE BJS SURVEYS AND THEIR SCOPE

Congress drew extensively on data provided by Human Rights Watch and JDI to reach findings on the extent of sexual abuse in incarceration

and incorporated these findings into PREA. They convey the best estimate of the extent of sexual abuse in incarceration that could be made
at that time:

Insufficient research has been conducted and insufficient data reported on the
extent of prison rape. However, experts have conservatively estimated that at
least 13 percent of the inmates in the United States have been sexually assaulted
in prison. Many inmates have suffered repeated assaults. Under this estimate,
nearly 200,000 inmates now incarcerated have been or will be the victims of
prison rape. The total number of inmates who have been sexually assaulted in
the past 20 years likely exceeds 1,000,000.[3]

A number of PREA provisions focus on the need for improved data
on the extent and nature of sexual abuse in incarceration. Accordingly,
the statute requires the BJS to "carry out, for each calendar year, a comprehensive statistical review and analysis of the incidence and effects of
prison rape."[4] From its reviews and analyses the BJS produces several
series of reports, and these are now among the most up-to-date, relatively consistent sources of information on sexual abuse in incarceration
in America. The BJS surveys also provided the data for the important
Regulatory Impact Assessment (RIA) for the PREA national standards
that the Department of Justice has issued, discussed later in this chapter
and in chapters 5 and 10.

It is particularly important that the BJS from the very beginning of
its program has included jails as well as prisons. Before the BJS surveys,
there had been very little scrutiny of sexual abuse in jails. In fact, the
Davis investigation of the Philadelphia system, discussed in chapter 1,
was the only study of any significance. The Human Rights Watch report, *All Too Familiar* (also discussed in chapter 1), makes it clear why
so little attention had been paid to jails. The report includes a survey
of prison conditions in Georgia and explains why it did not extend its
examination to jails:

To begin with, there are over 200 city and county jails in Georgia, each with
a separate set of responsible authorities (and thus, for purposes of litigation,
a separate set of potential defendants). In addition, jails hold a much more
transient population than do prisons—detainees may be held for very short
periods—so that, in the absence of constant monitoring, abuses are likely to remain concealed. In short, it would require a large and continuing investment of
resources to investigate jail abuses and to initiate legal action to remedy them.[5]

Essentially, it needed the powers and scope of action of a federal agency,
as well as federal funding, even to begin to undertake the investigation
of sexual abuse in jails on a nationwide basis.

Jails hold a variety of individuals who have not been convicted of any criminal offense, including many who are not accused of any crime at all. These individuals may be among the many people held in jails who are ill equipped to withstand jail conditions. "Large city jails tend to be noisy, crowded, and chaotic. . . . Jails hold many inmates who are among the most vulnerable to sexual abuse: nonviolent, first-time detainees lacking even basic prison savvy, often picked up for disorderly conduct, or failure to make bail—many never even charged with a crime. For many of these detainees, a couple of days in a local jail results in a lifetime of trauma."[6]

The BJS has also now begun to include community corrections facilities in its reporting program. Residents in these facilities are vulnerable to sexual abuse:

The Shea Farm Halfway House in Concord, New Hampshire, is a minimum-security facility for women transitioning back to the community after being incarcerated in State prison. In 2002, an officer who had been accused of sexual harassment against a woman corrections officer at another facility was transferred to become the night supervisor at Shea Farm. In this position, he had a significant amount of power over the approximately 45 women living there. He had the authority to lower their security classification, approve or limit overnight leave requests, telephone privileges, and/or visits with family members, and essentially, he had the ability to write the women up for disciplinary infractions and send them back behind bars. . . . [H]e used this power to repeatedly sexually abuse and violently assault residents.[7]

Individuals under nonresidential supervision in community corrections are also vulnerable to sexual abuse. These individuals, who generally live in their own home, "may report to a community corrections officer to update their status or for drug testing, or an officer may visit them at their home or workplace. These meetings may take place at predetermined times or randomly, and they can occur at any hour, day or night." In a Minnesota case, "a male community corrections officer, visiting a former prisoner's apartment to discuss her failure in a drug treatment program, instead requested and had sex with her." But few cases come to light. As a chief probation officer explains, "because community corrections staff work with significantly less direct supervision than their counterparts in secure correctional facilities, it is much easier for them to conceal sexual abuses, making the task of detecting and responding to abuse all the more difficult."[8]

Sexual abuse of individuals in community corrections is potentially a very large problem, with nearly five million adults under supervision in the community on either probation or parole (see chapter 1). The BJS does not have the resources to directly survey the great range of these facilities. But the BJS has now conducted a survey of former state inmates in which it asked each participant whether he or she had suffered sexual abuse in a local jail, state prison, or postrelease community corrections facility. The survey was carried out in 2008, and the BJS issued its report in 2012. Note that the Department of Justice takes the view that nonresidential supervision is outside the scope of its mandate under PREA, which is limited to sexual abuse in confinement facilities.[9]

The BJS does not have the resources to deal at all with the thousands of local lockups across the country that hold individuals who have been arrested. In its RIA for the PREA national standards, the Department of Justice recognizes that individuals held in these facilities may be in danger of sexual abuse, even though they are usually held for only a short period of time:

While the short amount of time detainees usually spend in lockup facilities, together with the typical physical layout of lockups, would suggest that lockup detainees face a lower risk of sexual abuse than inmates in other settings, we cannot ignore anecdotal evidence that sexual abuse can and sometimes does occur in lockup settings.

Furthermore, statistics indicating that 15% of sexual abuse victims in jails report having been abused by another inmate within the first 24 hours of their arrival at the jail suggest that sexual abuse can occur even in the briefest of detention stays. Nevertheless, we are currently constrained by an absence of data in determining the magnitude of that problem.[10]

THE BJS SERIES OF SURVEYS

There are three main series of BJS surveys of sexual abuse in incarceration under the PREA mandate, with corresponding reports. The first series, with which the BJS began its PREA mandate, consists of surveys of sexual abuse that correctional authorities have reported to the BJS. The second series consists of surveys of sexual abuse that inmates have reported.[11] This chapter will discuss these two series.

The third series consists of surveys of sexual abuse that former inmates have reported. One such report, as already referred to, was published in 2012. It is not clear when any further such reports are to be published, and so this series will be referenced only in passing.

An important development by the BJS was to move toward adopting uniform definitions of abusive sexual acts perpetrated on inmates.[12] These definitions initially classify each abusive sexual act according to whether the perpetrator is another inmate or a member of staff and then classify according to the type of act perpetrated.

The BJS definitions divide abusive inmate-on-inmate sexual acts into two categories: "nonconsensual sexual acts" and "abusive sexual contacts." The definition of nonconsensual sexual acts encompasses everything that is generally defined as rape. It includes rape with an object and nonconsensual oral sex. It also includes nonconsensual manual sexual stimulation. The acts within the definition of abusive sexual contacts are less invasive but nonetheless serious, nonconsensual contacts that have a sexual component.[13]

The BJS applies different criteria for sexual abuse of inmates by members of the staff of incarceration facilities. All sexual activity between staff and inmates is officially deemed to be sexual abuse and is illegal in all states and the federal system. As the Department of Justice explains, "the power imbalance in correctional facilities is such that it is impossible to know if an incarcerated person truly 'consented' to sexual activity with staff."[14]

Accordingly, the BJS defines a single, very broad category of "staff sexual misconduct." This category includes not only sexual acts perpetrated by staff on inmates but also invasion of privacy, indecent exposure, and voyeurism by staff, as well as sexually offensive or invasive touching by staff. It also includes staff requests for sexual acts. The BJS also recognizes "staff sexual harassment" of inmates as a separate category of sexual abuse. This encompasses repeated statements or comments of a sexual nature.[15]

The BJS is right to include noncontact abusive behavior such as voyeurism and sexual harassment within the definition of sexual abuse. Behavior of this kind contributes to creating an environment that encourages all forms of sexual abuse. As the legal scholar Kim Shayo Buchanan explains in an important social analysis of sexual abuse in incarceration, "sexual harassment and sexual assault fall along a continuum and tend to occur together."[16]

Sexual harassment is designed to humiliate and as a result encourages sexual abuse. The desire to humiliate appears particularly in the way that some male corrections officers have dealt with sanitary supplies for women inmates. In one reported case in a California state facility, "male guards threw a packet of sanitary napkins onto the floor, in response to a request for sanitary napkins, and the prisoner had to 'fish' for the packet by using a string, with which she was supposed to catch the packet and drag it along the floor into her cell. While she tried to get the napkin, the guards shouted encouragement and bet on whether she would be successful."[17]

Notably, a problem with the BJS definitions of sexual abuse is that the categories are too broad to reflect the range and complexity of sexual abuse. In particular, they are not well suited for developing a cost analysis of sexual abuse in incarceration. Accordingly, the Department of Justice has developed more nuanced definitions in its RIA. These are discussed later in this chapter and in chapter 5.

THE BJS SURVEYS OF SEXUAL ABUSE REPORTED BY CORRECTIONAL AUTHORITIES

For these surveys, the BJS reviews the records of allegations of sexual abuse that correctional authorities maintain. Every year the BJS mails survey forms to administrators at a representative sample of correctional authorities. The administrators may mail back a completed form or complete it online. A few simply do not respond to the survey. The BJS extrapolates the survey results to yield nationwide data, using standard and accepted statistical methods. This series of surveys is referred to as the *Survey of Sexual Violence* (SSV).[18]

The surveys in this BJS series are *incidence* surveys. That is, each survey provides information on the number of discrete incidents of sexual abuse reported during the period covered by the respective survey. To understand the way in which data on sexual abuse are presented, it is important to distinguish incidence surveys from *prevalence* surveys. Prevalence refers to the number or the proportion of inmates who report having been a victim of sexual abuse during the period covered by the report.[19] In chapter 1, the Struckman-Johnson study was a prevalence study; the Davis investigation provided information on both prevalence and incidence.

It is not possible to obtain prevalence information from incidence information without further data. The fact that a particular number of incidents of sexual abuse occurred does not tell us how many individuals were victims of sexual abuse, since some of the incidents may relate to the same individual victim. Similarly, it is not possible to obtain incidence information from prevalence information without further data. The fact that a particular number of individuals were victims of sexual abuse does not tell us how many incidents of sexual abuse occurred, since some of the victims may have suffered more than one incident.

The first BJS report on sexual abuse reported by correctional authorities, covering incidents reported during 2004, encompassed adult prisons (federal, state, and private), adult jails (public and private), and juvenile detention facilities (state, local, and private) within a single report. It also encompassed other facilities, including Native American county jails, military-operated facilities, and facilities operated by or for the Bureau of Immigration and Customs Enforcement. From 2005 onward, adult and juvenile facilities have been treated separately in this series of reports. The BJS has so far issued reports in this series on adult facilities for 2005, 2006, and 2007–2008, as well as a single report on juvenile facilities for 2005–2006.[20]

The reports inform that the total number of allegations of incidents of staff sexual misconduct reported to adult correctional authorities over the country as a whole remained at a constant level, proportionate to the number of inmates, from 2005 (the first year for which adult facilities were separately reported) to 2008 (the most recent year for which a report is currently available). The reports also show that from 2005 to 2008, allegations of incidents of inmate-on-inmate nonconsensual acts remained at a very nearly constant level, proportionate to the number of inmates. So too did allegations of incidents of staff sexual harassment. But allegations of incidents of inmate-on-inmate abusive sexual contacts more than doubled from 2005 to 2008, proportionate to the number of inmates.[21]

Note, though, that all of the data that this series of reports provides should be viewed with caution. From the beginning of the series the BJS has warned: "Administrative records alone cannot provide reliable estimates of sexual violence. Due to a fear of reprisal from perpetrators, a code of silence among inmates, personal embarrassment, and lack of trust in staff, victims are often reluctant to report incidents to correctional authorities."[22] The Department of Justice shares this view, as discussed shortly.

This caution also applies to the information that correctional authorities provide regarding their investigations of allegations of incidents of sexual abuse. The BJS survey asks the administrators of correctional authorities that respond to the survey to state the results of these investigations. Each allegation must be classified under one of four heads: *substantiated*, if the alleged incident is determined to have occurred; *unsubstantiated*, if the evidence was insufficient to make a final determination that it occurred; *unfounded*, if it was determined not to have occurred; and *investigation ongoing*, if a final determination had not been made at the time of data collection.[23]

In every category of sexual abuse, most allegations end up being dismissed as unsubstantiated. According to the most recent report, this is the outcome for more than half of all allegations of inmate-on-inmate nonconsensual sexual acts, inmate-on-inmate abusive sexual contacts, and staff sexual misconduct. For staff sexual harassment, nearly two-thirds of allegations are dismissed as unsubstantiated. Correspondingly few allegations of sexual abuse end up being substantiated.[24]

It is not surprising that only a small proportion of allegations of incidents of sexual abuse end up being substantiated. In incarceration facilities it is particularly difficult to obtain evidence to substantiate an allegation of sexual abuse. As explained in chapter 1, inmates have reason to fear retaliation from other inmates or from corrections officers and so are reluctant to testify to sexual abuse that they have witnessed. Also, in each incarceration facility the procedures for defining, reporting, recording, and investigating allegations of sexual abuse are set up by the authorities of the facility and operate under their close control. In many facilities these procedures are frankly unfair, to the point of being themselves abusive of inmates (see chapter 8).

The BJS recognizes that many allegations of sexual abuse that do not end up being substantiated are in fact true. Its report on sexual abuse in juvenile facilities for 2005–2006 notes that the rates of substantiated incidents of sexual abuse, proportionate to the number of inmates, are six times higher in juvenile than in adult incarceration facilities. The report explains that this "may largely be the result of more complete reporting of incidents and more thorough investigations when incidents of sexual violence involve youth."[25] The point is plain: the authorities in adult incarceration facilities often do not completely report and thoroughly investigate inmates' allegations; they would discover and substantiate far more incidents of sexual abuse if they did so.

The PREA national standards include a provision requiring an allegation of sexual abuse or sexual harassment to be deemed substantiated if the evidence on balance makes the allegation more likely to be true than not true. But it is not yet clear how far this and other provisions of the PREA national standards will actually be implemented (see chapter 10).

THE BJS SURVEYS OF SEXUAL ABUSE REPORTED BY INMATES

The BJS has continued its PREA mandate with surveys of sexual abuse that inmates have reported. Four reports in this series have appeared so far. There are two reports for 2007, one for state and federal prisons and one for local jails. Each of the other two reports covers the two-year period 2008–2009. One of these reports deals with adults in prisons and jails, and the other deals with juvenile facilities. The surveys on adult inmates are referred to as the *National Inmate Survey* (NIS) and the survey on juveniles as the *National Survey of Youth in Custody* (NSYC).[26]

The NSYC deals only with juveniles who are held in juvenile facilities. It excludes juveniles who are held in adult facilities. They are also not covered by the NIS. As a result, there is at present no survey at all of sexual abuse reported by the approximately 8,500 juveniles held in adult prisons and jails.[27]

The BJS Methodology

Inmates are selected at random for these surveys in a three-stage process. First, a sample of incarceration facilities is selected at random. Then, within each facility, a sample of inmates is selected at random. Finally, at the actual interview, inmates are assigned at random to receive either the questionnaire on sexual abuse or a survey on drug and alcohol use that has nothing to do with the BJS mandate. Neither the inmate nor corrections officers know in advance of the interview which questionnaire the inmate is to receive.

Surveys of inmates on the subject of sexual abuse need to ensure confidentiality and anonymity. If they do not do so, they are essentially worthless (see chapters 1 and 3). The BJS survey procedures take this reasonably well into account. The interviews take place in a private room in the incarceration facility. Before being interviewed, inmates are informed that participation is voluntary and that all information provided is held in confidence. The interviews are conducted on computer. At the beginning of the interview, the survey interviewer requests some limited, anonymous background information and enters this into the computer.

The interviewer then either leaves the room or moves away from the computer, and the survey proceeds as what is known as an ACASI (audio computer-assisted self-interview) survey, in which the inmate being interviewed completes the questionnaire on the computer using a touch screen and with the help of audio instructions delivered through headphones. As Allen Beck, staff member of the BJS, explains, "self-administration is key when you have very sensitive items, either behaviors or attitudes that you're trying to collect information on."[28] The questionnaire does not ask for any information that could personally identify the inmate being interviewed.

The aim of these measures is to overcome, or at least to reduce, the reluctance of inmates to attest to having suffered sexual abuse. Of course, it is still impossible to know how effective these measures have been. The BJS acknowledges that "some inmates may remain silent about sexual victimization experienced in the facility, despite efforts of survey staff to assure inmates that their responses would be kept confidential."[29]

It is also possible for inmates to make false reports of having suffered sexual abuse. But the questionnaire is set up with a view to eliminating the main incentives for an inmate to make a false report. On the one hand, an inmate cannot hope to reap any personal advantage from making a false report, because the questionnaire does not ask for any information that could personally identify the inmate being interviewed. On the other hand, an inmate cannot hope to cause trouble for a corrections officer or another inmate by accusing him or her of perpetrating sexual abuse. This is because if the inmate attests in the questionnaire to having been a victim of sexual abuse, the questionnaire does not ask for any information that could personally identify the perpetrator. In accordance with this, there is never any follow-up investigation of reported incidents of sexual abuse, however serious.

In addition, false reports are statistically likely to show inconsistent response patterns. The BJS therefore implements consistency checks on the interview responses. In every survey the results have shown very high levels of consistency. The 2008–2009 survey of adult prisons and jails is typical: about 94 percent of completed interviews had no inconsistent responses at all, and over 5 percent had only one.[30] Finally, the BJS extrapolates the survey results to yield nationwide data, using standard and accepted statistical methods.

These BJS surveys are primarily prevalence surveys, as they provide information on the number of inmates who reported being sexually abused. In fact, though, the surveys did collect some incidence data. Participants in the survey who reported having been sexually abused were asked follow-up questions regarding how many incidents of sexual abuse they had suffered. This is discussed later in this chapter.

THE DEPARTMENT OF JUSTICE RIA

As part of the process of developing national standards under PREA (discussed in part IV), the Department of Justice produced an RIA of the standards. This is essentially a monetary cost/benefit analysis of the standards. The "cost" side of the cost/benefit analysis is the monetary cost that incarceration facilities would incur by complying with the standards (see chapters 9 and 10). The "benefits" side of the cost/benefit analysis is the monetary value of the sexual abuse in incarceration that would be avoided if incarceration facilities complied with the standards.

For the computation of the benefits side of the cost/benefit analysis, the RIA had to make three assessments. First, it had to assess the prevalence of sexual abuse in incarceration. That is, it had to assess the number or the proportion of inmates who were victims of sexual abuse during a given period. The RIA assessments of the prevalence of sexual abuse are considered next in this chapter.

Second, the RIA had to assess the monetary cost of the sexual abuse that any given victim suffers. The reason is that the monetary benefit of avoiding sexual abuse is, obviously, the same as the monetary cost if the sexual abuse occurs. The estimates of the monetary cost of sexual abuse are considered in chapter 5.

Third, the RIA had to assess the reduction in levels of sexual abuse required to justify the cost side of the cost/benefit analysis. This is discussed in chapter 10.

The Department of Justice produced its assessments and estimates in cooperation with the BJS on the basis of data from the BJS surveys. Not all of these data are in the BJS reports. The RIA assessments now give the best available estimates of the prevalence and the cost of sexual abuse in incarceration.

Choice of Data Source

The RIA reviews the potential sources of data on the prevalence of sexual abuse in incarceration and reaches the conclusion that the BJS surveys are the only feasible sources. All other studies and surveys are too limited in scope, too dated, or of questionable methodology. The key question then is whether to draw on the SSV surveys (sexual abuse reported by correctional authorities) or the NIS/NSYC surveys (sexual abuse reported by inmates).[31]

The RIA expresses major concerns regarding the SSV surveys. One problem concerns the underlying data that correctional authorities provide to the BJS. There is considerable variation among correctional authorities regarding how they define and record allegations of sexual abuse. These variations in the underlying data necessarily feed through to the results of the SSV surveys and undermine their reliability.

Another problem with the SSV surveys is that, as already noted, victims of sexual abuse are often reluctant to report the abuse to correctional authorities. The RIA explains the consequences:

[T]he institution-reported data almost certainly undercount the number of actual sexual abuse victims in prison, due to underreporting by victims. . . . [F]or a variety of reasons, many sexual abuse victims do not report their abuse to institutional managers. Indeed, of the adult respondents to the inmate surveys, between 69% and 82% of inmates who reported sexual abuse in response to the survey stated that they had never reported an incident to correctional managers. Thus, the data drawn from institutional surveys almost certainly miss thousands of victims that the inmate surveys capture.[32]

Because of these problems with the SSV surveys, the RIA prefers to rely on the NIS/NSYC surveys, in which it expresses confidence: "the NIS and NSYC comprise the most rigorous and large-scale studies of prison rape prevalence ever undertaken, and the methodologies underlying these studies have been repeatedly peer-reviewed and endorsed by academics and experts from across the country. . . . We therefore stand behind the conclusions that BJS has drawn based on the NIS and NSYC."[33]

However, the RIA does recognize that, despite the precautions taken by the BJS in these surveys of inmate reports, there can still be underreporting of sexual abuse and also false reporting of sexual abuse. Accordingly, the RIA introduces modifying factors into its assessments to compensate for these possibilities, as explained later in this chapter.

Prevalence or Incidence Data

The NIS/NSYC surveys are primarily prevalence surveys, so in relying on them the RIA is largely limited to prevalence rather than incidence data on sexual abuse in incarceration. As the RIA recognizes, the danger in this is that it "risks understating the suffering, and the concomitant cost to society, of inmates who are repeatedly harmed by sexual predators."[34]

Bryson Martel, an African American man, testified before the National Prison Rape Elimination Commission (NPREC) regarding his experience in an Arkansas state prison: "Eventually, I was interviewed by an investigator from the State Police, and I made a report of every assault I survived in prison. I had to list all the inmates who sexually assaulted me, and I came up with 27 names. Sometimes just one inmate assaulted me, and sometimes they attacked me in groups. It went on almost every day for the nine months I spent in that facility."[35]

The number of incidents of sexual abuse that Martel suffered is certainly at least two hundred, is very probably over five hundred, and could well be over a thousand. His kind of experience in incarceration is far from unique (see chapter 4). Yet in a prevalence survey he is counted only as a single victim like any other.

The NIS/NSYC surveys did collect a limited amount of incidence data regarding how many incidents of sexual abuse victims had suffered. The RIA is able to use these data to take serial victimization into account in its estimates to a very limited extent, as explained next in this chapter. But, despite this, the RIA acknowledges that its decision to rely largely on prevalence data "is likely to introduce a conservative bias" into its estimates.[36]

Classification of Sexual Abuse: Adult Inmates

The RIA departs from the classification scheme that the BJS presents in its reports and adopts a scheme more suited to eventually assigning monetary costs to various types of sexual abuse in incarceration. This classification scheme takes into account a number of criticisms that advocacy groups combating sexual abuse in incarceration had made regarding a classification scheme that the Department of Justice had proposed earlier. The RIA classification scheme as it now stands is fairly satisfactory, given the limitations on available data and the need for analytical coherence and reasonable simplicity.[37]

The RIA classifies sexual abuse into six levels. Within this classification scheme, level 1 is the most serious level of abuse that a victim can suffer. Note that, in accordance with the RIA reliance on prevalence rather than incidence data, its classification scheme is based on *per victim* classification rather than *per incident* classification. Each victim of sexual abuse is classified as having suffered a certain level of sexual abuse. It may well be that the victim has suffered more than one incident of sexual abuse, but he or she is still counted once only within the RIA classification scheme as having suffered sexual abuse at a certain level. In fact, as will now be explained, it is part of the definition of some of the levels within the RIA classification scheme that the victim has suffered several incidents of sexual abuse.

Levels 1 and 2 sexual abuse both involve "nonconsensual sexual acts," which are defined as "unwanted contacts with another inmate or with a staff member that involved oral, anal, or vaginal penetration, or hand jobs." The difference between these two levels is that for sexual abuse to be classified as level 1 it must involve "injury, force, or high incidence." The RIA defines "high incidence" as meaning that the inmate victim has reported three or more events or incidents of sexual abuse. Sexual abuse is classified as level 2 if it involves "no injury and no force, and low incidence." The RIA defines "low incidence" as meaning that the inmate victim has reported a total of no more than two events or incidents of sexual abuse.

The earlier Department of Justice classification scheme had also divided nonconsensual sexual acts into two categories, but the division between the categories was based entirely on the level of coercion involved. The higher category was reserved for acts involving physical force or the threat of force. The lower category encompassed acts procured through pressure of various kinds, including bribes or blackmail. Advocacy groups objected to this distinction, arguing that the physical and psychological impact of sexual abuse is not necessarily greater when force rather than pressure is used and that in any event "prisons are inherently coercive environments in which there is no bright line between force, threat of force, pressure, and coercion."

The RIA recognizes the validity of these objections but at the same time is not willing to "ignore altogether the characterizations which the inmates themselves give to their experience." It explains:

[I]nmates . . . were asked to describe the extent to which their sexual interaction with another inmate or with a staff member was an act of force or an act of pressure or an act of volition. While the boundaries among the three may sometimes be difficult to ascertain, and while some inmates' subjective descriptions of the level of coercion or volition may be misguided or naïve, the inmate's choice of how to describe the sexual encounter is likely to provide at least some indication of the extent of harm the inmate suffered. This, in turn, will have a bearing on the cost of the event.

. . . Thus, we have maintained the distinction between force and pressure as one criterion for assigning victims into the higher or lower category of nonconsensual sexual acts, but we have added two additional criteria (presence vs. absence of physical injury and high vs. low incidence) to provide a more complete and more realistic distinction between the higher and lower categories.[38]

Level 3 in the RIA classification scheme is " 'willing' sex with staff." The RIA encloses the word "willing" in quotation marks within its definition of level 3 sexual abuse. This is appropriate, because the concept of willing sex between inmates and staff is obviously problematic. As the BJS and the Department of Justice recognize, "all sexual contacts between inmates and staff are legally nonconsensual."[39]

At the same time, in the BJS surveys these inmates themselves characterized their sexual contacts with staff as voluntary. As the legal scholar Brenda Smith points out, it is certainly feasible that an inmate might desire, seek, or even initiate a sexual interaction with a member of staff. This, though, does not change the fact that, as Smith insists, "prisoner/ prison staff [sexual] pairing epitomizes the inequality of power and the potential for abuse of that power."[40]

So although it is right to acknowledge that individuals continue to be sexual human beings with sexual volition during incarceration, because of the overwhelming power imbalance between staff and inmates it is still appropriate to classify these sexual contacts as sexual abuse. That is, as a matter of good policy, these sexual contacts must be regarded as nonconsensual. As Beck explains, "staff who engage in such activity, even though initiated by inmates, are acting improperly and considered predators."[41]

Levels 4 and 5 in the RIA classification scheme encompass inmate-on-inmate "abusive sexual contacts," which are defined as "unwanted contacts with another inmate that only involved touching of the inmate's buttocks, thigh, penis, breasts, or vagina in a sexual way." The difference between these two levels is that level 4 involves "injury or high incidence," but level 5 involves "no injury and low incidence." High incidence and low incidence are defined in the same way as with levels 1 and 2.

Level 6 in the RIA classification scheme encompasses "staff sexual misconduct touching only." This is defined as "contacts with a staff member that only involved touching of the inmate's buttocks, thigh, penis, breasts, or vagina in a sexual way."

Classification of Sexual Abuse: Juveniles in Juvenile Facilities

The RIA classification scheme for sexual abuse of juveniles in juvenile facilities differs from the scheme for adult inmates. This is in part a consequence of differences between the definitions and survey questions in the NSYC and those in the NIS. Also, the RIA classifies sex between a juvenile and a staff member as a higher level of abuse even when the juvenile regards it as willing, because of "laws against statutory rape and the generally deep-seated revulsion to sexual activity between adults and children."[42]

The RIA classifies sexual abuse of juveniles into five levels. Level 1 involves "serious sexual acts," which are defined as "unwanted contacts with another youth [inmate] or with a staff member that involve vaginal or anal penetration, oral contact with penis/vagina, or rubbing of penis/vagina." In addition, for serious sexual acts to be classified as level 1 sexual abuse, at least one of two criteria must be satisfied. One criterion is that any sexual abuse that involves "injury, force, or coercion" is classified as level 1, regardless of whether it occurs many times or only once. The other criterion is that if the serious sexual acts have been at least three in number (high incidence), and these acts have not been reported by the youth as "willing," then these serious sexual acts are classified as level 1 sexual abuse.

Levels 2 and 3 in the RIA classification scheme for juveniles also involve serious sexual acts. Level 2 sexual abuse consists of serious sexual acts with staff that are high incidence; that do not involve injury, force, or coercion; and that the juvenile has "reported as 'willing' or 'consensual.'"

Level 3 sexual abuse consists of serious sexual acts with another juvenile inmate or with a staff member that do not involve injury, force,

or coercion and that have occurred no more than twice (low incidence). This includes acts that the juvenile has "reported as 'willing' or
'consensual.'"

Levels 4 and 5 involve "other sexual acts," which are defined as "unwanted contacts with another youth [inmate] or any contact with staff
that only involved kissing other parts of the body, other touching, looking at private parts, and showing of sexual pictures." The only difference between them is that level 4 is high incidence and level 5 is low
incidence.

Cross Section and Flow

The NIS/NSYC surveys ask each participant inmate whether he or she
has been a victim of sexual abuse during the previous 12 months. If any
inmate has not been in incarceration for the whole 12 months prior to
taking the survey, his or her response necessarily covers only the period
that he or she has actually been in incarceration.

In the 2008–2009 survey of adult prisons and jails, the federal prison
inmates who participated in the survey had been incarcerated for an
average period of 9 of the 12 months prior to the interview. For state
prison inmates, the period was 7.9 months. For jail inmates, it was only
3.4 months.[43] And during the prior 12-month period preceding the survey, other inmates had of course been released from incarceration or
transferred to other facilities, so were not covered by the survey at all.
The Department of Justice explains the problems that result:

[T]he BJS inmate and youth surveys capture data only from a sampling of inmates who happen to be in the facility on the days the surveys are administered,
missing inmates who may have been in the facility during the twelve-month
period covered by the surveys but who were released or transferred before the
dates of the surveys. Put otherwise, the surveys take a cross-section, or snap-
shot, view of the prevalence of prison rape, without accounting for the flow of
inmates through a facility over the period covered by the study.
    This is a particular problem in jails and lockups, where many inmates remain
for very short durations. . . . The problem is less pronounced, but not negligible,
in prisons.

The Department of Justice accordingly concludes: "It would thus appear
inappropriate to rely on the figures from the BJS report without a flow adjustment, for that would under-report the baseline prevalence. We asked
BJS to provide estimates based on its survey data to take into account the
flow of prisoners, so that the baseline figures account for all inmates in
prisons, jails, and juvenile facilities during the reporting period."[44]

The BJS provided the Department of Justice with estimates taking flow into account for the single 12-month period of 2008, for both adult inmates and juveniles in juvenile facilities. These are the estimates that the RIA uses for its assessment of the prevalence of sexual abuse in incarceration, discussed later in this chapter.[45]

Modifying Factors

As noted earlier in this chapter, the RIA recognizes that, despite the precautions taken by the BJS in the NIS and NSYC, there can still be underreporting of sexual abuse and also false reporting of sexual abuse. Accordingly, the RIA introduces modifying factors into its assessments to compensate for these possibilities. It also introduces a modifying factor into its assessments to take into account that juveniles held in adult facilities are excluded from these surveys.[46]

However, there is no sure way to compensate for underreporting and false reporting. Because of this, the RIA provides three different assessments of the prevalence of sexual abuse in incarceration that take different approaches to dealing with underreporting and false reporting. It calls the first of these its *principal* assessment. This simply gives the data from the NIS/NSYC without any adjustment for underreporting or false reporting.

The RIA calls the second of its assessments its *adjusted* assessment. For this, it increases the count of reports of sexual abuse in each category by 15 percent, as a conservative approach to accounting for a share of the likely underreporting.

To account for false reporting, the RIA-adjusted assessment draws on the BJS surveys of sexual abuse reported by correctional authorities (SSV). Recall that correctional authorities provide information in these surveys regarding the results of their investigations into allegations of sexual abuse and that an allegation is classified as unfounded if the investigation determined that the alleged incident did not occur. The SSV provides information on the percentage of various categories of allegations of sexual abuse that are classified as unfounded. The RIA uses these percentages to reduce the count of reports of sexual abuse from the NIS/NSYC.[47]

Finally, the RIA presents its *lower-bound* assessment. For this, it increases the count of reports of sexual abuse in each category by a mere 5 percent, as an extremely conservative approach to accounting for a share of the likely underreporting. It also uses the percentages of unfounded allegations to reduce the count of reports of sexual abuse from the NIS/NSYC but does so in a purposefully unsophisticated way that sharply reduces the count.[48]

The RIA Assessments of the Prevalence of
Sexual Abuse in Incarceration

The lowest RIA assessments of the prevalence of sexual abuse in incarceration are its lower-bound assessments.[49] According to these, within a single year at least 70,500 inmates of adult prisons, 69,200 inmates of adult jails, and 9,500 juveniles in juvenile facilities suffer sexual abuse. In total, the lower-bound estimate is that at least 149,200 individuals suffer sexual abuse in incarceration within a single year. Since the RIA lower-bound prevalence assessments are drastically conservative, the actual number is surely substantially higher.

According to these lower-bound assessments, 55,400 individuals suffer level 1 sexual abuse—essentially, violent or repeated rape—within a single year. These comprise 25,600 inmates of adult prisons, 26,000 inmates of adult jails, and 3,800 juveniles in juvenile facilities. Again, the actual numbers are surely substantially higher than these drastically conservative lower-bound estimates.

Overall, the highest RIA assessments of the prevalence of sexual abuse in incarceration are its principal assessments. According to these, within a single year, at least 89,700 inmates of adult prisons, 109,200 inmates of adult jails, and 10,600 juveniles in juvenile facilities suffer sexual abuse. In total, this estimate is that at least 209,400 individuals (allowing for rounding errors) suffer sexual abuse in incarceration within a single year.

According to these principal assessments, 82,800 individuals suffer level 1 sexual abuse within a single year. These comprise 32,900 inmates of adult prisons, 45,600 inmates of adult jails, and 4,300 juveniles in juvenile facilities.

In sum, the number of individuals who suffer sexual abuse in incarceration in each single year is at least 149,200 and is probably substantially more than this. It may well be as high as 209,400. In fact, since this assessment is also based on very conservative estimates, the total number may be yet higher. The number of individuals who are violently or repeatedly raped is at least 55,400 and may well be as high as 82,800 or even more.

Chapter 3

Recent Developments

It is fair to acknowledge that some enlightened corrections administrators have for many years succeeded in curbing sexual abuse in their facilities. In 2001, even before PREA was enacted, Cahill explained:

I invite you to look at what Sheriff [Michael] Hennessey has done in San Francisco. For more than 20 years, he has had a protocol—the San Francisco protocol—designed specifically to reduce inmate rape. And it works. Rape in the San Francisco jail is a rare occurrence. He has designed the jail to increase visibility. He has trained the staff to be more vigilant, he separates the obviously nonviolent from the obvious predators. Male or female nurses interview each prisoner to see if they can handle themselves or if they're vulnerable and then assign them accordingly. I've seen it myself—from the inside. I've been a guest there a few times over the years for my civil disobedience.[1]

Hennessey served as San Francisco sheriff for thirty-two years until 2012. Administrators of this quality were rare until a few years ago.

In recent years there is evidence of positive developments in a number of corrections institutions across the nation. A 2008 report for the Department of Justice, jointly produced by staff of the Urban Institute and the Association of State Correctional Administrators, recognizes that achieving a continuing substantial reduction in sexual abuse of inmates depends on a commitment to cultural change at the most senior levels of correctional administration. Cultural change needs to be implemented with "strong, consistent leadership from the senior levels" of corrections staff and to be coupled with and supported by "policies that include staff training, investigation procedures, documentation procedures, victim services and prevention efforts."[2] Some corrections institutions have made these changes and as a result appear to have succeeded in virtually eliminating sexual abuse of their inmates.

Yet in many other corrections institutions there is no evidence of improvement or even of any awareness of the need for improvement. A common theme in these institutions is "the unwillingness of agency staff and correctional officers to change their attitudes and behaviors."[3]

In addition, there are negative developments. In particular, a number of correctional authorities have claimed that measures to substantially reduce sexual abuse would be too expensive or have simply denied the existence of sexual abuse in incarceration. A few academic writers have also relied on deeply flawed studies to deny that sexual abuse is at all prevalent in incarceration, as discussed later in this chapter.

POSITIVE DEVELOPMENTS IN SOME FACILITIES

From around 2007, signs have appeared that some jurisdictions and some officials are taking action against sexual abuse in incarceration. In that year, David Kaiser, president of Just Detention International (JDI), was able to note: "In facilities where the chief official cares about it, and ensures that his or her subordinates take it seriously, rates of sexual abuse go down dramatically." In 2009, Michela Bowman, then a project director for the prestigious Vera Institute for Justice, was quoted as saying that she has seen substantial attitude changes about prison rape within prisons themselves; that since enactment of PREA more grants have gone out and more programs have been initiated that target rape culture within facilities; and that in her frequent visits to prisons and jails she hears how facilities are giving a great deal of attention to the issue.[4]

Among the most positive developments has been a close collaboration between the Oregon Department of Corrections and JDI. In a jointly written 2009 newspaper article, Max Williams, director of the Oregon Department of Corrections, and Lovisa Stannow, executive director of JDI, describe a partnership between the two organizations in which they work together to identify strengths and weaknesses in the policies of the Department of Corrections, as well as in day-to-day practices at three Oregon prisons. The two authors detail concrete improvements that have resulted from their partnership.[5]

Positive developments of this kind are noted in the June 2009 report of the National Prison Rape Elimination Commission (NPREC):

[C]orrections leaders and their staff have developed and implemented policies and practices to begin to prevent sexual abuse and also to better respond to victims and hold perpetrators accountable when prevention fails. They have been aided by a range of robust Federal initiatives, support from professional corrections associations, and advocates who have vocally condemned sexual abuse in confinement. The landscape is changing. Training curricula for corrections staff across the country now include information about sexual abuse in confinement and how to prevent it.[6]

A 2011 report from JDI similarly describes cooperation with corrections officials over several years. This cooperation "has helped establish pilot programs at several prisons and has trained officials nationwide in sexual abuse awareness." The programs have entailed "bringing community rape crisis counselors into prisons and training inmates as peer educators on the Prison Rape Elimination Act." Jim Gondles, who has been executive director of the American Correctional Association for more than twenty years, acknowledges the need for this cooperation: "Working with JDI sometimes makes me want to pull my hair out—the little hair I have left—but it's still worth it. . . . We need to collaborate with advocates to make our prisons as safe as possible."[7] These are vital, positive steps in combating sexual abuse in incarceration.

LACK OF CHANGE IN MANY FACILITIES

In contrast to the facilities that are showing considerable success in combating sexual abuse, many incarceration facilities show no positive developments. They remain rife with sexual abuse and are resistant to change. A facility that illustrates what is still very wrong in many of America's incarceration facilities is Orleans Parish Prison (OPP) in Louisiana.

OPP is in fact a complex of six incarceration facilities that together hold about 2,500 inmates in a range of different categories. Some of the inmates are serving long terms of imprisonment for major felonies; others are serving short sentences for misdemeanors; yet others are being held before trial. Women inmates are held in a facility within the complex that also holds male inmates. Because of its range of categories of inmates, OPP has some characteristics of a prison and some of a jail. But because it is operated under the local control of a sheriff rather than by a state authority, it is classified as a jail.

In 2008, OPP was the subject of an investigation by the Civil Rights Division of the Department of Justice for suspected violations of the constitutional rights of inmates. The findings of that investigation were published in 2009 in the form of a letter from the attorney general to the sheriff responsible for OPP, cataloging a range of violations of the constitutional rights of inmates.[8]

In any incarceration facility, the most immediate safeguard needed as soon as an inmate arrives at the facility is an adequate classification system for assigning inmates to the appropriate housing and level of supervision. The Department of Justice found this to be wholly lacking at OPP: "The current classification system does not consider an inmate's prior convictions, prior assaultive behavior, or true potential for violence. . . . Under this system, there is very little to safeguard against housing predatory inmates with vulnerable inmates. Not surprisingly, we found a disturbingly high number of assaultive incidents in the multiple-occupancy cells."[9]

The Department of Justice also found inadequate staffing levels at OPP: "OPP operates its facility without a staffing plan or analysis to establish the minimum number of security staff needed to safely manage OPP's population. . . . We found several instances where staff failed to conduct daily rounds . . . and one officer had to monitor and supervise an entire floor for extended periods. During our review, we found the most densely populated facility . . . at OPP also was the most understaffed, which likely explains the high incidence of violence."[10]

In addition, a number of members of staff inflicted violence on inmates. A typical incident that the findings letter reports is: "While [E.E. was] lying asleep in his bed, two officers entered E.E.'s cell and beat him for nearly 10 minutes, before leaving the cell. E.E. sustained two black eyes and bruises on his upper, middle, and lower back." This incident also demonstrates the near impunity enjoyed by staff. After an officer who was not involved observed E.E.'s injuries and reported them, OPP conducted an investigation that "sustained allegations of abuse and recommended that both officers be suspended for 14 days."[11]

The Department of Justice findings letter demanded that OPP implement a range of remedial measures to address these concerns.[12]

The Department of Justice report did not focus specifically on sexual abuse, but the BJS 2008–2009 report on sexual abuse reported by inmates distinguishes OPP as having a particularly high rate of sexual abuse. Because of this, OPP was the subject of public hearings in September 2011 under the auspices of the Review Panel on Prison Rape, a body set up under PREA (see chapter 9).

Elizabeth Cumming, a New Orleans civil rights attorney with years of experience working on behalf of OPP inmates, gave sworn testimony before the panel regarding the causes of "the rampant sexual assault and violence levels we see at the jail."[13] She attested that "nothing has changed" in the three years since the Department of Justice conducted its investigation. She testified to continuing grossly inadequate staffing levels, as well as the continuing lack of an appropriate system for classifying and housing inmates that would safeguard vulnerable inmates.

Cumming also testified to an "essentially nonexistent" grievance system for reporting any kind of unsafe conditions, threats, or abuse: "When rapes do occur, the failures of the grievance system and the lack of staff supervision can mean that the rape will go unreported for days, even when the survivor is looking for a way to report the rape or to be moved to protective custody." In sum, Cumming testified to conditions that "all create a hostile environment for survivors of sexual assaults and perpetuate a culture in which sexual assault is accepted as a necessary part of incarceration."

STASIS OVERALL

The overall level of sexual abuse in incarceration nationwide appears to be little changed. At the September 2011 public hearings by the Review Panel on Prison Rape, the chair asked Beck the following question regarding developments since enactment of PREA in 2003: "Does your [BJS] data suggest that we're on a path to eliminate sexual misconduct in correctional facilities? Can you quantify what's happened at least between 2003 and 2011? Do correctional facilities across the country really get it?"

Beck's response in his sworn testimony was: "There is no indication that there's been a reduction in sexual victimization in prisons and jails since the passage of the Act. In fact, you know, we have stability in the levels of victimization, and we have stability in the kinds of victimizations being reported through self reports."[14]

NEGATIVE DEVELOPMENTS

A troubling recent negative development is that a number of correctional authorities and a few academic writers have taken to blatantly denying that sexual abuse is prevalent in incarceration in America. A 2009 book, *The Myth of Prison Rape*, by the academics Mark Fleisher and Jessie Krienert has been prominent in this denial.

Fleisher, an anthropologist, and Krienert, a sociologist, declare that they are interested only in the cultural idea of rape inside American prisons and not in the prevalence of rape. They report that inmates treat rape as not a matter of concern:

Inmates unequivocally stated that they did not worry about rape in prison. . . . Inmates we talked to resoundingly reported that prison was a safe place. . . . Inmates reported little reason to worry about or fear a physical or sexual attack inside the walls. . . . Inmates said that they don't fear or worry about rape because it is unlikely to occur inside prison. . . .

Inmate narratives provide strong verbal support for the low levels of reported worry or fear about rape inside prison. In strong opposition to popular culture and media-infused beliefs about violent prison sexual assault, inmates perceive prison as a place relatively free of worry.

On this basis, the authors claim that their work demonstrates that prison rape is uncommon: "When all interviews were analyzed we corroborated . . . [an earlier researcher's] finding that there was no epidemic of prison rape."[15]

Of course, there is now overwhelming independent evidence that the Fleisher and Krienert study reaches false and misleading conclusions. The series of BJS reports have made it clear that many incarceration facilities throughout America are in fact far from safe, and the discussion earlier in this chapter shows that a number of correctional authorities have recognized this. It is plain from the many accounts of continuing suffering from violent sexual abuse that a substantial number of inmates do worry about or fear a physical or sexual attack (see chapter 4). Accordingly, the only interesting question about the Fleisher and Krienert study is why the inmates whom they interviewed chose to say that they had no such worries or concerns.

The answer to this question is plain in the research design and methodology of the Fleisher and Krienert study. The authors inform: "Once inmates gave us their written consent to interview, they were explicitly warned to withhold information about previous and future institution rule violations and warned that prior or future incidents of violence of any type mentioned in the interview would be reported to the warden's office."[16]

This astounding warning guaranteed that no inmate would reveal anything about rape or other form of actual or threatened sexual abuse. It is well established—and was already well established at the time of the Fleisher and Krienert study—that surveys of inmates on the subject of sexual abuse are essentially worthless unless they ensure confidentiality and anonymity (see chapters 1 and 2). Fleisher and Krienert adopted a study methodology that ensured the very opposite of confidentiality and anonymity. This sufficiently explains the outcome of their deeply flawed study.

Note that, in any event, the Fleisher and Krienert study is too small to have any present-day significance. It interviewed a total of 564 inmates. This should be compared with the BJS surveys as Beck describes them in his sworn testimony before the Review Panel on Prison Rape: "We've perhaps had as many as 300 staff members on this collecting data nationwide. . . . We have completed two rounds of data collection in adult prisons and jails, one round in juvenile facilities. And so what this [current report] represents is the data collection that we conducted between October 2008 and December 2009 in 286 jails. We completed roughly 45,000 interviews in these 286 jails."[17]

The Department of Justice RIA, discussed in chapter 2, wholly ignores the work of Fleisher and Krienert in its assessment of the prevalence of sexual abuse in incarceration. This is appropriate.

Part II

The Cost of Sexual Abuse in Incarceration

Chapter 4

The Suffering of Victims

This chapter considers the cost of sexual abuse in incarceration in terms of the suffering that it generates. It presents accounts by victims and survivors of the violation that they have suffered and of the physical and psychological consequences of that violation. It also includes accounts by witnesses of sexual abuse.

These accounts are of events both before and after PREA was enacted. PREA has not changed the nature of sexual abuse in incarceration, so each of these accounts portrays the suffering of victims at the present day.

The words of victims and witnesses have not been expurgated. The approach that Davis took in regard to his 1968 investigation of the Philadelphia system of incarceration, discussed in chapter 1, remains appropriate. Davis wrote: "In an early draft of our report, an attempt was made to couch this illustrative material in sociological, medical, and legal terminology less offensive than the raw, ugly language used by the witness[es] and victims. This approach was abandoned. The incidents are raw and ugly. Any attempt to prettify them would be hypocrisy." Courts agree that the unexpurgated language must be used in these cases.[1]

WHO THE VICTIMS ARE

It is important to recognize that any inmate can become a victim of sexual abuse. The slightest lapse can result in victimization. For example, the words of an inmate describe the culture of men's incarceration facilities: "You can't show any fear, they pick up on that. You gotta show strength. . . . Never look down, like you're afraid to look 'em in the eye. . . . You gotta be a man all the time, and a man according to the standards in here." The NPREC report recognized the truth of this assessment.[2]

However, inmates with certain characteristics are more vulnerable to sexual abuse than others. Donaldson explains: "Victims are more likely to be young, small, non-violent, first offenders, middle-class, not 'street-wise,' obviously homosexual, not gang-affiliated, not part of the dominant ethnic group in that jail, without major fighting experience, and held in big-city jails. The more of these factors apply, the more likely the victimization. If most apply, rape becomes a probability."[3]

The 2009 report of the NPREC describes the characteristic vulnerability of a young, small inmate:

Rodney [Hulin] was 16 years old . . . and small even for his age, weighing about 125 pounds and standing just 5'2" tall. He had been convicted of second-degree arson with property damage totaling less than $500 as a result of setting a neighborhood dumpster on fire, and he had been sentenced to 8 years in adult prison. . . . [T]he first rape occurred almost immediately. . . . Despite Rodney's pleas to be moved out of the general population, after receiving medical treatment he was returned to the same unit where he had been raped.[4]

Boys are vulnerable, but girls are even more so. As the NPREC report explains, among youthful inmates "[s]imply being female is a risk factor. Girls are disproportionately represented among sexual abuse victims. . . . And they are much more at risk of abuse by staff than by their peers."[5]

Emotional vulnerability increases the risk yet further. A clinical psychologist with extensive experience working with incarcerated women reported that "officers often target 'like a radar' women with histories of sexual or physical abuse or prisoners in emotionally vulnerable positions, such as those who lack support from family or friends, who are alienated or isolated by other prisoners or staff, and younger women who are incarcerated for the first time." An investigation by the Department of Justice Office of the Inspector General into sexual abuse of inmates in federal incarceration "found that guards took advantage of vulnerable or psychologically weak inmates to have sex with them. Such inmates included those who had drug addictions, who previously were physically or sexually abused, who had mental health issues, who had little experience in the criminal justice system, who were awaiting deportation, or who had previously engaged in prostitution."[6]

The NPREC report recognizes two further categories of persons particularly vulnerable to sexual abuse in incarceration. "Individuals with severe developmental disabilities are at especially high risk of being sexually abused. Their naivety, tendency to misinterpret social cues, and desire to fit in make many developmentally disabled individuals vulnerable to manipulation and control by others."[7]

The other category is male-to-female transgender individuals: "most male-to-female transgender individuals who are incarcerated are placed in men's prisons, even if they have undergone surgery or hormone therapies to develop overtly feminine traits. Their obvious gender nonconformity puts them at extremely high risk for abuse." Certainly, prison officials are aware of this, and in fact the NPREC report notes a case of a male-to-female transgender individual being "deliberately placed in a cell with a convicted sex offender to be raped."[8]

SURVIVOR ACCOUNTS OF SEXUAL ABUSE

The accounts given here are a tiny selection from the range of available testimony.

Donaldson, a navy veteran and Quaker peace activist, was one of the first victims of rape in incarceration to speak publicly about what he had suffered. In 1973 he was arrested for trespassing at a pray-in on the White House lawn. He spent two days and nights in a Washington, DC, jail, during which he was gang-raped about sixty times.[9]

Marilyn Shirley was convicted of a drug offense and incarcerated in a federal prison for women in need of specialized medical and mental health services. She testified at public hearings before the NPREC in 2005, and an account of her testimony appears in the NPREC report:

One night in March 2000, a senior prison official, who was the only officer on duty at the time, awakened Shirley. He ordered her from her room and took her to the officers' station. There, he made a call asking for a signal if the supervisor approached the camp. After he hung up the phone, he began kissing and groping Shirley and pushed her into a supply room. . . . As she resisted, he became increasingly brutal, throwing her against the wall and slamming her head against it repeatedly. He then violently raped her, all the while warning that if she ever talked about it, no one would believe her. The assault ended only when the officer received a signal over the radio that someone was approaching. . . . She was terrified about what would happen if she reported the assault, only informing the camp administrator on the day of her release months later.[10]

In the Davis investigation report, "[a] witness describes the ordeal of William McNichol, 24 years old and mentally disturbed":

I looked up a couple of times. They had the kid on the floor. About 12 fellows took turns with him. This went on for about two hours.

After this he came back to his bed and he was crying and he stated that "They all took turns on me." He laid there for about 20 minutes and Cheyenne came over to the kid's bed and pulled his pants down and got on top of him and raped him again. When he got done Horse did it again and then about four or five others got on him. While one of the guys was on him, raping him, Horse came over and said, "Open your mouth and suck on this and don't bite it." He then put his penis in his mouth and made him suck on it. The kid was hollering that he was gagging and Horse stated, "you better not bite it or I will kick your teeth out."[11]

A California prison doctor was accused of sexually abusing several women inmates. The attorney for one of the inmates reports the inmate's medical visit to this doctor for a lump on her neck: "The doctor conducted a vaginal examination and, according to the prisoner, made remarks about how tight she was and how long it had been since she had sexual intercourse. A medical assistant was present during the exam, but she reportedly moved behind a screen and did nothing to stop the doctor. The prisoner stated that the doctor then 'played with her' and touched her in a sexual way. He never examined the lump on her neck."[12]

A typical letter to Human Rights Watch from a male inmate victim of repeated gang rapes reads:

[I have been] raped so many times I have no more feelings physically. I have been raped by up to 5 black men and two white men at a time. I've had knifes at my head and throat. I had fought and been beat so hard that I didn't ever think I'd see straight again. . . . I've requested protective custody only to be denied. . . . I have great difficulty raising food to my mouth from shaking after nightmares or thinking to hard on all this. . . . I've laid down without physical fight to be sodomized. To prevent so much damage in struggles, ripping and tearing. Though in not fighting, it caused my heart and spirit to be raped as well.[13]

Hope Hernandez was incarcerated in Washington, DC, for eight months before being eventually sentenced only to probation:

They put me on some medications. I had no idea what they were or what they would do to me. I ended up sleeping a lot and I was kind of in a daze. I was wearing a paper jumpsuit that was really just a piece of gauze with a zipper.

I needed a shower . . . but they weren't letting me out of my cell. Every time a new guard would come on shift, I would ask for a shower. I was promised a shower by guard after guard, but I never got one.

One night, in the middle of the night, this guard came into my cell and said I could go take a shower. He had a towel and a fresh paper jumpsuit and some shampoo. He led me to a room with locked doors that had a separate bathroom and a shower. He waited out in the hallway. . . . I got undressed and into the shower, and he came in. The next thing I knew he was standing in the shower stall and was engaging in intercourse with me. He pulled down his pants and turned off the shower and raped me. I couldn't do anything. It was like I was on a 30-second delay. I was heavily medicated and it was 2:30 or 3:00 in the morning. He had awoken me from a dead sleep.[14]

A female corrections officer in a Texas state prison repeatedly coerced Ivory Mitchell to perform oral sex on her by threatening him that "if he did not do what she demanded, she would report him for inappropriately touching her."[15]

Garrett Cunningham was raped in the prison laundry. His assailant was the corrections officer charged with supervising his work:

[T]he officer assaulted Cunningham as he finished his job in the prison's laundry, knocking him to the floor. The officer was literally twice his weight and could have easily overpowered him, but he handcuffed Cunningham and then violently raped him. Cunningham testified that, "When I screamed from the terrible pain, [the officer] told me to shut up. . . . After it was over, I was dazed. He took me to the shower in handcuffs, turned on the water and put me under it. I was crying under the shower and saw blood running down my legs."[16]

Amanda Hall was coerced into sexual activity with corrections officer Sergeant Leshawn Terrell. When she tried to refuse, Terrell became violent:

He demanded that she get on her knees and perform oral sex, and shoved his penis in her mouth. Forcing her to get up from her knees and bend over, he then anally raped her, telling her as he did so, "that's my pussy; you don't ever tell me no." Terrell's "slamming himself into" her was sufficiently violent that the rape tore Hall's rectum. . . . After the rape, Terrell left a bleeding Hall on the floor . . . and told her to "go clean [her]self up."[17]

Jesús Manuel Calderón-Ortiz, a minor, was awaiting trial in a state prison in Puerto Rico:

This institution did not take measures to separate and house inmates according to their safety needs and the security risks they posed. Calderón's housing unit consisted of a corridor of two-prisoner cells. One housing officer was assigned to Calderón's building on the day of the incident, and he remained at or near the "control," which is a separate enclosed area at the entrance to the housing unit. From this location, the officer could not supervise the inmates inside the cells. The only way he could do so was by patrolling the walkway or corridor. The officer on duty that day did not engage in such a patrol.

On the day of the incident, Calderón was lying on his bed inside his cell when four inmates from his housing unit approached him. They threw a blanket over his face, held him by force, and threatened to kill him if he said anything. They proceeded to sodomize him for approximately a half an hour to an hour. No officer intervened during the attack. After the attack, Calderón could not move and remained in his bed until he was taken to the hospital.

The charges against Calderón were later dismissed.[18]

Chapter 1 noted the case of Lucas, who "made an official complaint regarding the practice of allowing male inmates into her cell in the middle of the night. . . . [Her] cell door was opened while she was asleep and three men entered her cell, and restrained and handcuffed her from behind. She was then brutally beaten, raped, and sodomized."

Frank Mendoza testified at a Just Detention International (JDI) congressional briefing: "I lost my job at a law firm and was arrested for public drunkenness. . . . I had never been arrested before. I was scared of other inmates—I did not know at the time that I had more reason to fear the Los Angeles jail staff. The abusive officer entered my cell, beat me, and raped me."[19]

The case of Kerry Max Cook is well known. Cook was convicted of murder in Texas in proceedings tainted by the misconduct of police, prosecutor, and state forensic experts. DNA evidence later made available strongly indicates his innocence. He was eventually released after twenty years' incarceration, many of them spent on death row. Other inmates had sexually abused him from the outset: "After suffering repeat assault for years and experiencing a state of gender confusion and emotional trauma, Kerry cut off his penis as instructed by his abusers. He also cut open his scrotum and removed his testes. . . . One of his rapists carved the words 'good pussy' across his backside with a knife."[20]

Jackie Tates is a transgender woman incarcerated in a men's facility:

In Sacramento, the deputies were letting inmates into my cell to have sex with me against my will. The first time it happened, I tried to tell the inmate no. He showed me some autopsy photos. He said, "This is what happens to people who fuck with me."

I ended up submitting. I did what he told me to do. I orally copulated him, and he sodomized me. Thirty or forty minutes later, the deputy came onto the speaker and asked him if he was done. He said, "I'm done." The door clicked and let him out.

They must have let 12 or 14 inmates into my cell to have sex. One day, I said to a deputy, "If you're going to make me do this, could I at least have some condoms so I don't get AIDS?" He told me to shut the fuck up. The next day, he came in and threw 15 condoms at me. . . .

In September 2005, I was put into a "protective custody" tank with five or six other inmates. Two of them jumped me right away. They both made me suck them off. The deputy walked by and saw me fighting and struggling with them, but he didn't do anything.

The next day, the deputy made jokes about it. He asked me how much I charge for that.[21]

At Glades Correctional Institution, a Florida prison for men, "staff permitted regular, unsupervised showings of hard-core pornographic movies" during which "[s]ounds of inmates screaming and crying could be heard."[22]

Robin McArdle reports: "There was a deputy who used to sell drugs to the girls and then threaten to go to the parole board if they didn't suck his dick. He knew if you were dirty [using drugs], and if he turned you in, you would have to spend another year in prison."

She also recounts how she coped with sexual abuse by a corrections officer:

For me, being sexually abused as a child made me an easy target. It is in our file, and the guards can see that. We are easy targets because we learn from a young age to keep our mouths shut. There are repercussions to telling. It is brainwashed into us. It was almost the norm because of how I grew up. I just felt like "Well, here comes another one." It's hard to explain it unless you have been there. I have known it all my life since I was six years old. I just reverted back to being totally numb.[23]

INADEQUATE MEDICAL TREATMENT OF VICTIMS

Victims of rape and any violent sexual abuse need emergency and follow-up medical care. They may be physically injured in ways that are not apparent on visual inspection, so that proper medical care may require advanced visualization techniques using special scopes. Proper medical care may also require prophylactic drug therapies to prevent sexually transmitted diseases or pregnancy. Victims also generally require emotional support, including counseling and psychiatric support.[24]

Unfortunately, the care that victims of rape or other violent sexual abuse in incarceration actually receive does not meet these requirements. In fact, the great majority of victims receive no adequate care of any kind. In 2003, Congress declared in its PREA findings that "inmate victims often receive inadequate treatment for the severe physical and psychological effects of sexual assault—if they receive treatment at all."[25] A decade later, this remains true throughout most of America.

In part, this is simply one aspect of the general neglect of the medical and mental health needs of inmates throughout the American system of incarceration. In the key 2011 case of *Brown v Plata*, the Supreme Court recognizes the systemic inadequacy of the medical and mental health care provided to inmates. This case concerned California prisons, but there are similar systemic inadequacies in prison systems throughout America. The situation in jails appears to be even worse.[26]

The Supreme Court does not suggest that inmates are entitled to better care than the many Americans outside prison who lack adequate medical or mental health care. As a federal court explained earlier in the litigation that culminated in *Brown v Plata*, only a minimal standard is required: "The United States Constitution does not require that the state provide its inmates with state-of-the-art medical and mental health care, nor does it require that prison conditions be comfortable. California must simply provide care consistent with the minimal civilized measure of life's necessities."[27]

The Supreme Court explains this minimal standard: "As a consequence of their own actions, prisoners may be deprived of rights that are fundamental to liberty. Yet . . . [p]risoners retain the essence of human dignity inherent in all persons. . . . A prison that deprives prisoners of basic sustenance, including adequate medical care, is incompatible with the concept of human dignity and has no place in civilized society."[28] The court opinion upholds the findings of the federal trial courts that the California system falls dreadfully short of meeting even these minimal standards. Many of the systems of incarceration throughout America also fall dreadfully short.

The kind of conditions that a federal trial court in the litigation found were: "Inmates are forced to wait months or years for medically necessary appointments and examinations, and many receive inadequate medical care in substandard facilities that lack the medical equipment required to conduct routine examinations or afford essential medical treatment. Seriously mentally ill inmates languish in horrific conditions without access to necessary mental health care." Another trial court observed: "Many clinics did not meet basic sanitation standards. Exam tables and counter tops, where prisoners with infections such as Methicillin-Resistant Staph Aureus (MRSA) and other communicable diseases are treated, were not routinely disinfected or sanitized. Many medical facilities required fundamental repairs, installation of adequate lighting and such basic sanitary facilities as sinks for hand-washing."[29]

A federal court in this litigation also focused on the generally poor standard of medical staff in incarceration facilities. "Many of the . . . physicians have prior criminal charges, have had privileges revoked from hospitals, or have mental health related problems. . . . The Court Experts testified that the care provided by such doctors repeatedly harms prisoner patients. The Court finds that the incompetence and indifference of these . . . physicians has directly resulted in an unacceptably high rate of patient death and morbidity." This court described a number of incidents of lack of proper treatment, or lack of any treatment, or cruel treatment, each of which resulted in severe harm to inmates.[30]

A crucial way in which states have ensured that inmates receive insufficient medical and mental health care is to charge them for care at a level that they cannot pay. The NPREC report explains: "In the majority of States, legislatures have passed laws authorizing correctional agencies to charge prisoners for medical care—fees . . . that are beyond the means of many prisoners." It adds: "Correctional health care is seriously underfunded everywhere."[31]

It is in this context that the state of California enacted the Sexual Abuse in Detention Elimination Act (SADEA) in 2005. This act declares: "Thoughtful, confidential standards of physical and mental health care shall be implemented to reduce the impact of sexual abuse on inmates" and goes on to detail a range of fine-sounding specific provisions for treatment.[32] But these are fantasy. Thoughtful, confidential standards of physical and mental health care are conspicuously and notoriously lacking for inmates throughout the American incarceration system, whether they are victims of sexual abuse or not.

A federal court describes the quite typical level of care that Hall received after corrections officer Terrell raped her:

For nearly two years following the rape, Hall suffered pain and bleeding when she defecated. She repeatedly attempted to get medical treatment. . . . For nearly two years, rather than doing an examination to determine the source of her bleeding, the medical staff told Hall to use stool softeners, Milk of Magnesia, or hemorrhoid cream. Finally, after filing this federal lawsuit, Hall did receive a full medical examination, which revealed that she needed surgery to repair her torn rectum.[33]

In fact, inmate victims of sexual abuse may be in a worse situation than other inmates in need of care. They can have no expectation of confidentiality in medical treatment. They may even be required to give the name of the person—inmate or corrections officer—who perpetrated the abuse as a condition for receiving treatment. As a result, fear of being labeled a "snitch," and consequently being further abused, may effectively prevent inmates even from seeking medical care.

The PREA national standards prohibit medical care of inmate victims of sexual abuse being made contingent on naming the abuser or cooperating with any investigation. But it is not yet clear how far this and other provisions of the PREA national standards will actually be implemented (see chapter 10).

Victims who do seek medical treatment may suffer further abuse from substandard medical staff. Parsell explains in his testimony to the NPREC that because he feared being killed as a "snitch" he did not report being gang-raped by other inmates but found when he later sought treatment for rectal bleeding that everyone knew about the rapes anyway: "The guards knew what had happened. The prison doctors knew as well. When I saw the proctologist for my bleeding, I raised concern about the size of his rectal scope, and his reply was, 'Well, it's not any larger than what's been going up there.'"[34]

FAILURE TO INVESTIGATE SEXUAL ABUSE

It has long been true, and remains true years after enactment of PREA, that correctional authorities fail to investigate many of the cases of sexual abuse that are reported to them. JDI reports regarding the 534 letters it received in 2010 from survivors of sexual violence: "More than half (277) of these survivors stated that they reported the assault to prison officials, but an investigation was undertaken less than half the time (112)." Notably, federal incarceration facilities are no better than the overall average in this respect.[35]

The BJS report on its 2008 survey of former state inmates shows a similar overall pattern nationwide. In 37 percent of reported incidents of inmate-on-inmate sexual abuse, the correctional authorities made no response—that is, they did nothing. In many of the remaining cases there was no investigation. In fact, only 28.5 percent of inmate-on-inmate incidents of sexual abuse were even "written up" (officially recorded) by the correctional authorities. Correctional authorities were more responsive to reported incidents of sexual abuse by staff; they did nothing in only 14.5 percent of incidents. But only 46.3 percent of these incidents were even written up; the majority of these reported incidents could not result in any investigation.[36]

A typical case of a facility doing essentially nothing is that of a Texas inmate referred to as "S.M." who was raped countless times:

[B]ecause of his past assaults, S.M. was aware that proof of rape could be obtained by the use of a rape kit. He desperately wanted the prison authorities to collect evidence of the rape. Early in the morning, when his cellmate left the cell, he reported the rape to a guard, who told him that he would tell the sergeant what had happened. But for several hours, no one came to investigate. When S.M. was released from his cell for lunch, he found a sergeant and reported the rape. The sergeant handcuffed S.M. and left him on the recreation yard for an hour; finally around noon S.M. was brought to the infirmary and examined for rape. He was later informed that the examination showed no evidence of rape.[37]

In a lawsuit brought by inmates against the authorities of a Florida prison, the authorities even conceded the following facts: "Inmates raped Saunders in a small bathroom adjacent to the confinement area; he reported the incident but officials did not investigate and refused his request for a medical examination. . . . Inmates raped Aldred and Durrance in shower areas. Aldred reported the incident to an officer, but there was no investigation." The court found that generally "the procedures for investigating rapes, to the extent such procedures existed, were not followed. . . . [This] created an atmosphere of tolerance of rape . . . where inmates could rape other vulnerable inmates without concern of being detected or deterred."[38]

Mendoza reports the aftermath of being raped by a corrections officer. "When the officer on the next shift saw me naked and bloodied in my cell, he asked what had happened. I told him I was raped and he just told me to get dressed."[39]

Corrections officers may exert pressure on inmate victims of sexual abuse not to lodge a complaint that would require investigation. A typical case is that of Brian Lee Nestor, who was raped by another inmate of a minimum-security federal prison in New Jersey: "Nestor was devastated and in shock and was reluctant to report the rape for fear of retaliation by inmates and staff. When he finally told a lieutenant, the officer told Nestor that if he filed any paperwork or otherwise complained he would be transferred to a prison in the south."[40]

An individual referred to as "S.H." with two previous nonviolent felony convictions was convicted of burglary in Texas in 1994. At the age of twenty-four, he was sentenced to seventy-five years' imprisonment. He fell victim to repeated gang rape:

[S.H.] told a classification counselor that he was considered the "property" of a Hispanic gang, and a few days later the counselor sent a sergeant into the wing to investigate. S.H. told the sergeant what was happening and the sergeant responded that he was lying, then called him a "wimp" for not fighting the gang. The sergeant wanted to call out one of the Hispanic inmates to question him about S.H.'s allegations, an action that S.H. opposed, as he felt it would put his life in danger by branding him as a snitch. The sergeant said that this was the way he conducted investigations, and if S.H. disagreed with his methods, he could ask for the investigation to be dropped. Feeling he had no choice, S.H. dropped the investigation.[41]

In many cases, inmates who try to report sexual abuse are hampered by the unfairly convoluted grievance systems that correctional authorities have implemented. These are discussed in chapter 8.

A frequent consequence of the inadequacy of medical care and the failure to investigate in cases of sexual abuse is that forensic evidence is not collected. An expert explains the basic forensic procedure that ought to be followed in cases of sexual assault: "The collection of forensic evidence is a multistep process that can take 6 or more hours to complete and is best performed by specially trained personnel. The aim is to record the victim's report of the assault, collect and record evidence to support this report, and collect DNA."[42] Plainly, this procedure will rarely be followed in incarceration facilities. As a result, there will often be insufficient evidence for victims to bring a lawsuit or for perpetrators to be prosecuted.

PROTECTION AND PUNISHMENT OF VICTIMS

It has long been true, and remains true years after enactment of PREA, that correctional authorities fail to protect many vulnerable inmates from sexual abuse and many victims from further abuse. A major problem is that in many corrections facilities the general inmate housing is unsafe throughout. In such facilities, the only immediate way to protect an inmate from sexual abuse is to place him or her in "protective custody." But protective custody has severe detriments, "as it results in a loss of services and programs, can brand someone as a victim and/or a snitch, and often leaves the inmate with less access to outside support."[43]

Also, in many institutions protective custody entails isolation or near-isolation in what is known as "segregated housing" for extended periods under appalling conditions. A federal appellate court recounts the quite typical experience of an inmate, Morales, who "had been victimized as a consequence of his diminutive size, immature appearance and bisexual orientation. . . . [T]wo tough male . . . inmates were attempting to coerce [him] . . . by threats into becoming a male prostitute . . . for their economic gain and enjoyment. The head of the jail unit responded to this event by placing Morales in solitary confinement—also known as 'the hole.' "[44]

Many individuals suffer psychological damage from such isolation, particularly individuals who are already traumatized by sexual abuse. For example, in 1999 a federal trial court found the segregation units in the Texas prison system to be "virtual incubators of psychoses-seeding illness in otherwise healthy inmates and exacerbating illness in those already suffering from mental infirmities." Even worse, in some institutions segregation is not wholly secure, so that vulnerable inmates suffer psychological damage together with continuing sexual abuse.[45]

Even when safe alternatives are available, some correctional authorities still isolate vulnerable inmates in segregation. Plainly, this discourages inmates who cannot cope with isolation from expressing fears or filing reports of sexual abuse. JDI reports regarding the unsolicited letters it received in 2010: "Eighty-eight survivors [out of 277 who reported sexual abuse to corrections officers] stated that they were placed in segregation as a result of reporting, more than half of whom (46) were placed there involuntarily." The PREA national standards include provisions restricting the use of segregation when safe alternatives are available, but it is not yet clear how far these provisions will actually be implemented.[46]

The BJS report on its 2008 survey of former state inmates conveys the extent of segregation or isolation of inmates who report having been sexually abused. In 34.3 percent of reported incidents of inmate-on-inmate sexual abuse and 41.2 percent of reported incidents of sexual abuse by staff, the correctional authorities responded by moving the victim to administrative segregation/protective housing. In 24.3 percent of reported incidents of inmate-on-inmate sexual abuse and 35.2 percent of reported incidents of sexual abuse by staff, the correctional authorities responded by confining the victim to his or her cell.[47]

Yet some inmates clearly prefer isolation to the threat or actuality of sexual abuse. But many inmates who seek the protection of segregation are denied it: "Scott Howard was repeatedly raped, assaulted, extorted, and forced into prostitution by a large, notorious white supremacist prison gang while serving time in Colorado. Because he is openly gay, officials blamed Howard for the assaults and refused to protect him. Howard repeatedly requested safe housing but was told that he could enter administrative segregation only if he named the assailants." It is, of course, unlikely that segregation could have protected Howard for long from the retaliation that naming his assailants would invite.[48]

In fact, some inmates take extreme measures to ensure being isolated. "S.M. was only eighteen when he entered Texas prison; he was twenty-one when he was first raped. But from the very beginning predatory inmates targeted him. S.M.'s strategy for avoiding victimization was to violate prison rules—to refuse to shave, to cut his hair, or go to work—so that, as punishment, he would be kept safe in a locked cell. For three years, he managed to protect himself in this way."[49] An inmate who continuously violates rules in this way will receive no credit for good conduct in terms of a reduction of time spent in incarceration.

THE LONG-TERM SUFFERING OF VICTIMS

The subsequent history of some of the victims discussed earlier is known.

Donaldson recalled: "I spent a week in the Veteran's Hospital . . . getting my rectum sewn up." He contracted HIV through rapes in incarceration and died in 1996 at the age of forty-nine from AIDS-related infections. Martel also contracted HIV from rapes in incarceration and died in 2010 at age forty-seven.[50]

Shirley reports:

Now that I am out of prison, I am left with the devastating impacts of the rape. . . . I haven't been able to be intimate with my husband. . . . I have paralyzing panic attacks. I can't even hold my grandbaby because I'm afraid of having a panic attack and dropping her. . . .

I have awful nightmares and sometimes I wet the bed as a result. Sometimes my husband has to come and pull me out of the closet, where I go when I have these attacks. At the request of my therapist, I wear a rubber band around my wrist so that I can "snap" myself back to reality when I have panic attacks. I'm also on five different medications for these conditions. And, although my boss was very understanding about my situation, it got to a point where I could not work anymore. So I am now unable to work.[51]

Hulin hanged himself in his cell, at 17 years of age.[52]

Jackie Tates recalls: "Gay people, transgender people in this jail—they put us in compromising positions. They chain us to 12 inmates and throw us in the back of a van with no supervision. People get dragged into bathrooms. One of my friends got dragged into a bathroom—she walks with a walker now."[53]

Hernandez gave testimony to the NPREC about the lasting effects of being raped in incarceration. "Although it's been eight years, I'm still suffering from the effects of that rape. On the one-year anniversary of this rape, I kept seeing the guard's face over me. . . . I wanted to see something besides his face. . . . [M]y husband has tried to be intimate with me. All I could see was this guard's face flashing back in my mind, and I would become ill."[54]

The NPREC explains the aftermath of sexual abuse in incarceration.[55] Many victims suffer far-reaching, severely detrimental psychological effects that may last for years. Clinical depression and anxiety, sleep disturbances, and eating disorders are common. Many survivors of sexual abuse engage in self-mutilation. Many have suicidal feelings, and a substantial number actually attempt suicide. Some succeed.

There is strong evidence that victims of sexual abuse who suffer such psychological effects are more likely than the general population to develop a range of serious medical conditions. These include cardiovascular disease, ulcers, fibromyalgia, and a weakened immune system.

A number of women inmates raped by male corrections officers have become pregnant. They must either undergo abortion or continue the pregnancy to term, with the attendant risks and complications, physical and emotional, in either case.

There are many physical injuries. As well as injuries to vagina, rectum, and throat directly caused by forced penile penetration, victims suffer bruises, lacerations, broken bones, concussions, knocked-out teeth, and extensive injuries to internal organs.

Victims are exposed to the full range of sexually transmitted diseases. These include chlamydia, gonorrhea, hepatitis, herpes, human papillomavirus, pelvic inflammatory disease, syphilis, and trichomoniasis. They also include HIV and the development of AIDS.

Chapter 5

The Cost to Society at Large

Each year, large numbers of individuals return from incarceration into American society. In 2010, over seven hundred thousand individuals were released from prison. Far more were released from jails, which have a high turnover rate. The BJS estimates that around thirteen million individuals were released from jails in 2010. There is no estimate for the number released from lockups, but since lockups also have a high turnover rate the number is certainly large.[1]

Overall, over 95 percent of incarcerated individuals eventually return into society.[2] It is reasonable to suppose that over 95 percent of those among them who have suffered sexual abuse eventually return into society.

Individuals who have been damaged by sexual abuse in incarceration bring that damage with them when they return into American society. As a result, the damage that sexual abuse in incarceration causes imposes its cost on our society as a whole. This is true of the direct damage caused to the individual victims. These costs can be high. In testimony before the NPREC, Cahill explained:

Can you put a cost on an incident of prison rape? I have. I believe that one day I spent in jail has cost the government and the taxpayers at least $300,000. I've been hospitalized more times than I can count and I didn't pay for those hospitalizations, the tax payers paid. My career as a journalist and photographer was completely derailed, which means lost income tax and spending power. For the past two decades, I've received a non-service-connected security pension from the Veterans' Administration at a cost of about $200,000 in connection with the only major trauma I've ever suffered, the rape.[3]

In addition, there are further detrimental effects on the broader society. The findings of Congress in enacting PREA summarize some of these further effects:

Prison rape undermines the public health by contributing to the spread of [HIV and AIDS]. . . . Prison rape endangers the public safety by making brutalized inmates more likely to commit crimes when they are released. . . . Victims of prison rape suffer severe physical and psychological effects that hinder their ability to integrate into the community and maintain stable employment upon their release from prison. They are thus more likely to become homeless and/or require government assistance.[4]

This chapter discusses the various costs to society of sexual abuse in incarceration. Some of these costs can be quantified in monetary terms, but others are unquantifiable.

THE QUANTIFIABLE COSTS OF SEXUAL ABUSE IN INCARCERATION

PREA directs the attorney general to promulgate national standards for combating sexual abuse in incarceration (see part IV). As part of the process, the Department of Justice was required to produce a regulatory impact assessment setting out the costs and benefits of its proposed standards. This is the RIA that chapter 2 of this book has already referred to.

The RIA attempts to quantify in monetary terms the cost to society of sexual abuse in incarceration, to the extent that this is possible. Plainly, as the RIA itself recognizes, the result can be no more than an imperfect estimate of the monetary cost of some aspects of the harm that this sexual abuse generates. But, despite this, the RIA was obliged to make the best possible estimate.

In general, there are two quite different methodologies used to ascribe a monetary cost to acts that cause harm, including both crimes and civil torts. One is an ex post model of inquiry, the other is an ex ante model. The ex post model is the so-called willingness-to-accept (WTA) model. The approach of the WTA model is to ascribe a monetary value to each of a range of harms that a crime or civil tort has generated and then to assess the total cost as the sum of the values ascribed to the various factors.[5]

The WTA model is used in court verdicts and settlements to place a monetary value on the harm suffered by victims of crimes and torts.

It will normally include a range of factors that can be reasonably well computed, such as actual and prospective expenses for medical and mental health care. It will also normally include factors that are not so readily computed but for which American society has developed generally accepted valuations. These factors include pain and suffering and, more broadly, diminution in quality of life of the victim.

Because this range of factors focuses on compensating the victim for the harm that he or she has suffered, the WTA model is often known as the victim compensation model. But in fact this model can incorporate broader social costs of crimes and torts as well as victim compensation costs. For example, when the harm is the result of crime, the WTA model can incorporate the cost of investigating and prosecuting the crime. When a perpetrator is convicted, the WTA model can include the cost to society of incarcerating him and also his lost employment income.

The ex ante model is the so-called willingness-to-pay (WTP) model. The WTP model has been widely used to quantify in monetary terms social costs and benefits that do not have a clear market value, particularly environmental costs and benefits. The approach of this assessment model is to use carefully designed surveys to determine how much people would be willing to pay to obtain a benefit or to avoid loss of a benefit. In the context of surveys regarding how much people would be willing to pay to avoid crime, the WTP model arguably manages to incorporate the broad value that people place on living in a society with less crime.

Both the WTA and the WTP models are widely used in the social sciences. When both models are applied in the same context, each of the two resulting estimates serves as a check on the other. This is the case with the RIA, which draws on two empirical studies for its assessment, one of these being a WTA study and the other a WTP study. There are in fact no studies attempting to place a cost specifically on sexual abuse in incarceration. The RIA therefore draws on studies that attempt to place a cost on sexual abuse generally and then adjusts the conclusions of those studies to reflect as best as possible the circumstances of sexual abuse in incarceration.

The WTA Assessment

The WTA study that the RIA draws on is by Dr. Ted Miller and colleagues of the Pacific Institute for Research and Evaluation on behalf of the Minnesota Department of Health. The Miller report draws on national as well as specifically Minnesota data, so the circumstances that

it examines are representative of America as a whole. Its cost estimates
are based on Minnesota costs, which are close enough to average costs
in America as a whole for the Miller report to provide a fair WTA assessment of the cost of sexual abuse in America. The RIA applies the
appropriate multiplier to all the Miller estimates to translate them to
2011 dollars.[6]

The Miller report computes cost estimates for the victim's medical
care, mental health care, lost work, property damage, suffering and lost
quality of life, sexually transmitted diseases, pregnancy, suicide acts,
and substance abuse. It also includes cost estimates for victim services,
criminal justice investigation and adjudication, sanctioning, and perpetrator's earnings loss.

The RIA adjustments to the Miller estimates for the circumstances of
incarceration take a generally conservative approach. The RIA simply
deletes the amounts for the victim's lost work and property damage as
inapplicable in the incarceration context. It also deletes the perpetrator's
earnings loss. Its reasoning is that if the perpetrator is another inmate
this loss is inapplicable in the incarceration context, and if the perpetrator is a correctional staff member this loss is essentially incorporated
into the "sanctioning" cost element.[7]

For each of the other items in the Miller report, the RIA first makes an
adjustment appropriate to level 1 sexual abuse in adult prisons and jails.
Recall from chapter 2 that level 1 sexual abuse in adult prisons and jails
consists of "nonconsensual sexual acts" involving "injury, force, or high
incidence" (high incidence being three or more events reported). Level 1
sexual abuse of juveniles in juvenile facilities consists of "serious sexual
acts" involving "injury, force, or coercion" or "high incidence." These
definitions—essentially, violent or repeated rape—are similar enough
for the RIA to be able to treat level 1 sexual abuse of adults and of juveniles in juvenile facilities together in a single analysis, with variations
as needed.

For the cost of medical care, the RIA saw no reason to adjust the
Miller estimates and so uses them without adjustment both for adults
and for juveniles in juvenile facilities.[8] Note that the RIA is correct to include the appropriate sum for medical care even though correctional authorities often fail to provide even the most basic and essential medical
care (see chapter 4). The point is that the economic benefit of basic, essential medical care is far greater than its cost. Correctional authorities
that fail to provide inmates with adequate medical care likely increase
the social cost of any physical harm that the inmates have suffered, as
well as the later cost of medical treatment after the inmates are released
into the community.[9]

For the cost of mental health care, the RIA was persuaded that the harm that sexual abuse causes to mental health is far greater in the incarceration context than in the general population. It concludes that "the exacerbation of preexisting mental health conditions and the phenomenon of serial victimization almost certainly increase the cost of therapeutic responses by at least 100%." Accordingly, it uses twice the Miller estimate as its own estimate. For juveniles in juvenile facilities it is persuaded that the increase in cost due to incarceration is yet greater and accordingly uses the Miller estimate multiplied by 2.25 as its own estimate.[10]

Note that the RIA is correct to include the appropriate sum for mental health care, just as for medical care, even though correctional authorities often fail to provide the necessary mental health care. Again, the point is that the economic benefit of the necessary mental health care is far greater than its cost. So correctional authorities that fail to provide inmates with necessary mental health care likely increase the social cost of harm to the mental health of the inmates, as well as the later cost of mental health care after the inmates are released into the community.

For the cost of suffering and lost quality of life, the RIA considers the argument "that rape victims in prison experience even *greater* pain and suffering than victims in the community at large due to the fact that they cannot escape from their perpetrators and may fear retaliation should they report their victimization." But, consistent with its conservative approach, the RIA ultimately decides to use the Miller estimate without adjustment, both for adults and for juveniles in juvenile facilities.[11]

For the cost of sexually transmitted diseases resulting from sexual abuse, the RIA takes into account that the prevalence of these diseases is far higher in incarceration facilities than in the general population. There is evidence that the prevalence is not quite as high in juvenile as in adult facilities. Accordingly, the RIA uses, as its own estimate, twice the Miller estimate for adult facilities but somewhat less than twice the Miller estimate for juveniles in juvenile facilities.[12]

For the cost of pregnancy resulting from sexual abuse, the RIA needed to take into account that "the vast majority of rape victims outside prison confines are female, . . . [but] in confinement settings, the overwhelming percentage of victims are male, and only about 5.25% of prison rapes involve male perpetrators on female victims." Accordingly, the RIA uses 10 percent of the Miller estimate as its own estimate, both for adults and for juveniles in juvenile facilities.[13]

For the cost of suicide acts, the RIA takes into account that more than one in six victims of sexual abuse in incarceration actually attempts suicide. The RIA concludes "that because suicide acts are more prevalent among detained populations than they are among the population as a whole, Miller's estimate of the monetized value of rape-related suicide impacts should be adjusted upward in the prison context." The RIA ultimately decides to use "a multiplier of 1.25 for this purpose as a very conservative estimate of the differential impact of suicide acts." This multiplier applies both to adults and to juveniles in juvenile facilities.[14]

For the cost of the remaining items—substance abuse, victim services, criminal justice investigation and adjudication, and sanctioning—the RIA ultimately saw no reason to adjust the Miller estimates and so used them without adjustment, both for adults and for juveniles in juvenile facilities.[15]

The RIA needed to make a further adjustment to take into account juveniles held in adult facilities. Recall that these juveniles are not included in any BJS surveys and that the RIA accordingly introduces a compensatory modifying factor into its computations of the prevalence of sexual abuse in incarceration.[16]

The RIA assessment next takes account of the fact that a number of victims of sexual abuse in incarceration suffer more than one incident of sexual abuse. The Miller report, dealing with the same issue, had applied a multiplier of 1.26 to its estimates to account for repeated sexual abuse, in accordance with data provided by the National Crime Victimization Survey. The RIA considered the argument that serial sexual abuse is likely a greater problem in incarceration than in the general population: "Prison rape victims are often unable to avoid subsequent interactions with their assailants, and are also more likely than victims in the general population to be targeted by multiple perpetrators." But the RIA also considered that some of the cost impact of multiple acts of sexual abuse is already captured in the factors for mental health care and for suffering and lost quality of life. Overall, it explained that "there is no evidence that there is a one-to-one relationship between the number of incidents and the costs incurred by the victim."[17]

The RIA ultimately decided to take multiple incidents of sexual abuse into account only for victims of sexual abuse classified as high incidence. Recall from chapter 2 that high incidence is among the criteria used in defining sexual abuse at levels 1 and 4 for adults and at levels 1, 2, and 4 for juveniles in juvenile facilities. For victims of sexual abuse at high incidence, the RIA applies a multiplier of 3 to the cost estimates. Since high incidence means three or more abusive sexual acts reported, this is plainly a very conservative approach.[18]

The RIA now applies these various adjustments to compute its WTA cost assessments for each victim of level 1 sexual abuse in incarceration.

For adult prisons and jails, the assessment for each victim is $480,000. For juveniles in juvenile facilities, the assessment for each victim is $675,000.[19]

Next, the RIA applies the same kind of analysis for each of the other levels of sexual abuse. In effect, its analysis for level 1 sexual abuse serves as a template for the analyses at the other levels.

Recall from chapter 2 that level 2 sexual abuse in adult prisons and jails consists of nonconsensual sexual acts that involve no injury and no force and are "low incidence" (no more than two events reported). Also, level 3 sexual abuse of juveniles in juvenile facilities consists of serious sexual acts with another juvenile inmate or with a staff member that do not involve injury, force, or coercion and are low incidence. These definitions are similar enough for the RIA to be able to analyze level 2 sexual abuse of adults and level 3 sexual abuse of juveniles in juvenile facilities in the same way.

This analysis differs from the level 1 analysis in just two factors. One is that the RIA entirely deletes the cost estimate for medical care on the ground that, by definition, these victims have not suffered any physical injury.[20] This is surely an error. Many of these victims have suffered penetrative sexual abuse. In every such case, a medical examination is needed to ascertain that there has been no physical injury and to determine whether prophylactic drug therapy is needed to prevent sexually transmitted diseases or pregnancy (see chapter 4). In any event, the elimination of the cost estimate for medical care makes the RIA assessment yet more conservative.

The other difference from the level 1 analysis is that for victims of sexual abuse at low incidence, the RIA does not make any adjustment at all to the cost estimates to account for multiple incidents of sexual abuse. Since low incidence includes cases in which two abusive sexual acts were reported, this is a very conservative approach.[21]

The RIA now computes its WTA cost assessment for each victim of level 2 sexual abuse in adult prisons and jails as $160,000. For each victim of level 3 sexual abuse of juveniles in juvenile facilities, the RIA assessment is $225,000.[22]

Recall from chapter 2 that level 3 sexual abuse in adult prisons and jails consists of " 'willing' sex with staff." Also, level 2 sexual abuse of juveniles in juvenile facilities consists of serious sexual acts with staff that are high incidence; that do not involve injury, force, or coercion; and that the juvenile has reported as "willing" or "consensual." These definitions are similar enough for the RIA to be able to treat level 3 sexual abuse of adults and level 2 sexual abuse of juveniles in juvenile facilities together in a single analysis, with variations as needed.

The RIA again entirely deletes the cost estimate for medical care, both for adults and for juveniles in juvenile facilities. Again, this is surely an error, for the same reasons as before. But, in any event, the result is simply to make the RIA assessment yet more conservative.

For adult victims of level 3 sexual abuse, the RIA does not make any adjustment to take multiple incidents of sexual abuse into account, even for those victims who reported a high incidence of events. The RIA explains:

We do not use a serial victimization multiplier here, even for victims who reported a high incidence of "willing" sex with staff, because doing so would elevate the unit cost of this category above the unit cost of category [level] 2. We do not believe this would be appropriate, since it would not be logical for sexual activity that the inmate self-describes as "willing" to have a greater cost than sexual activity that the inmate describes as "nonconsensual."

As a result, all the cost estimates for adult prisons and jails are the same for level 3 as for level 2. Accordingly, the WTA cost assessment is the same, $160,000.[23]

For victims of level 2 sexual abuse of juveniles in juvenile facilities, the RIA takes a different approach:

For juveniles, the situation is somewhat more complicated, since our hierarchy distinguishes between "willing" sex with staff with a high incidence [Category 3] and "willing" sex with staff when there is low incidence [included in Category 4 along with other "serious sexual acts" of low incidence]. The sole distinction between these two levels relates to high vs. low incidence of the sexual conduct. Unlike for adults, we view this as a meaningful distinction for juveniles because of their greater vulnerability and because of the strong societal aversion to sexual activity between adults and youth.

Accordingly, the RIA applies the multiplier of 3 for high-incidence sexual abuse to the cost estimates for level 2 sexual abuse of juveniles in juvenile facilities. The WTA cost assessment then computes to $672,000.[24]

For the remaining levels of sexual abuse of adults and of juveniles in juvenile facilities, the RIA assessed relatively low, very conservative estimates. These do not have a significant effect on the eventual total cost assessments.[25]

The WTP Assessment

The WTP study that the RIA draws on is by Prof. Mark Cohen and colleagues. "This study was based on a national survey which asked people how much they would be willing to pay in additional taxes to reduce the prevalence of crime in their community by 10%; from these survey responses and other data, Cohen then extrapolated the value to society of avoiding one incident of each type of crime studied." The study found that communities were willing to pay on average $310,000 (as translated to 2011 dollars) to prevent one incident of "rape and sexual assault."[26]

The RIA considered whether the Cohen study, which dealt with crime in the general population, would apply to the incarceration context. One issue was whether people would value a reduction in crime less if it occurred in a relatively distant incarcerated population rather than in their own community, where it could affect "their own household, their families, friends, or coworkers." But the RIA noted that "the number of incarcerated persons in the United States is very large (estimated at 2.4 million in prisons, jails, and juvenile facilities), and the number of people who are arrested and who pass through jail or a lockup each year is even larger (estimated at 13.4 million)." Consequently, the RIA concluded that sexual abuse in incarceration personally affects a large enough proportion of the population to make the Cohen WTP study relevant to the general population.[27]

Certainly, the RIA insists that sexual abuse of an inmate matters just as much as sexual abuse of an individual in the general population: "One of Congress's purposes in enacting PREA was to counteract the cultural tendency to take prison rape for granted; this tendency is in turn largely driven by the diminished value some in society may place on the tribulations of prisoners. . . . Congress has rejected this devaluation."[28]

Another issue that the RIA considered was whether it should "adjust Cohen's figures to take into account the fact that in the general population the vast majority of sexual abuse victims are female, whereas in the confinement setting the victims are overwhelmingly male." The RIA strongly rejects this, correctly concluding that "all sexual abuse is equally unacceptable, regardless of the victim's gender, custody status, or criminal history."[29]

A remaining problem for the RIA in applying the Cohen study is that this study asked its respondents how much they would pay to reduce the prevalence of rape and sexual assault but did not define these crimes for the respondents. "Respondents were instead asked to respond based on their personal understanding of the crimes." So it is not clear how to correlate the results of the Cohen study with the levels of sexual abuse that the RIA carefully defines. Also, the Cohen study did not distinguish between adult and juvenile victims although, as the RIA recognizes, "the cost to society is higher when the victim is a juvenile."[30]

Accordingly, the RIA is willing to use the WTP cost estimate from the Cohen study ($310,000) as an alternative to its cost estimate derived from the Miller study for adult victims of level 1 sexual abuse ($480,000). But the RIA concludes that the Cohen study "does not provide a useful mechanism for assigning cost values" to sexual abuse of adults at any other level or of juveniles at any level. As a result, the RIA WTP assessments are the same as its WTA assessments, except for the estimates for adult victims of level 1 sexual abuse.[31]

The Total Assessment Range

From these analyses, the RIA now has the information needed to produce its assessments of the overall cost of sexual abuse in incarceration. For each level of sexual abuse, two items of information are necessary: an estimate for the prevalence—the number of victims—of sexual abuse at that level and an estimate for the cost per victim of sexual abuse at that level. Multiplying these together then gives an estimate for the total cost of sexual abuse at that level.

However, recall from chapter 2 that the RIA developed three assessments of the prevalence of sexual abuse in incarceration. Its principal assessment draws directly on the data from the BJS surveys of sexual abuse reported by inmates. Its adjusted assessment conservatively accounts for the possibility of underreporting by inmates and also draws on the BJS surveys of sexual abuse reported by correctional authorities to take account of possible false reporting by inmates. Its lower-bound assessment is extremely conservative, taking the possibility of underreporting by inmates into account only to the smallest degree and making drastic allowance for possible false reporting by inmates.

As a result, for each level of sexual abuse the RIA produces three assessments of the total cost of the abuse. In fact, for level 1 sexual abuse of adults the RIA produces six assessments of the total cost, since there are two estimates of the cost per victim (WTA and WTP), each of which can be multiplied by any of the three assessments of the prevalence of level 1 sexual abuse.

The lowest RIA assessment of the total cost of sexual abuse in incarceration comes from the lower-bound assessment for the prevalence of sexual abuse in incarceration coupled with the WTP estimate of the cost per victim for level 1 sexual abuse. The assessment is $11.6 billion for adult prisons, $10.6 billion for adult jails, and $4.7 billion for juvenile facilities. The total of these is $26.9 billion. This is the lowest official assessment by the Department of Justice for the quantifiable costs of sexual abuse in incarceration *in each single year*.[32] Since the RIA lower-bound prevalence assessments are drastically conservative, the actual quantifiable costs are surely substantially higher.

The cost of level 1 sexual abuse—essentially, violent or repeated rape—makes up the greater part of this assessment. For adult facilities this cost is $16.2 billion and for juvenile facilities it is $2.6 billion, the total of these being $18.8 billion. This is the lowest assessment for the quantifiable costs of level 1 sexual abuse in incarceration in each single year.[33] Again, the actual quantifiable costs are surely substantially higher than these drastically conservative lower-bound estimates.

The highest RIA assessment of the total cost of sexual abuse in incarceration in each single year comes from the principal assessment for the prevalence of sexual abuse in incarceration, coupled with the WTA estimate of the cost per victim for level 1 sexual abuse. The assessment is $20.6 billion for adult prisons, $26 billion for adult jails, and $5.2 billion for juvenile facilities. The total assessment (allowing for rounding errors) is $51.9 billion.[34]

Again, the cost of level 1 sexual abuse makes up the greater part of this assessment. For adult facilities this cost is $37.8 billion and for juvenile facilities it is $2.9 billion, the total of these being $40.7 billion.[35]

In sum, the assessment of the total quantifiable cost of sexual abuse in incarceration in each single year is at least $26.9 billion and is probably substantially more than this. It may well be as high as $51.9 billion. In fact, since this assessment is also based on very conservative estimates, the total cost may be yet higher.

Note that none of these assessments encompasses sexual abuse in the vast number of lockups and community corrections facilities nationwide (see chapter 2). In principle, the costs for lockups and community corrections facilities should be quantifiable to the same extent as the costs for prisons and jails. But they cannot currently be quantified since no information is available on the prevalence of sexual abuse in these facilities.

COSTS NOT READILY QUANTIFIABLE OF SEXUAL ABUSE IN INCARCERATION

Sexual abuse in incarceration imposes a range of costs on society that cannot be readily expressed in monetary terms. It is possible to cover only a sampling of them.

Spread of Disease

More than four centuries ago it was recognized that persons kept in incarceration can be the source of disease in the wider population, although there was as yet no clear sense of how diseases were spread. In Oxford, England, in 1577, a virulent outbreak of "a malignant disease known as the jail-fever" was seen as emanating from the assizes (court proceedings) then being held. The outbreak caused the death of the judge, the sheriff, and about three hundred others. The court proceedings became known as the Black Assize.[36]

The English philosopher-scientist Francis Bacon, who had investigated the Black Assize, wrote in the early seventeenth century: "The most pernicious infection, next the plague, is the smell of the jail, when prisoners have been long and close and nastily kept; whereof we have had in our time experience twice or thrice; when both the judges that sat upon the jail, and numbers of those that attended the business or were present, sickened upon it, and died."[37]

Typhus was then one of the more common diseases under the general rubric of jail-fever. Typhoid fever also spread readily in incarceration facilities, from where it infected the general population. Tuberculosis was also rife and highly contagious in the environment of incarceration, with airborne infectious particles passing easily from one inmate to another. Tuberculosis infection also passed from incarceration facilities to the general population, although in earlier centuries the slower onset of symptoms after initial infection impeded recognition of tuberculosis as a disease incubated in incarceration.

By the mid-eighteenth century, contagion was better understood. In England there was particular concern with disease in the strategically important navy arising from pressing newly released prisoners into service on board ship. The Scottish physician James Lind, who had been physician at a naval hospital in England, focused on this danger in an influential essay. Among his various insightful proposals to prevent the communication of disease within the navy was that newly released prisoners should be in effect quarantined for two weeks on a river boat before being equipped with new clothes (their old clothes having been destroyed) and allowed into the general population of seamen.[38]

John Howard, the eighteenth-century English reformer after whom the Howard League for Penal Reform is named, was familiar with jail-fever from Lind and other contemporaries and from his own experience of prison inspection as a sheriff. In fact, he eventually died of typhus contracted on a prison visit in eastern Europe. In a book of continuing influence, he argued persuasively that the danger of disease spreading through the general population was good reason to improve the conditions of incarceration.[39]

Unfortunately, the lessons learned at great cost centuries ago are often not heeded today. Tuberculosis remains rife in incarceration facilities.

The disease spreads easily in overcrowded, inadequately ventilated conditions of incarceration. Many cases are multidrug resistant. Nationwide, the incidence of tuberculosis is four to five times higher in incarceration facilities than in the general population. In some regions of the country the incidence in incarceration facilities is as much as ten times higher than in the general population of the region.[40]

MRSA (methicillin-resistant *Staphylococcus aureus*) is a recently emerged, very dangerous disease that is also rife in incarceration, where it spreads easily. An explanation comes from Robert Daum, a pediatrician at the University of Chicago Comer Children's Hospital, who has investigated MRSA outbreaks:

Inmates . . . get bored. They touch each other. They touch things that others have touched. They get MRSA on their hands. . . . Once the bacterium gets there, it's likely to stay. They don't shower as often as the general population, and they don't have the best soaps—you have to be very careful what chemicals go into a jail. And if their one uniform fits, they don't want to send it back into the general jail laundry system, so they wash it with cold water in the cell sink.[41]

Tuberculosis and MRSA can pass easily from one person to another during sexual contact, consensual or nonconsensual. In addition, the incidence of the entire range of specific sexually transmitted diseases is many times higher in incarceration facilities than in the general population.[42] Certainly, sexual abuse makes a substantial contribution to the high level of sexually transmitted diseases in incarceration facilities.

Overall, nationwide, very little is done to prevent disease spreading within incarceration facilities. Some prison systems have instituted programs to vaccinate against contagious diseases for which vaccines are available (such as hepatitis B) and to diagnose and treat other contagious diseases. But many prison systems have no such programs and so leave many diseases among their inmates undiagnosed and untreated. There are far too few such programs to meet the needs of the rapidly shifting populations of jail systems.[43]

In the late 1990s, a report to Congress by the National Commission on Correctional Health Care drew on a range of studies to assess the number of inmates with particular communicable diseases released from incarceration in a single year. Over half a million inmates returned to society with latent tuberculosis infection. Almost half a million returned to society with at least one sexually transmitted disease. About a hundred thousand or more returned to society HIV positive. An estimated 38,500 returned to society with AIDS. The incarcerated population is now over a third more than it was in 1996–1997, so the numbers of inmates returning to society with communicable diseases, including sexually transmitted diseases, are surely yet higher.[44]

Individuals who have returned to society from incarceration encounter severe difficulties in obtaining adequate treatment for their health problems. Many return to society without proper medical referrals from the correctional authorities and without an ongoing supply of prescription medications. Many find that they have been removed from the Medicaid rolls and face a long waiting period for recertification. As a result, there may be interruption in taking medication for communicable diseases, leading to development of drug resistance.[45]

The inevitable result is that communicable diseases spread from incarceration facilities into the general population. This is well recognized and documented for tuberculosis and the range of sexually transmitted diseases.[46] A well-documented example of MRSA spreading from incarceration facilities into the general population occurred in Cook County, Illinois, in the mid-1990s. Daum and his colleagues "noticed a rising tide of MRSA cases in children who had no risk factors—they had not been recently hospitalized and had no chronic conditions." On investigation, they "found that about 60 percent of their patients had close relatives or friends who had recently spent time in jail. That was the common thread they were looking for." Further investigation discovered the source of this MRSA outbreak in the Cook County jail system. Notably, over one hundred thousand individuals—one in every fifty of the approximately five million residents of Cook County—pass through this jail system each year.[47]

Certainly, sexual abuse makes a substantial contribution to the spread of communicable diseases from incarceration facilities to the general population. These include highly contagious diseases such as tuberculosis and MRSA, as well as the full range of specifically sexually transmitted diseases, including HIV/AIDS.[48]

This spread of disease imposes costs on society. Individuals in the general population who acquire a contagious disease need treatment, which imposes a cost. While they are suffering the effects of the disease their work efficiency may be diminished, which imposes a cost. The disease may make them less able to undertake a range of socially beneficial activities, which again imposes a cost on our society. These costs may not be readily quantifiable, but they are certainly substantial.

Increased Crime

It is a matter of plain fact that some victims of sexual abuse in incarceration become abusive and violent in their turn. The result is an increase in crime in the community when these victims are released. In his testimony before the Massachusetts legislature, Donaldson explains:

If there is hope for anyone in the prison system, anyone at all, hope that they will learn to live normal lives of respectability, who is it? It is precisely those most likely to be sexual assault targets: the young, the first-termers, the non-violent, the middle-class. Precisely the ones whose lives are most likely to be ruined by prison rape. What do you think rape is teaching them? I'll tell you: hate, rage, might makes right, violence rules, real men prove it by raping others, and society really doesn't gives a shit what happens to its most vulnerable members. That's some lesson, and they'll absorb it in their bones and practice it faithfully on the streets of your and their home town.[49]

This increase in crime imposes costs on society. Note that there is no point in theorizing—or moralizing—about whether victims of sexual abuse in incarceration who turn to crime should be held individually responsible for doing so or whether the system of incarceration should bear the blame. In terms of the social cost of sexual abuse in incarceration, the only point here is that some individuals who would likely not have become abusive and violent do become abusive and violent following sexual abuse in incarceration. Their abuse and violence cause damage, which imposes a cost on American society. If they are held individually responsible and again incarcerated, both the loss of their productive labor and the cost of incarcerating them are costs on society. Regardless of theories about the underlying causes of criminal behavior, the plain fact is that sexual abuse in incarceration imposes a cost on society in terms of subsequent criminal behavior by some victims of the abuse. Again, these costs may not be readily quantifiable, but they are certainly substantial.

Chapter 6

The Moral Cost to American Society

This chapter explores how sexual abuse in the American incarceration system diminishes the moral stature of our justice system and our society as a whole. This imposes a severe cost on our society in addition to the costs considered in chapters 4 and 5.

PREA and the national standards promulgated under PREA have declared a commitment to combat sexual abuse in incarceration, but this commitment has not yet been fulfilled, and it is not clear how far it will be fulfilled. The present reality is that sexual abuse continues to pervade the American system of incarceration. Accordingly, as philosophy professor Kwame Anthony Appiah observes regarding this, "the full extent of the punishment prisoners face isn't detailed in any judge's sentence."[1] In addition, the justice system and the general society exploit the existence of systemic sexual abuse in incarceration in reprehensible ways, as explained next.

SEXUAL ABUSE USED FOR CONTROL OF INMATES

It is well established that correctional authorities at times directly and intentionally employ sexual abuse to control inmates.

In 2001, the then attorney general of California, Bill Lockyer, made a revelatory comment. At a press conference about Enron Corporation chairman Kenneth Lay, Lockyer held Lay responsible for the California electricity crisis at the time and declared: "I would love to personally escort Lay to an 8-by-10 cell that he could share with a tattooed dude who says, 'Hi, my name is Spike, honey.' " A commentator noted: "as the chief law enforcement officer of the largest state in the nation, he not only has admitted that rape is a regular feature of the state's prison system, but also that he considers rape a part of the punishment he can inflict."[2]

The practice to which Lockyer referred is well attested and prevalent. For any of a range of reasons, officers will place a vulnerable inmate with a far stronger inmate, and particularly with an inmate with a history of perpetrating sexual abuse. Plainly, the expectation is that the stronger inmate will sexually abuse the inmate that has been placed with him.

There are major studies attesting to such practices. One such study finds: "Corrections officers and prison administrators . . . threaten to expose prisoners to a greater threat of rape in order to evoke good behavior, to punish, or to squeeze out information. . . . [P]risoners . . . have been thrown into cells with known . . . rapists, and left there as retaliation for having disrespected or hit an officer." Another finds: "Young men were used as 'gifts' from prison officials to inmate leaders who helped them keep the institution quiet. . . . The situation has not changed dramatically in recent years."[3]

The case of Eddie Dillard is attested not only by the testimony of Dillard himself but also by that of Roscoe Pondexter, one of the corrections officers originally involved in what happened to him. Dillard, a small but nevertheless unpleasant young man imprisoned for assault with a deadly weapon, had kicked a female corrections officer:

Dillard was transferred to the cell of Wayne Robertson, better known as the "Booty Bandit." For a time, his vocation was beating, torturing and sodomizing fellow inmates while prison guards looked the other way. This psychopathic serial rapist was the guards' resident enforcer, one whose specialty was reining in abrasive young toughs.

Dillard protested the transfer, pointing out that Robertson was a known predator. "Since you like hitting women, we've got somebody for you," came the reply. . . . For the next several days Robertson beat, raped, tortured and humiliated Dillard, tearing open his rectum in the process. Guards and other inmates listened to the echoes of the young man screaming, crying for help and begging for mercy. . . . Robertson . . . received new tennis shoes and extra food for his services.[4]

In a federal lawsuit, an inmate who had himself been involved with two other inmates in perpetrating sexual abuse swore an affidavit that the other two inmates "had an arrangement with . . . the Officer in Charge . . . to let them have sex with any new kid they wanted to have sex with in return for information of contraband on the Unit."[5]

As one more example drawn from the many documented cases of this kind, that of Cahill following his arrest is noteworthy. The "jailer put him in a cell with known sexual predators, telling them . . . that if they 'took care of him' they'd get extra rations of jello. For the next twenty-four hours Tom [Cahill] was gang-raped. He has never fully recovered from this."[6]

SEXUAL ABUSE IN INCARCERATION USED AS THREAT BY PROSECUTORS

It is well attested that prosecutors use the threat of sexual abuse in incarceration to induce defendants to surrender a range of their legal rights and privileges.

A notorious case (mentioned in the introduction) was an extradition proceeding before the Supreme Court of Canada. The Canadian courts considered an extract from the transcript of a 1997 interview on Canadian television. The interviewer is Linden MacIntyre, and the interviewee is Gordon Zubrod, an assistant U.S. attorney and the prosecutor responsible for requesting extradition from Canada in the case in question:

MacIntyre: . . . For those accused who choose to fight extradition, Gordon Zubrod warns they're only making matters worse for themselves in the long run.

Zubrod: I have told some of these individuals, "Look, you can come down and you can put this behind you by serving your time in prison and making restitution to the victims, or you can wind up serving a great deal longer sentence under much more stringent conditions," and describe those conditions to them.

MacIntyre: How would you describe those conditions?

Zubrod: You're going to be the boyfriend of a very bad man if you wait out your extradition.

MacIntyre: And does that have much of an impact on these people?

Zubrod: Well, out of the 89 people we've indicted so far, approximately 55 of them have said, "We give up."[7]

The Canadian extradition judge interpreted this as a threat of sexual abuse and consequently denied the extradition request. The Supreme Court of Canada agreed: "As for the comments made by the prosecuting attorney: 'You're going to be the boyfriend of a very bad man if you wait out your extradition,' referring to the harsher conditions under which a prison sentence would be served, that statement . . . bears precisely the meaning given to it by the extradition judge. No less sinister interpretation is plausible."[8]

Shortly after the Canadian extradition judge's denial of the extradition request, and while the appeal from that denial was pending, Zubrod reportedly "apologized for his inappropriate comment" in the Canadian television interview.[9] But there was no apology for the actual practice that Zubrod's comments revealed and certainly no denial of the existence of that practice. Also, there is no reason to doubt the capacity and commitment of the office of the U.S. attorney in following through on its threats.

Officials no longer make public statements revealing practices based on sexual abuse. An obvious reason is that such statements can be immediately counterproductive: the Supreme Court of Canada unanimously upheld the extradition judge's denial of the extradition request, basing its decision entirely on the implications of Zubrod's interview comments. No American prosecutor is likely to make that mistake again.

Another reason why such public statements are no longer heard is that, following enactment of PREA, the culture of government reference to sexual abuse in incarceration has changed. No American government official would now suggest publicly that he even tolerates sexual abuse in incarceration, far less that he favors the infliction of it as part of punishment. But although the culture of government reference to sexual abuse in incarceration has changed, the culture of actual, pervasive sexual abuse in incarceration has not substantially changed (see part I) and it is not yet clear how far and how fast it will change (see chapter 11).

Most negotiations between prosecutors and defendants take place during plea bargaining. A common situation is that prosecutors will try to persuade a defendant to plead guilty to certain charges in return for concessions. These concessions may relate to other charges that the prosecution is willing to drop and may also relate to the sentencing hearing. The concessions at the sentencing hearing may entail reduction in the likely sentence and also agreement on the kind of incarceration facility in which the sentence will be served.[10]

The prospect of sexual abuse in incarceration will be an important tool for the prosecution in these negotiations. The jurist Jeremy Waldron notes "the regular leverage of prison rape and other phenomena by prosecutors in the course of plea bargaining." The reported level of sexual abuse varies widely from one incarceration facility to another, and prosecutors and defense counsel alike will be perfectly aware of which facilities are better or worse in this respect. So even if sexual abuse is not mentioned in the negotiations, the threat of it remains strong and must severely weaken the negotiating position of many defendants. As Waldron again notes, American prison conditions "are well known to be de facto terrorizing . . . and we know that prosecutors freely make use of defendants' dread of this brutalization as a tactic in plea bargaining."[11]

The influential journalist Martin Wolf has noted: "Plea-bargaining is effective because of . . . the justified terror of what might happen in prison . . . and the possibility of obtaining a far lighter sentence by agreeing to pleas of guilty. . . . [T]he US judicial system has a potent machine for extracting pleas of guilty to lesser charges." In explicit support of this view, an experienced California attorney wrote: "Judges are the last to care about jail and prison conditions . . . because those conditions add to the pressure on defendants from whom they and the prosecution seek pleas."[12]

SEXUAL ABUSE IN INCARCERATION
USED AS ENTERTAINMENT

Sexual abuse in incarceration, and in particular anal rape of male inmates, is a staple topic of American popular culture. It is portrayed as entertainment in movies, television shows, and board games. It is also used as a marketing theme for a range of products.

An illustration is the television realist-drama *OZ* that ran through six series from 1997 to 2003. All the series of *OZ* repeatedly and graphically depicted pervasive anal rape of male inmates in a prison setting. In *OZ*, "prisoner rape functions as a central plot device and creates an environment in which our darkest suspicions about life in prison are confirmed." The program was so widely viewed that other highly popular television programs (including *Saturday Night Live*, *The Simpsons*, *South Park*, and *The Wire*) were able to refer to, feature, or parody it, relying on broad viewer awareness of it.[13]

Astonishingly, American popular culture often portrays this anal rape, both threatened and actual, as amusing. For example, anal rape of male inmates is a theme of the recent popular movies *Big Stan* and *Let's Go to Prison*, both of which have been publicized as comedies.[14] The original movie poster for *Let's Go to Prison* shows a part of the blue-tiled floor of a shower. Next to the drain, at the center of the poster and filling most of its width, lies a yellow bar of soap, flecked with suds. On the soap is written in large orange letters, "LET'S GO TO PRISON." Along the lower edge of the poster is written, "welcome to the slammer 2006." The reference here, common in American popular culture, is that a man bending over to retrieve dropped soap in communal prison showers is likely to be anally raped.

This theme—that dropped soap in men's incarceration facility showers results in anal rape—also appears in a board game entitled *Don't*

Drop the Soap that has been on the market since 2008. The game is set in a men's incarceration facility and relies on anal rape for its value as entertainment. Within the game the danger of rape stems particularly from a gang called "the Aryans," a name that recalls a gang called the "Aryan Brotherhood" in the OZ television series. A goal of the game is: "Fight your way through 6 different exciting locations [in incarceration] . . . avoid being cornered by the Aryans in the Shower Room." John Sebelius, the creator and marketer of the game, reportedly claims that *Don't Drop the Soap* "is simply intended for entertainment."[15]

As a further example, a decorative motif on the theme of anal rape adorns a range of products available on the American market. A typical version, marketed under the rubric of "humor," shows two black circles, one quite small and the other very much larger. Under the small circle appear the words, "This is Your Ass Hole"; under the large circle appear the words, "This is Your Ass Hole in Jail." Among the various items available for purchase emblazoned with this decoration are buttons, messenger bags, tote bags, T-shirts, and sweatshirts. It is available on a range of children's clothing including T-shirts, sweatshirts, and baseball jerseys, as well as on infant clothing including creepers, T-shirts, and bibs. It is also available on teddy bears.[16]

THE MORAL COST

The pervasive sexual abuse of inmates in the American system of incarceration is a systemic moral wrong. The exploitation of sexual abuse of inmates by officials such as corrections officers and prosecutors is a further moral wrong. The exploitation of sexual abuse of inmates by the general culture constitutes yet a further systemic moral wrong. These wrongs diminish the moral stature of American society as a whole, because they are committed in the name of our society and because our society is responsible for them.

American society is morally responsible for the safety of those that it incarcerates. Warren Burger, as chief justice of the Supreme Court, declared: "[W]hen a sheriff or a marshall takes a man from the courthouse in a prison van and transports him to confinement for two or three or ten years, *this is our act.* We have tolled the bell for him. And whether we like it or not, we have made him our collective responsibility. We are free to do something about him; he is not." As two members of the court have commented: "It is society's responsibility to protect the life and health of its prisoners."[17]

The court as a whole has recognized this responsibility: "Having incarcerated persons with demonstrated proclivities for antisocial criminal, and often violent, conduct, having stripped them of virtually every means of self-protection and foreclosed their access to outside aid, the government and its officials are not free to let the state of nature take its course."[18] Although the court appears here to focus on protecting vulnerable inmates from other, abusive, inmates, it equally recognizes that the government and its officials are not free to allow abusive corrections officers to prey on vulnerable inmates.

The commitment to combat sexual abuse in incarceration declared in PREA and the national standards promulgated under PREA has not yet been fulfilled. Until it is fulfilled, American society, and particularly its justice system, remains guilty of failing to meet its responsibilities.

Plainly, some individuals bear particular moral responsibility for sexual abuse of inmates and the further exploitation of that sexual abuse. There are shades and degrees of moral responsibility, and some degree of moral responsibility must attach to individuals closely connected with the legal and justice system whose policies, actions, or failures to act allow sexual abuse to flourish in incarceration facilities. This category includes legislators and executive officials, prosecutors, and judges. These individuals know that sexual abuse is pervasive throughout the incarceration system. They control, or at least can influence, the circumstances that allow this to continue.[19]

The individuals who exploit sexual abuse in incarceration as entertainment also bear some degree of moral responsibility. They support what philosophy professor Larry May calls "a climate of attitudes" that sustains a cavalier approach toward combating this abuse. Even ten years after enactment of PREA, many people, including many in authority, do not take the problem seriously enough to devote the necessary resources to combat it. In this context, the individuals who produce or consume media that rely on sexual abuse in incarceration as entertainment "demonstrate a kind of moral recklessness."[20]

However, the main point is not to document the moral failings of specific individuals. Rather, the main point is the failings of our society to fulfill its moral responsibilities and the moral cost that this imposes on all of us.

We like to take pride in our society. As individuals, we are broadly encouraged to take moral pride in the accomplishments of American society, even if we are not in any way personally involved in those accomplishments. So, for example, school systems enthusiastically support the annual Americanism Essay Contest for schoolchildren sponsored nationwide by the Elks organization. In 2011, under the contest theme of "Why I Am Proud to Be an American," fifth-grade student Tanner Lundberg was a first-place winner in a local Minnesota branch of this contest:

I'm proud that people volunteer to join our military. Our soldiers risk their lives every day. While they are serving our country they only get to see their families for a short time. These soldiers protect us from danger and help us to continually be free.

Being an American makes me proud because we care for and help people all over the world. We protect people that are unfairly attacked for their beliefs. We support countries that are in need by providing medicine, food, clothing and shelter. Our country is always helping people that are less fortunate.[21]

However, there is a counterpart to this claim to a personal moral share in the accomplishments of American society. It consists of willingness to accept a personal moral share in the failings of our society. It would be morally dishonest to claim a moral share in the accomplishments while denying any moral share in the failings.

The continuing existence of pervasive sexual abuse in incarceration is a failing of our society. The use of sexual abuse to control inmates is a failing of our society. The use of threats of sexual abuse to gain negotiating advantage over defendants is a failing of our society. The cultural treatment of anal rape as entertainment, willfully oblivious to the devastating injuries that it inflicts and the diseases that it transmits, is a failing of our society.

The counterpart of pride is shame. The counterpart of feeling pride as an American "because we care for and help people all over the world" is feeling shame as an American because of these failings of our society. If it is appropriate for an individual who is not in any way personally involved to feel pride, then it is equally appropriate for that individual to feel shame.[22]

In blunt terms, the society in which we would wish to take unmitigated pride is, in part, a source of shame. This is a moral cost on all of us and on our society as a whole.

Part III

Combating Sexual Abuse in Incarceration through the Courts

Chapter 7

State and Comparable Federal Lawsuits

There are various possible ways of attempting to combat sexual abuse in incarceration through the judicial process, federal or state. This chapter and chapter 8 consider the most important of these ways and assess their limitations.

This chapter deals with the typical range of lawsuits in state courts, as well as with lawsuits of similar kinds in federal courts. Chapter 8 deals with the specific category of claims under the federal Constitution brought in federal court.

THE SYMPATHETIC TRIAL JUDGE

When an individual has been found guilty of a criminal offense, it is the task of the trial judge to determine the appropriate sentence.[1] To do so, she first refers to the *sentencing guidelines* for her jurisdiction. Each jurisdiction—that is, each state as well as the federal system—has its own sentencing guidelines. Sentencing guidelines are specific and detailed, with a view to reducing disparities in sentencing within the given jurisdiction as far as possible. Typically, sentencing guidelines specify the sentence to within a small range, based on two factors: the seriousness of the offense and the criminal history of the offender.

Despite the desire for uniform sentencing within each jurisdiction, under a variety of circumstances trial judges are able to impose a sentence below the normally applicable sentencing guidelines range. A reduction in sentencing from the guidelines specification is known as a

downward departure. In the 1990 case of *US v Lara* dealing with the
federal guidelines, the defendant was a young man of "diminutive size,
immature appearance and bisexual orientation." He had been convicted
of drug offenses for which the normally applicable guidelines sentence
range was imprisonment for ten to twelve-and-a-half years. But the
trial judge had taken into account the "extreme vulnerability" of the
defendant to sexual abuse in incarceration and imposed a sentence of
five years' imprisonment, the mandatory minimum under the statute.
The federal government appealed against the sentence, but the appellate
court held that such extreme vulnerability to sexual abuse in incarceration justified this substantial downward departure.[2]

The same federal appellate court reached a similar decision the following year in the case of *US v Gonzalez*. The defendant had been
convicted of drug offenses. The trial judge "noted that Gonzalez was
extremely small and feminine looking, and that, although he was nine-
teen, he had the appearance of a fourteen or fifteen year old boy." Taking this into account, the trial judge imposed a sentence of thirty-three
months' imprisonment, which was one-third of the lower end of the
normally applicable guidelines sentence range. The appellate court rejected the federal government's appeal against this downward departure
in the sentence.[3]

Cases of this kind are obviously problematic. A dissenting judge
on the appellate court that decided *US v Gonzalez* protested that the
downward departure defied logic, as a thirty-three-month sentence with
frequent sexual assaults would still be inhumanely long. One way of
viewing these cases is on the basis that the courts assumed that the defendants would serve their sentences in protective custody. Because of
the severe detriments of protective custody, a shorter period in protective custody could be seen as equivalent to a longer period in the general
population of the facility.[4] But in fact the courts exercise no control
over whether any particular inmates serve their sentences in protective
custody.

Otherwise, logic would suggest that an extremely vulnerable defendant should not be incarcerated at all. In one case, a state trial judge did
place a convicted defendant on probation rather than sentence him to
imprisonment, on the ground of his extreme vulnerability. The defendant was fifty-two years old and not much over five feet tall. The judge
said in court: "I shake to think what might happen to you in prison."[5]
Although the judge did not specify sexual abuse, this was clearly at least
part of her concern. The prospect of sexual abuse was also plainly at
issue in a federal trial decision in which the court allowed: "Sentencing can be deferred to allow this young, nonviolent offender—whose

physical and mental fragility renders him particularly susceptible to abuse in prison—further time to demonstrate rehabilitation under the strict control of Pretrial Services."[6]

There are not many decisions of this kind. In any event, they can at best only be minor palliatives for a few individuals. They do not effectively combat the continuing, pervasive sexual abuse in incarceration.

PROSECUTING PERPETRATORS

Sexual abuse of any person is a criminal offense in every state. So a corrections officer who sexually abuses an inmate, or an inmate who sexually abuses another inmate, commits a criminal offense. In addition, in all states and in the federal system a corrections officer who engages in any kind of sexual act with an inmate commits a criminal offense, regardless of consent on the part of the inmate (see chapter 2).

A person who commits a criminal offense may be prosecuted and punished if convicted. Since at least the 1990s, there have been instances of prosecutors proceeding against corrections officers who sexually abused inmates. For example, the NPREC report notes: "In Pennsylvania, from 1998 through 2005, corrections officials worked with district attorneys to convict 10 staff members of sexual misconduct."[7] These prosecutions must be seen as positive steps in combating sexual abuse in incarceration, despite the fact that they result in confining yet more individuals to corrections systems that may well be abusive.

The problem in terms of combating sexual abuse in incarceration is that the number of prosecutions has been very small. The NPREC report observes:

Despite that fact that most incidents of sexual abuse constitute a crime in all 50 States and under Federal law, very few perpetrators of sexual abuse in correctional settings are prosecuted. Only a fraction of cases are referred to prosecutors, and the Commission repeatedly heard testimony that prosecutors decline most of these cases. Undoubtedly, some investigations do not produce evidence capable of supporting a successful prosecution. But other dynamics may be at play: some prosecutors may not view incarcerated individuals as members of the community and as deserving of their services as any other victim of crime.

The report also explains: "In smaller jurisdictions where the correctional facility is a major employer, a 'company town' mentality may predominate, with prosecutors reluctant to take on cases in which the defendant is a corrections officer."[8]

This report appeared in 2009, but in fact there were by then some signs that the situation might be beginning to change, at least in some

parts of the country. An Ohio case decided in 2008 conveys some sense
of progress. Former corrections officer Johnny Fortson was convicted of
sexual abuse of three female inmates of a prerelease center. The abuse
included three counts of rape of one of the inmates. He was sentenced
to seven years' imprisonment and required to register as a sex offender
for life after his release.

Fortson's defense gave a sense of the attitudes toward inmate victims
of sexual abuse that, until quite recently, prevailed widely in general society as well as in justice systems throughout the country. His attorney
"suggested that the victims were not real rape victims because they were
hardened criminals, the opposite of ladylike, and all were classless."
But, as a possible indication of changing times, the trial judge chastised
Fortson and his attorney for this and "called the women courageous for
standing up to an intimidating prison culture that discourages inmates
from reporting misconduct when they have been victimized."[9]

A series of prosecutions for sexual abuse of women inmates at Coffee Creek Correctional Facility in Oregon also conveys a sense of attitudes that may be changing.[10] This facility, the only prison for women
in Oregon, was designed in the late 1990s to replace the former Oregon
women's prison. Construction began in 2000, and the facility opened in
2001–2002. Yet although this relatively new facility was designed and
built in an era of growing recognition of prevalent sexual abuse in incarceration, its design was fundamentally insecure in terms of safeguard-
ing inmates from sexual abuse. There were—and still are—many blind
spots. Among them are long, windowless tunnels that are not regularly
patrolled and have no surveillance cameras, many windowless rooms,
and isolated maintenance buildings scattered throughout the extensive
grounds of the facility and not regularly patrolled.

Sexual abuse began almost as soon as the facility opened. In 2004,
Jeffrey Barcenas, a command-level corrections officer who had engaged
in sexual relations with an inmate, Amanda Durbin, was convicted of
first-degree official misconduct, a misdemeanor, and sentenced to six
months in jail and five years' probation. Christopher Randall, the prison's food-services coordinator, who had also engaged in sexual relations with Durbin as well as with another inmate, was also convicted
of misdemeanor official misconduct and sentenced to forty-five days in
jail and five years' probation. Notably, both men committed the sexual
abuse in enclosed, lockable areas that were not patrolled and to which
they had privileged access; in the case of Randall, the area was the prison's meat locker.

Durbin initially reported the abuse to two male corrections officers,
but they refused to believe her. However, a female prison counselor

did believe her and encouraged her to document and retain evidence of the abuse. The criminal convictions resulted, as did a substantial financial settlement from the state for Durbin (discussed shortly). Following this, both the Department of Corrections and the major labor union representing corrections officers supported a legislative measure that was enacted in 2005, increasing the penalties for sexual abuse of inmates. The statute divides sexual abuse roughly along the lines of the BJS distinction between nonconsensual sexual acts and abusive sexual contacts. The former, when perpetrated by a corrections employee or contractor on an inmate, is a felony punishable by up to five years' imprisonment; the latter is a misdemeanor punishable by up to one year of imprisonment.[11]

In 2005, a few months after Barcenas and Randall were convicted, Paul Golden entered employment at Coffee Creek Correctional Facility as supervisor of inmates working in the grounds of the facility. He repeatedly sexually abused at least seventeen inmates, a number of them in a shed in the grounds that they called the "rape shed." Following investigations, he was eventually compelled to resign in 2008 and convicted on multiple counts the following year. Although some of the convictions were misdemeanors, the trial judge declared that it was "appropriate to have the sentence reflect the number of victims" and sentenced Golden to eleven-and-a-half years' imprisonment plus three years of postrelease supervision and registration as a sex offender.[12]

Since then, three other employees of Coffee Creek Correctional Facility—Kaleo Rick, Darcy MacKnight, and Troy Austin—have been convicted on various charges of sexual abuse of inmates. Currently, two more are facing charges.[13] Overall, it appears that correctional authorities in Oregon are treating sexual abuse of women inmates by corrections officers as a serious matter. The substantial financial settlements for Durbin and for the victims of sexual abuse by Golden and others (discussed shortly) may have helped to focus the mind of the state authorities on the seriousness of sexual abuse of inmates. In any event, the Oregon Department of Corrections is currently one of the most committed in America in terms of combating sexual abuse in incarceration (see chapter 3).

Sexually abusive corrections officers are also being effectively prosecuted in other parts of the country. These include some egregious offenders who had been sexually abusing inmates with apparent impunity. A notorious case was that of Mike Burgess, who for years used his power as an Oklahoma sheriff and member of a team controlling a drug court to sexually abuse numerous female inmates. In 2009, Burgess was sentenced to seventy-nine years' imprisonment.[14]

However, in much of America correctional authorities and state prosecutors continue to treat sexual abuse by corrections officers lightly. In Hall's action for civil damages for sexual abuse by corrections officer Terrell, the federal trial court sharply criticized the Colorado corrections and prosecutorial authorities for their typical failure to take sexual abuse of inmates seriously:

For five months, . . . Sergeant Leshawn Terrell, Hall's supervisor in her work assignment . . . , coerced her into having a sexual relationship with him. When Hall finally summoned the courage to refuse his advances . . . Terrell brutally raped and sodomized her, causing her lasting physical and emotional injury.

Almost inconceivably, . . . Terrell was permitted, in his criminal prosecution, to plead guilty to a class 1 misdemeanor: unlawful sexual contact where the "[t]he actor knows that the victim does not consent." He was sentenced to sixty days' imprisonment in the Denver County Jail, to be followed by five years of sex offender probation.[15]

Overall, most of the prosecutions of corrections officers that have so far taken place entail sexual abuse by male corrections officers of female inmates, with somewhat fewer prosecutions of sexual abuse by female corrections officers of male inmates. There are relatively few prosecutions of sexual abuse by corrections officers, male or female, of inmates of the same sex.[16]

It is very rare for a prison inmate to be prosecuted for sexual abuse of another prison inmate. The issues that the NPREC report noted—difficulty in obtaining evidence and prosecutorial reluctance to view inmates as members of the community—are particularly significant in such cases. In addition, the NPREC report heard testimony that "overburdened prosecutors choose not to prosecute crimes when committed behind bars by individuals already serving a long sentence."[17] The prospect of a further sentence may not be much of a deterrent for such individuals, so as far as the criminal justice system is concerned they can perpetrate sexual abuse with impunity.

Yet one prosecution of such an inmate did occur in 2009, when an Idaho court sentenced Cody Thompson to life imprisonment without parole for orally and anally raping his cellmate the previous year. Thompson was six feet tall and a documented member of the Aryan Knights gang. He had a long criminal history that included nine felonies, some of them violent. He was serving a thirty-year sentence. The inmate that the prison authorities assigned as his cellmate was five feet three inches tall and younger and suffered from mental illness. Following the trial verdict, the director of Idaho Department of Corrections declared: "This case shows Idaho is serious about eliminating prison rape."[18] But the fact that such an obviously vulnerable inmate was ever assigned as Thompson's cellmate wholly undermines this claim.

In fact, there are still far too few prosecutions to effectively deter either corrections officers or inmates from perpetrating sexual abuse on vulnerable inmates. Trawling through reports of prosecutions makes it clear that, in any given year so far, all the prosecutions for sexual abuse in incarceration taken together have related to no more than a few thousand victimized inmates in total. But every year at least one hundred and fifty thousand inmates suffer sexual abuse (see chapter 2). Even making every possible allowance, it is certain that for more than 95 percent of inmates who suffer sexual abuse, their abuse goes wholly unpunished. In sum, although in recent years criminal prosecution has gone beyond mere token action, it does not yet amount to effective action against prevalent sexual abuse in incarceration.

CIVIL LAWSUITS IN STATE COURTS

Sexual abuse of any person, whether or not incarcerated, is not only a criminal offense but also a *tort*—an injurious act for which the individual who suffered injury can bring a civil (as opposed to a criminal) lawsuit. The lawsuit could be for monetary damages or for an injunction (an order to someone to do or cease doing something). So, at least in principle, an inmate in a corrections facility could bring a tort lawsuit in a court of the state in which the facility is located. The lawsuit could be brought against a sexually abusive corrections officer or other inmate. In some cases, it could be brought against the corrections institution or the government entity that controls the corrections institution, which might be a local government entity or the state itself.

Of course, monetary payment cannot entirely compensate an individual for having been sexually abused. This is particularly clear if the abuse has taken the form of rape that caused serious injury and infected the victim with a variety of diseases, including HIV. But monetary payment in the form of compensatory damages, and possibly also punitive damages in egregious cases, is the only redress that society generally makes available to tort victims through civil lawsuits.

The prospect or the actuality of having to pay monetary damages to victims of sexual abuse can also focus correctional authorities and staff on amending the policies and behavior that have permitted or facilitated sexual abuse of inmates and so resulted in liability. Note that when damages are awarded against an individual officer, it is usually the corrections institution or government at some level that pays. Generally, corrections officers are indemnified against damages awards by statute or in their employment contracts, although this indemnification may not cover intentional or malicious wrongful acts. There is very little publicly available information regarding payments in individual cases. However, overall it is reasonable to assume in the cases discussed in this chapter and the next that the actual perpetrators of sexual abuse probably were not indemnified but that corrections officers whose derelictions allowed sexual abuse to take place probably were indemnified.[19]

In some cases, individual and institutional defendants in lawsuits for sexual abuse in incarceration have agreed to pay sums in settlement of the lawsuit without going through the trial process. This has particularly happened when corrections officers have already been convicted of blatant and pervasive sexual abuse of inmates, making it likely that the inmates will succeed in the civil lawsuit.

For example, the continuing sexual abuse of inmates at the Coffee Creek Correctional Facility resulted in settlements. In 2004, Durbin accepted an out-of-court settlement of $350,000 from the state for the sexual abuse perpetrated by Barcenas and Randall. In 2012, Oregon state authorities paid a total of $1.2 million to seventeen current and former inmates in settlement of lawsuits that they had brought regarding sexual abuse by Golden and others.[20]

Among more substantial settlements is the $10 million that Custer County commissioners agreed in 2010 to settle a lawsuit brought by fourteen female inmates alleging sexual abuse by former sheriff Burgess, who had previously been convicted. The chairman of the commissioners bemoaned: "Ten million dollars is a lot of money, and it's a shame the people of Custer County will have to pay."[21]

A series of lawsuits brought in the Michigan courts illustrates both the difficulties and the potential for redress entailed in civil lawsuits in state courts. In 1996, Tracy Neal and five other women inmates brought a lawsuit against the Michigan Department of Corrections (MDOC) and many of its officers, alleging numerous acts of sexual abuse since 1991. The ensuing litigation, which developed as a class action and ultimately involved more than five hundred women inmates and former inmates, spanned more than thirteen years with more than twenty appellate proceedings. It eventually resulted in a $100 million settlement to be paid by the state of Michigan.

The 1996 lawsuit was brought in a context of growing awareness of pervasive sexual abuse of inmates in Michigan women's corrections facilities. A Department of Justice investigation in 1995 had found a "pattern or practice of sexual abuse of women inmates by guards . . . including rapes." The Human Rights Watch Report *All Too Familiar* "revealed that rape, sexual assault or abuse, criminal sexual contact, and

other misconduct by corrections staff are continuing and serious problems within the women's prisons in Michigan [and] have been tolerated
over the years at both the institutional and departmental levels."[22]

In this context, the allegations in *Neal v Michigan Department of
Corrections* were indeed all too familiar:

[P]laintiffs' complaint alleged that the MDOC assigns male officers to the housing units at all women's facilities without providing any training related to
cross-gender supervision; that women are forced to dress, undress, and perform basic hygiene and body functions in the open with male officers observing;
that defendants allow male officers to observe during gynecological and other
intimate medical care; that defendants require male officers to perform body
searches of women prisoners that include pat-downs of their breasts and genital areas; that women prisoners are routinely subjected to offensive sex-based
sexual harassment, offensive touching, and requests for sexual acts by male
officers; and that there is a pattern of male officers requesting sexual acts from
women prisoners as a condition of retaining good-time credits, work details,
and educational and rehabilitative program opportunities. The complaint also
alleged that the inmates were subject to retaliation for reporting this gender-
based misconduct.[23]

The lawsuit took the form of a claim under the Michigan Elliott-Larsen
Civil Rights Act (ELCRA), which bars gender-based discrimination in
places of public service in the state. The MDOC disputed whether their
facilities were places of public service within the meaning of ELCRA,
but the Michigan Court of Appeals eventually held that they were. That
is, the court held that the women inmates were covered by ELCRA.[24]

The government of Michigan promptly enacted an amendment to
ELCRA providing that "public service does not include a state or county
correctional facility with respect to actions and decisions regarding an
individual serving a sentence of imprisonment." It took five years before
the Michigan Court of Appeals considered this amendment and ruled
that any claims based on wrongs that occurred after the date on which
the amendment came into effect must be dismissed.[25]

However, in 2007 the ELCRA amendment came before a federal court
for consideration. The court delivered a stinging rebuke to the Michigan
government: "Given the state's abhorrent and well-documented history
of sexual and other abuse of female prisoners, the court finds this
amendment particularly troubling. . . . The ELCRA amendment denies
prisoners the basic protections against discrimination that all others are
afforded under Michigan law. . . . Accordingly, the court concludes that
the ELCRA amendment violates prisoners' equal protection rights and
is unconstitutional."[26]

After over a decade of obstructive litigation and legislation, the lawsuits were at last starting to go to jury trial. Different lawsuits had been consolidated together, and there were now over five hundred women inmate and former-inmate plaintiffs. There were to be a substantial number of trials, each with a small group of plaintiffs.

The MDOC's trial preparation included wholesale destruction of relevant documents. The trial court for the first group of ten plaintiffs found as follows:

[The MDOC] destroyed or failed to retain documents including, but not limited to, grievances filed by women prisoners complaining of sexual harassment, privacy violations and sexual misconduct by MDOC staff; grievance logs and reports; telephone monitoring logs; minutes of staff meetings for facilities housing women prisoners; and other monthly reports, log books and documents relevant to plaintiff's claims and defendants' defenses. Defendants took such action despite their knowledge of plaintiffs' request for such documents, this court's orders for the production of these documents and the MDOC's own practice of requiring maintenance of documents related to pending litigation.

Accordingly, the court instructed the jury that it should accept the plaintiffs' claims based on the missing documents as true, unless the defendants could prove otherwise.[27]

At that first trial, in early 2008, the jury awarded the ten women damages totaling over $15.5 million. Notably, after the verdict was delivered a member of the jury made a statement in court to the plaintiffs: "We the members of the jury, as representatives of the citizens of Michigan, would like to express our extreme regret and apologies for what you have been through."[28]

A year later, the jury in another trial awarded eight women plaintiffs a total of $8.4 million in damages. By 2009, the courts had rejected the MDOC's appeal from the first trial award and the total of the two awards, including interest accrued over many years, amounted to over $46 million. There were many more trials to come, with likely similar outcomes. The state was finally ready to abandon its appeals, avoid further trials, and settle all the claims for a total of $100 million, to be paid over several years.[29]

This, though, was a rare success for victims of sexual abuse in incarceration. One important reason why these successes are rare is that plaintiffs rarely have the resources for such extensive litigation against the vastly greater resources of a state. Plaintiffs in this Michigan case needed, and were fortunate to have, a committed team of ten attorneys who expended over thirty thousand hours of their time and advanced more than half a million dollars in out-of-pocket costs during the thirteen years of the litigation. The attorneys were indeed eventually paid from the settlement funds, but if the case had been lost they would have received nothing—and been left to bear the out-of-pocket costs.[30] Not many attorneys are able or willing to take risks on this scale.

Plaintiffs in these cases also need the internal resource of courage that must be maintained over many years. Attorney Deborah LaBelle, whose law office handled the Michigan litigation, explains: "It took a number of years for the women to come together and agree to support each other. They had to be willing to face the inevitable retaliation that would result in filing the litigation as they would still be imprisoned with the men charged with sexually assaulting them and under the authority of the administration that was charged with deliberate indifference to their safety." Indeed, a 1998 Human Rights Watch report attested to extensive ongoing retaliation against Michigan women inmates.[31]

So it is hardly surprising that, overall, the total amount paid in lawsuit verdicts and settlements is minuscule compared to the total societal cost of sexual abuse in incarceration (see chapter 5). Overall, civil lawsuits in state courts have so far amounted to little more than token action against the nationwide problem of pervasive sexual abuse in incarceration. Note also that any effect of these civil lawsuits has been limited to sexual abuse by corrections staff. It is virtually unknown for an inmate to obtain compensation or an injunction in the state courts regarding sexual abuse by another inmate.

Chapter 8

Federal Constitutional Lawsuits

The federal Constitution includes provisions that purport to protect incarcerated individuals against abuse. These provisions apply whether the individual is an inmate of a federal prison, a state prison, a local jail, or any other incarceration or detention facility. Under certain circumstances, a sexually abused inmate can bring a lawsuit in federal court to invoke these constitutional provisions. The involvement in this area of the federal courts, with their relatively high level of political independence, has in the past been crucially important.[1] But this is now a complex area of the law, and even the limited account presented in this chapter, which is confined to the issues that are relevant here, will require several stages of analysis.

The procedure for an inmate to bring a lawsuit in federal court depends on whether he is incarcerated in a federal facility or in a facility operated at the state or local level. The discussion in the text focuses on inmates of state or local facilities; key issues regarding inmates of federal facilities are referenced in the endnotes.

SECTION 1983 LAWSUITS

In general, an inmate of a facility operated by a state or a local government who wishes to bring a lawsuit in federal court regarding her treatment in incarceration must do so under the rubric of a particular federal statute: section 1983 of title 42 of the United States Code. This statute was enacted as part of the Civil Rights Act of 1871, primarily to provide a civil remedy against abuses being committed in the southern states. The states themselves were not taking action against these abuses—in many cases the states were actively supporting them—and so a federal remedy was needed.

The relevant part of section 1983 provides that "every person who under color of any statute, ordinance, regulation, custom, or usage, of any state or territory or the District of Columbia, subjects, or causes to be subjected, any citizen of the United States or other person within the jurisdiction thereof to the deprivation of any rights, privileges, or immunities secured by the Constitution and laws, shall be liable to the party injured in an action at law, suit in equity, or other proper proceeding for redress."[2]

Since the phrase beginning "under color of any statute, ordinance, regulation, custom, or usage" is unwieldy, it is often convenient to say simply that section 1983 deals with deprivation of rights by persons acting "under color of law." The concept of "under color of law" is crucial in section 1983 jurisprudence. What it means is that for section 1983 to permit a lawsuit against a defendant, the defendant must have held government authority (whether at the state, city, county, municipal, or any equivalent level) and must allegedly have used that authority to deprive someone of constitutional rights.[3]

Persons with government authority can act under color of law *whether they act in accordance with their authority or misuse it*.[4] To understand this, consider the example of a corrections officer who sexually abuses an inmate. Certainly, this violates the inmate's constitutional rights, as discussed later. But the law of every state categorically forbids corrections officers to sexually abuse inmates. How then can a corrections officer be acting under color of law when he is actually violating the law? The point is that although he is indeed violating state law, he is only able to do so because he is a corrections officer enjoying the trust and wielding the power of that government office. If he were not a corrections officer, he would not be in a position to sexually abuse the inmate. This is why he is acting under color of law when he sexually abuses the inmate.

The judgment of a federal trial court in a section 1983 lawsuit brought by Priscilla Chavez, a former inmate of a Utah state prison, against former corrections officer Louis Poleate illustrates this: "Mr. Poleate took Ms. Chavez, then 18 years old, from her cell, telling her that he was going to take her to the infirmary. Instead, Mr. Poleate took her to a secluded gatehouse, which was not under surveillance by prison officials. Once there, Mr. Poleate brutally and viciously raped Ms. Chavez over a period lasting an hour and a half. During the rape, Ms. Chavez' hands and feet were in shackles."[5] Only Poleate's position as a corrections officer with authority over Chavez entitled him to shackle her and order her to accompany him from her cell. Only his position as a corrections officer with authority over her placed her in a position where she could not protest without risking official punishment for disobedience or resist without risking official punishment for assaulting a corrections officer, until it was too late for her to protest or resist. Because of these and associated factors, he was acting under color of law when he raped her.

Note that section 1983 does not itself provide any substantive rights. It provides nothing more than a route into federal court. In legal terminology, it provides a federal "cause of action" for persons claiming that they have been deprived of substantive rights that the Constitution provides.[6]

EXHAUSTION OF ADMINISTRATIVE REMEDIES

Incarcerated individuals face a particular barrier on the route to bringing a section 1983 lawsuit. A 1996 federal statute, the Prison Litigation Reform Act (PLRA), was enacted specifically to reduce the number of lawsuits brought by inmates. One provision of the PLRA bars inmates from bringing a section 1983 lawsuit "until such administrative remedies as are available are exhausted." The administrative remedies referred to are the grievance procedures that the correctional authorities have instituted. This enactment has been very effective in reducing the number of inmate lawsuits.[7]

In fact, though, it is quite common in a variety of contexts for legal systems to require exhaustion of administrative remedies before permitting access to the courts. But it is normal to accompany requirements of this kind with provisions assuring that the administrative remedies are reasonable and fair. Prior to enactment of the PLRA there was such a provision: an inmate could not be required to exhaust administrative remedies before bringing a section 1983 lawsuit in federal court unless the court considered it "appropriate and in the interests of justice" for him or her to do so, and the available remedies met standards set by the Department of Justice. However, the PLRA abandoned this provision. Its plain terms require inmates to exhaust whatever administrative remedies are "available," without regard to what these remedies might entail.[8]

An experienced civil rights attorney expresses the view of many commentators regarding the current situation: "The exhaustion provision of the PLRA puts the potential civil rights defendants in charge of defining the procedural hurdles that a prisoner must clear in order to sue them. This produces a perverse incentive for prison officials to implement complicated grievance systems and require hyper-technical compliance with them in order to shield themselves from prisoners' lawsuits. That has become the main purpose of many grievance systems." As law professor and civil rights expert Margot Schlanger comments, in corrections institutions "the sky's the limit for the procedural complexity or difficulty of the exhaustion regime."[9]

In 2006, the Commission on Safety and Abuse in America's Prisons issued its report. This commission was cochaired by a former federal appellate chief judge and a former attorney general. It included senior prison officials as well as human rights workers and former prison inmates among its members. Its report, entitled *Confronting Confinement,* explains: "if the grievance procedures are meaningless or unnecessarily cumbersome or strict, an exhaustion rule simply undermines access to justice." This report calls on Congress to change the exhaustion rule in the PLRA. The NPREC report declares that "the PLRA requirements present such serious hurdles that they block access to the courts for many victims of sexual abuse" and includes in its recommendations a reasonable and fair standard for exhaustion of administrative remedies.[10]

Many correctional authorities have imposed very severe filing deadlines in their grievance procedures. The American Bar Association House of Delegates approved a report of its Criminal Justice Section that focused on the effect of these deadlines on victims of sexual abuse:

The deadlines for filing a prison grievance typically are very short, usually no more than fifteen days and in some states as little as two to five days. . . . In effect, . . . the exhaustion requirement imposes a statute of limitations on many prisoners that ranges from a few days to a few weeks. . . . [S]ome constitutional violations are so egregious (e.g., rape by a correctional officer) or stigmatizing (e.g., failure to protect from a homosexual assault) that a prisoner-victim will need more time than that allotted for the filing of a grievance to overcome the trauma of the event before seeking administrative or legal redress.[11]

The PREA national standards include provisions prohibiting filing deadlines for sexual abuse grievances and requiring that inmates be allowed assistance in filing a grievance. But it is not yet clear how far these provisions will actually be implemented (see chapter 10).

LAWSUITS AGAINST OFFICIALS IN THEIR PERSONAL CAPACITY

A corrections officer who sexually abuses an inmate is personally responsible for his own actions in depriving the inmate of his constitutional rights. Under certain circumstances, the correctional authorities and other authorities might also be responsible, but this is another matter, discussed shortly. The point here is that the abused inmate can sue the abusive officer personally under section 1983 (assuming that she has exhausted administrative remedies). The standard terminology is that the officer can be sued "in his personal (or individual) capacity." In fact, a section 1983 lawsuit against an official in his personal capacity should declare in the documents filing the lawsuit that it is brought against the official in his personal capacity.

If the court awards the inmate damages against the officer in a section 1983 lawsuit brought against him in his personal capacity, he and he alone is liable for payment of those damages. The court cannot hold the correctional authority or any other authority liable.

In some cases, the officer might not end up paying the damages himself. State law or city, county, or municipal regulations might indemnify him against damages awarded against him, or his employment contract with the correctional authority might indemnify him. But it is also possible that none of these provisions will indemnify him against damages awarded against him. In particular, officials might not be indemnified regarding actions that are clear violations of state laws or correctional authority policies. In any event, as far as the court is concerned, the individual officer remains personally liable.[12]

Similarly, if the court grants the inmate an injunction against the officer in a section 1983 lawsuit brought against him in his personal capacity, he and he alone is liable for obeying the injunction. So, for example, if the officer resigns and another officer fills his position, the injunction does not apply to the new officer.

An obvious problem with an award of damages against an officer in his personal capacity is that he might not be able to pay it. It is possible to attach his assets, if any, and, if he is still employed, to garnish his wages to the limited extent that the law permits. But beyond this there is little prospect of collecting the damages award. In her section 1983 lawsuit against Poleate in his personal capacity, Chavez was awarded over $1.4 million, including $1 million in punitive damages; no public information is available as to how much she has actually received.[13]

If the individual perpetrator or perpetrators of the abuse cannot pay a damages award, the victim often has no redress. Although sexual abuse in incarceration takes place in a tightly controlled institutional setting, it is often not possible for the victim to obtain redress from the institution, as discussed shortly. It is also often not possible for the victim to obtain redress from superior officers whose laxity has allowed sexual abuse to flourish in incarceration.

A 2010 federal appellate court decision in a section 1983 case illustrates this. Ron Ball, sheriff of Hot Spring County, Arkansas, had hired Joseph Fite as a jailer and shortly afterward transferred him to be road deputy. Ball permitted Fite to operate in this law enforcement capacity almost completely unsupervised, despite giving him virtually no training.

Fite came into contact with Summer Parrish while frequenting the J-Mart, a convenience store at which Parrish was employed. Parrish, who was having some legal troubles, sought Fite's advice in solving those problems. After advising her, Fite asked Parrish if she would go on a date with him. Parrish declined the offer.

Subsequently, Fite learned that Parrish had several outstanding warrants for her arrest. . . . Fite drove to the J-Mart, arrested Parrish, and transported her to the county jail. While en route to the county jail, Fite informed Parrish that he would not have arrested her if she had simply agreed to go out with him.

Once they arrived at the jail, Fite bet Jason Farr, a jailer, that he could get Parrish to reveal her breasts. In furtherance of his scheme, Fite told Parrish that he could get her fines reduced if she would show him her breasts. After some trepidation, Parrish eventually complied with the request, raised her shirt, and exposed her breasts. Fite then grabbed Parrish's exposed breast.[14]

Parrish obtained a damages award against Fite in his personal capacity. But she failed to obtain a damages award against Sheriff Ball in his personal capacity for his own failure to train and supervise Fite. Referring to precedent, the court set out the applicable standards:

For Sheriff Ball to have violated Parrish's constitutional rights by failing to supervise Fite, Parrish must show that Sheriff Ball:

1. Received notice of a pattern of unconstitutional acts committed by subordinates;
2. Demonstrated deliberate indifference to or tacit authorization of the offensive acts;
3. Failed to take sufficient remedial action; and
4. That such failure proximately caused injury to [Parrish].

The court added: "a reasonable supervisor in Sheriff Ball's position would not know that a failure to specifically train Fite not to sexually assault a woman would cause Fite to engage in that very behavior."[15]

The court is, of course, correct that Ball could not have precisely anticipated the specific abuse that Fite would perpetrate on a vulnerable detainee and therefore could not have tailored a training program to Fite's particular abusive propensities. But Ball could have anticipated that letting people loose on the public as sheriff's deputies without training or supervision might quite likely lead to some form of abuse of someone. The court's decision and the doctrine on which it is based finesse this key issue and consequently license a great range of powerful police and corrections officials to be irresponsible in their hiring, training, and supervising decisions.

LAWSUITS AGAINST OFFICIALS IN THEIR OFFICIAL CAPACITY

Suppose that Jane Doe, the warden of a hypothetical Ruritania County jail system, has been implementing a policy that puts inmates at increased risk of sexual abuse. Inmates who have suffered sexual abuse as a result of this policy may wish to bring a lawsuit under section 1983, seeking damages for the past abuse resulting from the policy and an injunction against continuation of the policy. The question, though, is whom they can name as defendant in the lawsuit.

Since Doe herself has implemented the policy and has the authority to discontinue it, the inmates can certainly sue her in her personal capacity. But this may not meet their needs. Unless the county indemnifies Doe, she may not have enough money to pay an award of damages. Also, if she resigns and a new warden, John Roe, is appointed, an injunction that was obtained against Doe in her personal capacity would not be valid against Roe.

The key is that the inmates can sue Doe *in her official capacity* as warden of Ruritania County jail system. Bringing a lawsuit against an official in her official capacity is a formal legal structure that allows the lawsuit to be in effect brought against the office in question—in this case, the office of warden—whoever holds that office.

A section 1983 lawsuit against an official in her official capacity should declare in the documents filing the lawsuit that it is brought against the official in her official capacity. Note that it is possible to bring a section 1983 lawsuit against an official in both her personal and her official capacities; in fact, it is usual to do so.

If now the court issues an injunction against Doe in her official capacity requiring her to discontinue the policy in dispute, then this injunction applies to the office of warden. This means that the injunction applies to anyone who is currently in charge of the Ruritania County jail system. So if Doe resigns and Roe takes over as warden, the injunction remains valid against Roe.

If the court makes an award of damages against Roe in her official capacity, she is not required to pay the money from her own pocket.

Rather, the money is to be paid from the funds of the entity of which she is an official—in this case, the Ruritania County jail system.

What then is the difference between bringing a lawsuit against Doe in her official capacity and bringing a lawsuit against the Ruritania County jail system? In fact, there is no substantive difference. It is accepted in the law that bringing a lawsuit against an official of a government entity in his official capacity is just another way of bringing a lawsuit against the government entity. Generally, the entity must be given notice of the lawsuit and an opportunity to respond to it.[16] In fact, it is usual for section 1983 lawsuits to take the precaution of naming every possible person as a defendant: every official involved, in his personal capacity and in his official capacity, as well as the government entity or entities of which they are officials.

STATE SOVEREIGN IMMUNITY

Private individuals cannot bring a lawsuit in federal court against a state unless the state explicitly consents to be sued. If a private individual files a lawsuit naming a state as one of the defendants, the court will strike the state out of the list of defendants, either at the request of the state or on the court's own initiative. If the state is the only defendant, the court will dismiss the entire lawsuit. Another way of putting this is that, in regard to lawsuits in federal court, each of the states has *sovereign immunity*.

In earlier years, this doctrine was seen to derive from the Eleventh Amendment to the federal Constitution, which reads: "The judicial power of the United States shall not be construed to extend to any suit in law or equity, commenced or prosecuted against one of the United States by citizens of another state, or by citizens or subjects of any foreign state." This appears to leave open the possibility that an individual could bring a federal lawsuit against his own state, but the 1890 Supreme Court decision in *Hans v Louisiana* rejected this possibility. In any event, according to the modern doctrine of the court, "sovereign immunity [of the states] derives not from the Eleventh Amendment but from the structure of the original Constitution itself."[17]

However, there is an important proviso, known as the *abrogation doctrine*. This doctrine, according to a unanimous Supreme Court decision, is that the Fourteenth Amendment to the federal Constitution empowers Congress to abrogate (or remove) the immunity of the states to federal lawsuits in order to enforce the provisions of the Fourteenth Amendment.[18] In fact, the purpose of section 1983 is primarily to provide a civil remedy against violations of the Fourteenth Amendment, so it was within the power of Congress in enacting section 1983 to abrogate state sovereign immunity for section 1983 lawsuits. But this principle does not determine whether Congress actually did so. Rather, the Supreme Court determines whether Congress actually did so. That is, Supreme Court decisions interpreting section 1983 determine the extent to which states have immunity against section 1983 lawsuits.

This is a crucial matter for inmates of a state incarceration facility wishing to bring a section 1983 lawsuit. If the state were to enjoy immunity against section 1983 lawsuits, then so also would the prison system that the state operates. In addition, every official of the state prison system would then enjoy immunity against being sued in his official capacity under section 1983. This is because, as we have seen, bringing a lawsuit against an official in his official capacity is just another way of bringing a lawsuit against the government entity of which he is an official.[19]

The Supreme Court has decided that states have immunity against section 1983 lawsuits for monetary damages. In formal legal terms, the court has held that neither a state nor a state official acting in his official capacity is a "person" within the meaning of "every person" in the language of section 1983, when sued for monetary damages.[20]

However, in a convoluted twist of formal legal doctrine, the Supreme Court has decided that state officials acting in their official capacity do not have immunity against section 1983 lawsuits for injunctions regarding their future conduct. According to the court's doctrine, a state official who is doing or about to do something that would violate Fourteenth Amendment rights or a federal statute protecting Fourteenth Amendment rights does not stand for the state in doing so. His act "is simply an illegal act upon the part of a State official in attempting, by the use of the name of the State, to enforce a legislative enactment which is void because unconstitutional."[21]

This doctrinal twist can be seen as a narrow but important exception to the general rule that a lawsuit against an official in his official capacity is equivalent to a lawsuit against the government entity of which he is an official. A state can never be named as a defendant in a section 1983 lawsuit, regardless of whether the lawsuit is for monetary damages or for an injunction. But a state official in his official capacity can be named as a defendant in a section 1983 lawsuit, as long as the lawsuit is only for an injunction regarding the future conduct of the official.

LAWSUITS AGAINST LOCAL AUTHORITIES
AND THEIR OFFICIALS

Many government entities at a local level operate incarceration facilities. These entities include cities, counties, and municipalities. In general, the legal system does not regard these entities as equivalent to the state itself. Despite this, for a number of years Supreme Court doctrine gave all local government entities immunity from section 1983 lawsuits.

This doctrine of local government immunity eventually created inconsistencies and became difficult to support. In a 1976 case, the Supreme Court reviewed the legislative history of the 1871 Civil Rights Act and, on the basis of its historical analysis, directly overruled its previous holdings and declared new doctrine under which local government entities do not have immunity against section 1983 lawsuits. So in a section 1983 lawsuit it is possible to name as defendants a local authority itself, an incarceration facility that the local authority operates, as well as officials of both the local authority and the incarceration facility in their official capacities. These parties may be named as defendants in lawsuits for monetary damages as well as for injunctions regarding future conduct.[22]

However, there is an important limitation. In a section 1983 lawsuit against a local government entity, whether for monetary damages or an injunction, the entity is liable only for deprivations of constitutional rights that occur as a result of the entity's *policy or custom*. The Supreme Court has made it clear that if an official of a local government entity violates a person's constitutional rights in a way that does not result from a policy or custom of the entity, the entity is not legally liable in a section 1983 lawsuit.[23]

There are indeed cases where an affirmative local government policy has instructed officials to behave in a way that, it turns out, violates people's constitutional rights. There are also cases where local government has been lax with its officials in ways that have quite predictably led to violations of people's constitutional rights. Under circumstances that the Supreme Court has narrowly prescribed, that laxness can amount to a government policy resulting in liability in a section 1983 lawsuit. The court's doctrine is that a local government entity can be liable in a section 1983 lawsuit for *failure to train* its officials:

It may seem contrary to common sense to assert that a municipality will actually have a policy of not taking reasonable steps to train its employees. But it may happen that, in light of the duties assigned to specific officers or employees the need for more or different training is so obvious, and the inadequacy so likely to result in the violation of constitutional rights, that the policymakers of the city can reasonably be said to have been deliberately indifferent to the need. In that event, the failure to provide proper training may fairly be said to represent a policy for which the city is responsible, and for which the city may be held liable if it actually causes injury.[24]

It is difficult to win a claim of failure to train. In the section 1983 lawsuit brought by Parrish for sexual abuse perpetrated by Fite, she sued Ball, the sheriff, in his official capacity (in addition to his personal capacity, as discussed earlier) for his failure to train Fite. This was equivalent to suing the county of which Ball was sheriff, so the court had to decide "whether Hot Spring County itself caused the sexual assault by its alleged failure to train Fite." The court's decision was that "even though Fite should have been more properly trained . . . Fite's intentional sexual assault of Parrish is too remote a consequence of such a failure [to train] to meet the rigorous causation standard necessary to hold the county liable."[25]

So ultimately the only redress for Parrish was whatever she could obtain from the damages award against Fite personally. The county entirely avoided responsibility for a system of government that allowed its sheriff to let Fite loose on the public as a deputy without training or supervision, regardless of whatever abusive propensities he might exhibit. The court's decision and the doctrine on which it is based license local government police and correctional authorities to be irresponsible in their hiring, training, and supervising decisions.

LAWSUITS AGAINST PRIVATE CORRECTIONS CORPORATIONS AND THEIR OFFICERS

Private corporations now operate many incarceration facilities on behalf of federal, state, and local government. The corporations and their officers are regarded as acting under color of law in their treatment of inmates.

Section 1983 lawsuits may be brought against corporations operating state and local facilities and their officers for alleged deprivations of the constitutional rights of inmates. Case law has not yet made it clear whether the "policy or custom" doctrine that limits the liability of local government entities also applies to limit the liability of private corrections corporations.[26]

THE SUBSTANTIVE CONSTITUTIONAL RIGHTS OF INMATES

Section 1983 does not provide any substantive rights but only a route into federal court for persons claiming that they have been deprived of substantive rights that the Constitution provides. The question now is what substantive constitutional rights inmates have to freedom from sexual abuse.

The main source of inmates' substantive constitutional rights is the guarantee against cruel and unusual punishments in the Eighth Amendment to the federal Constitution. On its face, this applies to the federal government but makes no mention of the states. The same is true of all of the first eight amendments to the Constitution, these being collectively dubbed the Bill of Rights in this context. However, starting from the end of the nineteenth century, the Supreme Court has applied a range of the provisions of the Bill of Rights to the states, in a process that has become known as the *incorporation doctrine*. The court has made the provision against cruel and unusual punishments applicable to the states in this way.[27]

This Eighth Amendment provision is applicable to inmates that are incarcerated following conviction of a criminal offense. The Fourteenth Amendment to the federal Constitution extends the same rights to anyone being held without having been convicted of an offense, including pretrial detainees.[28]

During much of the history of the American republic, this Eighth Amendment provision was considered to apply only to the sentence as declared in the relevant legislation and pronounced by the judge. A 1910 Supreme Court decision in a case involving the identical provision in the constitution of the Philippine Islands (then under American control) illustrates how it was applied. An officer of the Philippines government had been convicted of making two false entries in a wages cashbook. Under a provision carried over from the Spanish criminal code, he was sentenced to fifteen years' incarceration, chained at wrist and ankle at all times, and at "hard and painful labor." In addition, he was subjected for life "to the surveillance of the authorities," forbidding him to change his abode without written permission. He was also disqualified for life from voting and holding public office, and lost his retirement pay. Added to this, he was fined an amount more than six times larger than the total of his false cashbook entries. The court held that these penalties were so severe and disproportionate to his offense as to constitute cruel and unusual punishment.[29]

In the final quarter of the twentieth century, the Supreme Court began to recognize that not only the sentence as the judge pronounced it but also the conditions under which the sentence was served could constitute "punishment" under the terms of the Eighth Amendment. The court set out as its doctrine that "when the State by the affirmative exercise of its power so restrains an individual's liberty that it renders him unable to care for himself, and at the same time fails to provide for his basic human needs—e.g., food, clothing, shelter, medical care, and reasonable safety—it transgresses the substantive limits on state action set by the Eighth Amendment and the Due Process Clause [of the Fourteenth Amendment]."

The court, though, insists that not every failure to provide for the basic human needs of inmates constitutes "punishment." Rather, there must be some level of intent or neglect on the part of corrections officers that makes conditions of incarceration become punishment. The standard that the court established was that "deliberate indifference" on the part of corrections officers to any of the basic human needs of inmates would, if it resulted in serious harm, constitute cruel and unusual punishment under the Eighth Amendment.[30]

The deliberate indifference standard is important in cases of sexual abuse in incarceration. In the key 1994 case of *Farmer v Brennan*, Dee Farmer, a young male-to-female transsexual, was incarcerated in a men's facility and repeatedly raped by other inmates. The ensuing lawsuit claimed that the correctional authorities "placed petitioner [Farmer] in its general population despite knowledge that the penitentiary had a violent environment and a history of inmate assaults, and despite knowledge that petitioner, as a transsexual who 'projects feminine characteristics,' would be particularly vulnerable to sexual attack. . . . This allegedly amounted to a deliberately indifferent failure to protect petitioner's safety and thus to a violation of petitioner's Eighth Amendment rights."[31]

The court restates its established doctrine that "prison officials must ensure that inmates receive adequate food, clothing, shelter, and medical care, and must take reasonable measures to guarantee the safety of the inmates." It then adds: "In particular . . . prison officials have a duty to protect prisoners from violence at the hands of other prisoners. . . . Prison conditions may be restrictive and even harsh, but gratuitously allowing the beating or rape of one prisoner by another serves no legitimate penological objective."[32]

Yet, according to the court, the harm alleged by Farmer would constitute a violation of the Eighth Amendment only if it resulted from the deliberate indifference of corrections officials. The court explains this standard: "We hold . . . that a prison official cannot be found liable under the Eighth Amendment for denying an inmate humane conditions of confinement unless the official knows of and disregards an excessive risk to inmate health or safety; the official must both be aware of facts from which the inference could be drawn that a substantial risk of serious harm exists, and he must also draw the inference."[33]

The final phrase of this quotation—"he must also draw the inference"—is essential to the court's doctrine. It insists on what the court calls a "subjective" element in terms of the state of mind of the prison official against whom suit is brought. The court drives the point home: "an official's failure to alleviate a significant risk that he should have perceived but did not, while no cause for commendation, cannot under our cases be condemned as the infliction of punishment."[34]

As Schlanger explains, the deliberate indifference requirement establishes "extremely defendant-friendly standards [which], joined with judge and jury suspicion and dislike of incarcerated criminals, have made inmate cases extremely hard to win." She observes that, in practice, inmates will not win section 1983 lawsuits unless they can prove that corrections officers showed reckless or callous disregard for their rights.[35]

The 2009 case of *Palton v Jackson* illustrates the difficulties that the deliberate indifference requirement imposes on sexually abused inmates.[36] Arkansas corrections officer Antonio Remley forced inmate Jason Palton to perform oral sex on him on four occasions and also anally raped him. After the second sexual assault, Palton reported the assaults to Thomas Hurst, the deputy warden who was in charge of security at the facility. Palton requested to speak with Hurst, but Hurst never found time to meet with him. Yet Remley was informed that Palton had reported the two sexual assaults. In fact, Remley even confronted Palton with the reports on the third occasion that he sexually assaulted him.

There were various breaches of security throughout. Surveillance cameras that would have recorded the sexual assaults were not functioning. Cell doors that should have been locked were left unlocked. Regulations required that two correctional officers should be on guard at night, but only one—Remley—was actually on guard.

After the fourth sexual assault, Remley was less careful than usual to clean up, and Palton was able to save some of Remley's semen. This evidence led to Remley being convicted of sexual assault and sentenced to five years' incarceration.

Palton brought a section 1983 lawsuit against Remley, Hurst, and several other corrections officers. Palton's claim against the officers other than Remley and Hurst failed because he could not establish that they were deliberately indifferent to the substantial risk that Palton would be sexually assaulted and the need to protect him from such assaults. He did succeed in establishing that Hurst was deliberately indifferent to the risk and the need to protect him from it. Palton was awarded $10,000 in compensatory damages against Remley and Hurst jointly, $250,000 in punitive damages against Remley, and $1,000 in punitive damages against Hurst.

Since employees are not normally indemnified against awards of punitive damages, any liability of the Arkansas corrections system was limited to $10,000. So virtually the entire damages award was against Remley, the corrections officer who was directly responsible for the sexual abuse. The award of $250,000 in punitive damages against Remley might seem reasonable, but of course it is questionable whether it would ever be paid.

Hurst was the only senior corrections officer found liable. Although his derelictions allowed Remley to continue sexually abusing Palton, he faced a liability of merely $11,000—and possibly as little as $1,000 if the correctional authorities indemnified him against the compensatory damages award. The Arkansas corrections system demonstrated how little it is concerned with eliminating sexual abuse in incarceration by promoting Hurst the following year.[37]

Overall, the deliberate indifference requirement has made it difficult for inmates to establish liability for sexual abuse higher in the corrections hierarchy than an individual low-ranking officer. It is even quite common for the trial judge in a section 1983 lawsuit to grant summary judgment in favor of defendant corrections officers on the ground that there is not enough evidence that they were subjectively aware of the risk of the plaintiff inmate suffering sexual abuse.[38]

THE CIVIL RIGHTS OF INSTITUTIONALIZED PERSONS ACT

The Civil Rights of Institutionalized Persons Act (CRIPA) is a federal statute aimed at protecting inmates from the most serious and harmful unconstitutional practices of correctional authorities. Under the statute, the attorney general (essentially, the Department of Justice) rather than inmates themselves is authorized to bring a federal lawsuit.[39]

When the Department of Justice suspects an incarceration facility of being in violation of CRIPA standards, it first launches an investigation through its Special Litigation Section. The NPREC report explains the process: "The investigations culminate in 'finding letters' that include recommendations for specific reforms that can then become the basis of court-filed civil complaints. . . . [T]he Special Litigation Section takes a problem-solving approach and tries to work cooperatively with agencies under investigation. The strength of the evidence gathered and the threat of costly litigation is usually enough to compel reforms; the lawsuits are most often settled, usually with a settlement agreement filed simultaneously with the court complaint."[40]

A CRIPA investigation can be effective in reducing sexual abuse in incarceration. The problem is that there are far too few investigations, in part because of a lack of resources. The report *Confronting Confinement* observes: "The Department of Justice has the powers it needs to effectively investigate civil rights violations in correctional facilities; it must be given the resources and the mandate to vigorously employ them." Three years later, the NPREC report notes the continuing lack of investigations and "urges the Department of Justice to provide adequate resources to the Special Litigation Section." The most recent of the annual reports that the Department of Justice transmits to Congress describing its activities under CRIPA show that the situation remains unchanged.[41] Because of this continuing lack of investigations, there is currently no possibility of CRIPA making any substantial overall contribution to the reduction of sexual abuse in the American incarceration system.

Part IV

The Prison Rape
Elimination Act

Chapter 9

The First Ten Years

The federal Prison Rape Elimination Act of 2003 (PREA) is a complex statute with a range of provisions to set up programs and establish entities to investigate and report. It ultimately envisages a structure established under the authorization of the Department of Justice, with standards and regulations applying nationwide to eliminate sexual abuse in incarceration.

THE PREA PROVISIONS IN DETAIL

The first section of PREA consists of its title and table of contents. The second section presents the findings of Congress in enacting the statute. This section recognizes "the epidemic character of prison rape" and gives an estimate for the number of incidents of sexual abuse occurring in incarceration. It observes that some categories of inmates are more vulnerable than others. It also discusses the costs in terms of spread of disease, increased violence, and other factors that sexual abuse in incarceration imposes on society at large.[1]

The third section of the statute is its statement of purposes. Here, the statute declares its intent to "establish a zero-tolerance standard for the incidence of prison rape in prisons in the United States" and "make the prevention of prison rape a top priority in each prison system." To do so, it intends to "develop and implement national standards for the detection, prevention, reduction, and punishment of prison rape" and to make corrections officials more accountable for their role in maintaining those standards. This section also recognizes the need for improved data based on standardized definitions as well as for efficient and effective federal grant programs to further the goals of the statute.

The substantive provisions of PREA are in sections 4 through 9. The final section, section 10, consists of definitions of terms used in the statute. This final section declares that the term "prison" in the statute is meant to include any confinement facility of a federal, state, or local government. It includes juvenile facilities, local jails, and lockups. It includes facilities administered by private organizations on behalf of government. In addition, section 10 makes it clear that the term "rape," used throughout the statute, is meant to include all forms of sexual abuse.

Section 4 is devoted to statistics, data, research, and reports. It directs the BJS to carry out annual surveys and produce reports, as explained in chapter 2. It provides guidance to the BJS regarding what considerations and what views it should take into account and even what sampling and survey measures it should use.

This section establishes the Review Panel on Prison Rape within the Department of Justice to assist the BJS in accomplishing its goals. The main task of the Review Panel is to hold annual public hearings that scrutinize the prisons with the highest incidence of prison rape and the prisons with the lowest incidence of prison rape. As the statute explains, these hearings aim to identify common characteristics of victims and common characteristics of perpetrators of prison rape and to identify common characteristics of prisons and prison systems with either a high incidence or a low incidence of prison rape. Accordingly, the Review Panel is able to summon corrections officials, victims of sexual abuse in incarceration, and staff of organizations representing victims and has subpoena power to compel them to appear and testify. The discussions in chapters 2 and 3 included testimony given before the Review Panel and indicate the scope of its work.

In addition, this section requires the attorney general to submit an annual report to Congress and the secretary of health and human services on the activities of the BJS and the Review Panel. The report is to present the data on sexual abuse in a way that allows for accurate comparisons among different incarceration facilities.

To fulfill its provisions, this section authorized annual appropriations of $15 million for seven years beginning with 2004.

Section 5 involves the National Institute of Corrections, an agency established by act of Congress within the Bureau of Prisons.[2] Section 5 of PREA tasks the National Institute of Corrections with providing information, training, and education to the range of federal, state, and local authorities responsible for preventing, investigating, and punishing sexual abuse in incarceration. It also requires the National Institute of Corrections to submit an annual report to Congress and the secretary of health and human services summarizing the activities of the Department of Justice in this area. To fulfill its provisions, this section authorized annual appropriations of $5 million for seven years beginning with 2004.

Section 6 provides for grants to states "for personnel, training, technical assistance, data collection, and equipment to prevent and prosecute prisoner rape." An individual grant under this section must be at least matched by other funding and is limited to $1 million. To fulfill its provisions, this section authorized annual appropriations of $40 million for seven years beginning with 2004.

Sections 4, 5, and 6 together authorized annual appropriations of $60 million in total. This is the maximum amount that the statute authorized the federal government administration to expend. The actual appropriations have been less. Specifically, the appropriation in each of 2006, 2007, and 2008 was about $18 million.[3]

Section 7 established the NPREC as a body tasked with undertaking a comprehensive study of the penological, physical, mental, medical, social, and economic impacts of prison rape. To aid in accomplishing this and producing the subsequent report, the NPREC was to hold public hearings and receive testimony, as it considered advisable. It had subpoena power to compel individuals to appear and testify before it. This section authorized the appropriation of "such sums as may be necessary to carry out" the tasks of the NPREC.[4]

The statute specified a range of matters for the NPREC to include in this study. It was to assess the pathological and social causes of prison rape. Under this rubric, it was to assess the characteristics of inmates most likely to commit and of inmates most likely to be victims of prison rape. Also under this rubric, it was to assess the relationship of prison rape to prison facility construction and design, to the safety and security of prison facilities, to prison conditions, to prison violence, and to levels of training, supervision, and discipline of prison staff.

The study was also to assess the impact of prison rape on individuals, families, and social institutions in the broader society and on the economy generally. This was to include an assessment of the contribution of prison rape to recidivism and increased incidence of sexual assault. In addition, it was to include an assessment of the contribution of prison rape to the spread of sexually transmitted diseases, particularly HIV.

The study was also to assess the need for improved research and data. In particular, it was to assess existing federal and state systems for reporting incidents of prison rape, including an assessment of whether existing systems provide adequate assurance of confidentiality, impartiality, and the absence of reprisal. As chapter 2 discussed in the context of the BJS reports, these are important issues that greatly affect the reliability of the data.

The study was then to review the effectiveness of existing federal, state, and local facilities, policies, and practices in terms of preventing, detecting, and punishing prison rape. Finally, the study was to consider and assess various proposals for prison reform.

The statute required the NPREC to complete its work, including the submission of a report based on its study, within two years. The statute then provided that after submitting its report the NPREC would automatically terminate.

The NPREC report was to include the findings and conclusions of the study and also to recommend "national standards for enhancing the detection, prevention, reduction, and punishment of prison rape." The statute specified a range of matters that these recommended national standards were to cover. Essentially, they encompassed all matters within the range of the study. But there was a crucial limitation: "The Commission [NPREC] shall not propose a recommended standard that would impose substantial additional costs compared to the costs presently expended by Federal, State, and local prison authorities." The standards that the NPREC recommended will be discussed shortly. The cost limitation will be discussed later in this chapter and in chapter 10.

Section 8 deals with implementation into law. This section requires the attorney general within one year after receiving the NPREC report to "publish a final rule adopting national standards for the detection, prevention, reduction, and punishment of prison rape." The attorney general must give due consideration to the NPREC-recommended national standards and may also take other opinions and proposals into account. But the statute requires that the national standards must ultimately be based on the attorney general's independent judgment.

Again, there is the crucial limitation: "The Attorney General shall not establish a national standard under this section that would impose substantial additional costs compared to the costs presently expended by Federal, State, and local prison authorities." The national standards and this cost limitation will be discussed in chapter 10.

This section mandates that once the attorney general publishes and adopts national standards, they immediately apply to the federal Bureau of Prisons. But they do not become mandatory for the states. This section does provide that any state that fails to meet the national standards may lose 5 percent of the federal grant funds that the state would otherwise receive for correctional purposes. However, the wording of this provision is complex, and states may well be able to avoid losing any federal grant funds even if they fail to meet the national standards (see chapter 10). In any event, the possible loss of 5 percent of federal grant funds for correctional purposes is the only incentive that PREA provides for states to comply with the national standards.

Note that this provision does not apply to jail systems or other facilities under local rather than state control. PREA provides no incentive whatsoever for facilities under local control to comply with the national standards.

Section 9 deals indirectly with accreditation of incarceration facilities. Under this provision, organizations that provide accreditation must adopt accreditation standards that accord with the national standards adopted under section 8. If they fail to do so, they receive no new federal grants.

THE WORK OF THE NPREC

PREA was signed into law in September 2003. There was some delay in making appointments to the NPREC, which held its first meeting in July 2004 under the chairmanship of Reggie B. Walton, a federal district judge.

PREA required the NPREC to complete its study and submit its report by July 2006. But the task was far greater than Congress had anticipated in enacting PREA, and the NPREC was not able to conclude its tasks and submit its comprehensive report until June 2009.

The Approach of the NPREC

The NPREC reviewed the existing literature on sexual abuse in incarceration and conducted new studies to resolve some of the unanswered questions about causality and intervention.[5] It convened public hearings and committees of experts around the country. It drew on the knowledge and experience of corrections leaders, survivors of sexual abuse in incarceration, health-care providers, researchers, legal experts, advocates on behalf of inmates, and academics.

The NPREC allotted two sixty-day periods of public comment, in which it received written comments from hundreds of institutions and individuals. It convened roundtable discussions involving representatives of the Bureau of Prisons, associations of corrections professionals, advocacy groups, law enforcement associations, large and small correctional facilities, community corrections agencies, and survivors of sexual abuse in incarceration. It also conducted case studies at eleven incarceration and community corrections facilities of different types, with each study including a facility inspection and interviews with a range of staff.

The NPREC took care to include corrections officials at all stages, including development of the standards. In fact, corrections officials made up the great majority of the expert committees that the NPREC drew on. On various points of disagreement between corrections officials and others on those committees, the NPREC mostly adopted the view of the corrections officials. Nonetheless, JDI officers Kaiser and Stannow recall the process as one in which "advocates [on behalf of inmates] and corrections officials on the expert committees were willing collaborators in a joint venture."[6]

The NPREC was concerned with the accuracy and credibility of its sources of information, so it particularly relied on court decisions and on sworn testimony that it received. The report notes that several incidents of sexual abuse described in it occurred many years ago. But it expresses the belief that these incidents illustrate continuing problems and challenges in correctional facilities today. This is a fair assessment, as PREA has not changed the nature of sexual abuse in incarceration (see chapter 4).

The NPREC delivered its report with recommended national standards in June 2009 and terminated in August 2009.

The Findings of the NPREC Report

Parts I and II of this book have already discussed much of the material that makes up the findings of the NPREC report.[7] But these findings are a good assessment of the severe national problem of pervasive sexual abuse in incarceration and the possible means of eliminating that abuse:

1. Protecting prisoners from sexual abuse remains a challenge in correctional facilities across the country. Too often, in what should be secure environments, men, women, and children are raped or abused by other incarcerated individuals and corrections staff.

2. Sexual abuse is not an inevitable feature of incarceration. Leadership matters because corrections administrators can create a culture within facilities that promotes safety instead of one that tolerates abuse.

3. Certain individuals are more at risk of sexual abuse than others. Corrections administrators must routinely do more to identify those who are vulnerable and protect them in ways that do not leave them isolated and without access to rehabilitative programming.

4. Few correctional facilities are subject to the kind of rigorous internal monitoring and external oversight that would reveal why abuse occurs and how to prevent it. Dramatic reductions in sexual abuse depend on both.

5. Many victims cannot safely and easily report sexual abuse, and those who speak out often do so to no avail. Reporting procedures must be improved to instill confidence and protect individuals from retaliation without relying on isolation. Investigations must be thorough and competent. Perpetrators must be held accountable through administrative sanctions and criminal prosecution.

6. Victims are unlikely to receive the treatment and support known to minimize the trauma of abuse. Correctional facilities need to ensure immediate and ongoing access to medical and mental health care and supportive services.

7. Juveniles in confinement are much more likely than incarcerated adults to be sexually abused, and they are particularly at risk when confined with adults. To be effective, sexual abuse prevention, investigation, and treatment must be tailored to the developmental capacities and needs of youth.

8. Individuals under correctional supervision in the community, who outnumber prisoners by more than two to one, are at risk of sexual abuse. The nature and consequences of the abuse are no less severe, and it jeopardizes the likelihood of their successful reentry.

9. A large and growing number of detained immigrants are at risk of sexual abuse. Their heightened vulnerability and unusual circumstances require special interventions.

The NPREC Recommendations for National Standards

The NPREC report included four sets of recommended national standards, each applicable to a specific incarceration setting: adult prisons and jails, juvenile facilities, community corrections facilities, and lockups. These standards were to apply to federal, state, and local facilities. The overall structure and layout of the standards in the NPREC report strongly influenced the Department of Justice in setting out both its proposed and its final national standards.[8]

However, the Department of Justice raised objections to a number of the specific provisions that the NPREC had included in its recommended national standards. Its objections were largely on the ground of cost. These provisions particularly included several in the first section of the NPREC-recommended national standards, entitled *Prevention and Response Planning*. Specifically, provision PP-3 required staff to provide the supervision necessary to protect inmates from sexual abuse. Provision PP-4 restricted staff of the opposite gender (except in case of emergency) from performing strip searches, pat-down searches, and visual body cavity searches and from viewing inmates who are nude or performing bodily functions.[9] Provision PP-7 required the use of video monitoring systems and other appropriate technology to supplement sexual abuse prevention, detection, and response efforts. It also required an assessment, at least annually, of the feasibility of and need for new or additional monitoring technology.

Overall, the NPREC acknowledged that the cost limitation imposed by PREA prevented it from making certain further proposals. At the press conference announcing the release of the report, Chairman Walton explained:

One of the restrictions in the legislation that did put some limitations on what the Commission did and could do was the fact that Congress said that we could not make recommendations that would have a substantial fiscal implication. We believe that we have accomplished that objective. There were many things that we could have recommended and things that clearly could have made a difference if money was not an issue, but obviously it is, and we had a proscription against making recommendations that would substantially increase the fiscal outlay of running our prisons and jails. Obviously, if you had single bunking, that would go a long way, but that would be expensive. Obviously, if we could redesign and reconstruct prisons, that are some—the old prisons that are difficult to police, that would make a difference.[10]

THE DEPARTMENT OF JUSTICE REVIEW OF THE NPREC-RECOMMENDED NATIONAL STANDARDS

Following publication of the NPREC report, the Department of Justice established an internal working group to review each of the NPREC-recommended national standards and to work toward preparing draft national standards.[11] Representatives of a wide range of divisions within the Department of Justice served in the working group. They included officials from the federal marshals, prison, and prosecutorial services as well as from the divisions dealing with civil rights, violence against women, and a number of justice programs. BJS officials also participated.

In early 2010, the working group held a number of listening sessions at which various individuals and groups provided preliminary input. The participants included representatives of state prisons, local jails, juvenile facilities, community corrections programs, lockups, state and local sexual abuse associations and service providers, national advocacy groups, survivors of sexual abuse in incarceration, and former members of the NPREC.

From March to May 2010, the Department of Justice accepted public input on the NPREC-recommended national standards. It received many hundreds of comments from a range of individuals and organizations. These included currently and formerly incarcerated individuals, county sheriffs, state correctional authorities, social service providers, and advocacy organizations.

The Booz Allen Hamilton Analysis for the
NPREC-Recommended Standards

The NPREC did not provide any cost analysis of its recommended national standards. The Department of Justice commissioned a cost impact analysis from the consulting firm of Booz Allen Hamilton. This firm selected a sample of correctional systems across the country: thirteen state prison systems, sixteen jail jurisdictions, ten juvenile agencies, four lockup facilities, and six community confinement jurisdictions. It assembled a team of experts who conducted on-site meetings with representatives of each of these forty-nine corrections agencies and reviewed documentation that those agencies provided. The report of its study appeared in June 2010.[12]

This Booz Allen Hamilton analysis has been criticized on a number of grounds. It relied on a small, nonrandom sample of facilities. Its cost estimates drew largely on estimates given by corrections professionals, bringing a danger of bias in the form of exaggerated costs. The Department of Justice acknowledges these issues with the Booz Allen Hamilton estimates and declares that it "has subjected those estimates to rigorous analysis and validation, eliminating where appropriate estimates that seem biased, speculative, [or] unreliable." But, despite this assurance, it remains possible that the Booz Allen Hamilton cost estimates are exaggerated.[13]

The Booz Allen Hamilton analysis focused largely on the particular provisions in the NPREC-recommended standards that were detailed previously in this chapter. It found the main potential sources for increased costs to be provisions PP-3 (providing supervision necessary to protect inmates from sexual abuse), PP-4 (restricting staff of the opposite gender from performing strip searches, etc.), and PP-7 (requiring the use of video monitoring systems). In fact, it estimated that these three provisions would together account for 99 percent of total up-front costs and 85 percent of total ongoing compliance costs of implementing the NPREC-recommended standards.[14]

In the RIA, the Department of Justice adopts a unified form for all of its assessments for implementing national standards. As a federal government agency, it is obliged to limit all of its cost/benefit analyses to a time frame based on reasonable judgments about the foreseeable future. Accordingly, it uses a fifteen-year time horizon. That is, it considers the cost of implementing national standards as if they were spread uniformly over a fifteen-year period, starting from 2012 and going out to 2026.[15]

Using this approach, and based on the Booz Allen Hamilton analysis, the Department of Justice was able to assess the nationwide costs of implementing the NPREC-recommended standards for prisons, jails, lockups, confinement in community corrections, and juvenile facilities. It assessed the projected costs at just under $6 billion per year.[16]

Recall that in the RIA the Department of Justice assesses the quantifiable costs of sexual abuse in incarceration as between the highly conservative lower-bound estimate of $26.9 billion and the more realistic, though still conservative, estimate of $51.9 billion. This is the quantifiable cost in each single year. So the NPREC-recommended national standards called for an annual expenditure to eliminate sexual abuse in incarceration that is certainly no more than about 22 percent of the quantifiable annual cost of this abuse and is more likely to be only about 12 percent of that cost or even less.[17]

Government agencies must conduct a cost/benefit analysis for any proposed regulations expected to have a significant impact, taking into account both quantitative and qualitative costs and benefits. Plainly, the benefit of any given regulation that might be adopted under PREA is the reduction in sexual abuse that results from the regulation. But the problem is that any quantitative estimate of how much sexual abuse any given regulation will prevent is to a considerable degree speculative. This issue will be considered further in the context of the final PREA national standards promulgated by the Department of Justice.[18]

THE DEPARTMENT OF JUSTICE'S DRAFT NATIONAL STANDARDS

In January 2011 the Department of Justice published its own draft proposals for PREA national standards. At the same time, it published a cost/benefit analysis of those proposed standards, which resulted from further work by the firm of Booz Allen Hamilton. It also requested public input on a number of specific questions on the draft proposals as well as on the proposals and analysis generally. It received over one thousand comments that, as was the case with the comments on the NPREC-recommended national standards, represented a wide range of viewpoints.[19]

Taking these comments into account along with a further analysis by Booz Allen Hamilton, the Department of Justice finally published its PREA national standards in May 2012. These entirely supersede the draft proposals, and so this book will not consider the draft proposals in any detail. But there will be some references to them in regard to how particular provisions developed from the NPREC-recommended standards through to the final PREA national standards (see chapter 10).

Chapter 10

The National Standards

The Department of Justice issued the final PREA national standards in 2012. They largely follow the same structure and layout as the NPREC-recommended national standards. There are four sets of regulations, designated as subparts A through D of the national standards. Subpart A deals with adult prisons and jails. Subpart B deals with lockups. Subpart C deals with community confinement facilities, defined as any "community correctional facility . . . in which offenders or defendants reside as part of a term of imprisonment or as a condition of pre-trial release or post-release supervision."[1] Subpart D deals with juvenile facilities.

Each of these subparts is divided into categories similar to those in the NPREC-recommended national standards. There are two further subparts within the national standards: subpart E deals with auditing and corrective action, and subpart F deals with state compliance.

THE PROVISIONS OF THE NATIONAL STANDARDS

The following discussion encompasses the chief provisions in the national standards. The category headings are those of the national standards.

Prevention Planning

Within this first category of regulations, the first provision is aimed at ensuring that correctional authorities pay appropriate attention to the prevention of sexual abuse in their facilities. A key requirement is that each authority—the regulations use the equivalent term "agency"—is required to employ a PREA coordinator or designate an existing employee as PREA coordinator. This individual must be an upper-level official "with sufficient time and authority to develop, implement, and oversee agency efforts to comply with the PREA standards."[2]

This PREA coordinator operates at the administrative level of the correctional authority. But many correctional authorities operate more than one incarceration facility. Where this is the case for adult prisons and jails and for juvenile facilities, the regulations impose the further requirement that "each facility shall designate a PREA compliance manager with sufficient time and authority to coordinate the facility's efforts to comply with the PREA standards."[3]

This category of regulations also includes provisions dealing with supervision and monitoring of inmates. Recall that the NPREC-recommended national standards included a provision dealing with staff supervision of inmates (PP-3) and a provision dealing with the use of video monitoring and other technology (PP-7) and that the Booz Allen Hamilton report focused on these provisions as particularly costly. The Department of Justice draft standards combined the supervision and monitoring of inmates into a single provision, "in recognition that direct staff supervision and video monitoring are two methods of achieving one goal: Reducing the opportunity for abuse to occur unseen." Former members of the NPREC expressed concern that combining these provisions deemphasizes the specific need for staff supervision to protect inmates from sexual abuse. Nevertheless, the national standards similarly combine the supervision and monitoring of inmates into a single provision.[4]

The Department of Justice posed a number of questions regarding whether specific staffing levels should be required. This drew many comments, a number of which expressed concern regarding the potential cost of implementing specific staffing levels. Accordingly, the final regulation provides general guidelines rather than setting any specific level of staffing. For adult prisons and jails, the regulation requires every facility to "develop, document, and make its best efforts to comply on a regular basis with a staffing plan that provides for adequate levels of staffing, and, where applicable, video monitoring, to protect inmates against sexual abuse."[5]

However, the counterpart provisions for lockups and for community confinement facilities do not require any "best efforts" to be made. The regulation simply requires every such facility to "develop and document a staffing plan that provides for adequate levels of staffing, and, where

applicable, video monitoring, to protect inmates against sexual abuse."
This omission is not a legislative oversight; the Department of Justice
explicitly declares, without giving any reason, that these facilities "are
exempt from the 'best efforts' language."[6]

For lockups and community confinement facilities as well as for adult
prisons and jails, the regulation does require each facility to take a range
of factors into account in developing its plan for staffing levels and video
monitoring. Also, if a facility fails to comply with the staffing plan that
it has developed it must "document and justify all deviations from the
plan." In addition, each facility must review the effectiveness of its plan
at least once a year.[7]

The corresponding regulation for juvenile facilities is more stringent.
It requires certain specified minimum staff-to-inmate ratios, although
because of cost considerations it delays implementing this requirement
until October 2017. It goes beyond any "best efforts" language, requiring every facility to "comply with the staffing plan except during limited
and discrete exigent circumstances, and . . . fully document deviations
from the plan during such circumstances."[8]

There are also regulations regarding juveniles held in adult prisons
and jails and in lockups. Essentially, these regulations aim to prevent
these juveniles being in unsupervised contact with adults but without
depriving them of exercise, education, or work opportunities. The Department of Justice decided not to impose a general ban on holding
juveniles in adult facilities because of the major legislative changes that
this would require in a number of states but declares that it "reserves the
right to reexamine this question if warranted."[9]

This first category of regulations also includes provisions imposing restrictions on staff of the opposite gender searching inmates and viewing
them nude or performing bodily functions. This corresponds to provision PP-4 in the NPREC-recommended national standards, which the
Booz Allen Hamilton report also focused on as being particularly costly.
Provision PP-4 in fact wholly prohibited cross-gender strip searches and
visual body cavity searches except in the case of emergency. It likewise
restricted cross-gender pat-down searches and cross-gender viewing of
inmates nude or performing bodily functions, except in the case of emergency or other extraordinary or unforeseen circumstances.[10]

The Department of Justice draft national standards included a similar
provision to PP-4 for juvenile facilities but not for adult facilities. The
concern was that the reorganization required to prohibit cross-gender
viewing and searching in adult facilities would be costly to implement.
There was also concern that it would require changes in the correctional
workforce that would reduce opportunities for hiring and promotion,

violate collective bargaining agreements, and could even violate federal and state equal employment opportunities laws.[11]

The national standards also include a similar provision to PP-4 for juvenile facilities. For adult facilities, the national standards adopt a compromise position. There are strong restrictions on male staff searching female inmates and viewing them nude or performing bodily functions but no equivalent restriction regarding male inmates. The Department of Justice explains that a very large proportion of female prison and jail inmates have been sexually abused by men prior to incarceration and so would likely be traumatized by being searched or viewed by male staff. The Department of Justice position also represents a compromise regarding costs. Restricting female staff from searching and viewing male inmates would be much more costly, simply because there are so many more male than female inmates. This compromise, though, takes no account of the sexual abuse that female staff perpetrate against male inmates.[12]

Responsive Planning

The provisions within this category of regulations are aimed at ensuring that correctional agencies establish procedures for responding to incidents and allegations of sexual abuse and sexual harassment. These procedures must include offering victims of sexual abuse access to forensic medical examinations without cost and, where possible, making available a victim advocate from a rape crisis center. Other categories of the regulations, discussed shortly, provide more information on what these response procedures must entail.

There must also be procedures for ensuring that administrative or criminal investigations are carried out for all allegations of sexual abuse and sexual harassment. Again, other categories of the regulations, discussed shortly, provide more information on how these investigations must be performed.[13]

Training and Education

Within this category of regulations there are provisions dealing with training and educating corrections staff, volunteers, and contractors who have contact with inmates. The training and education must encompass a range of issues related to preventing, detecting, and responding to sexual abuse and sexual harassment. For staff members there must be periodic refresher training. There must be proper documentation of the participation of staff, volunteers, and contractors in training and education.

This category also includes regulations requiring inmates to be educated on various issues regarding sexual abuse and sexual harassment. These encompass information on the right to be free from sexual abuse and sexual harassment and to be free from retaliation for reporting incidents. Inmates must also be informed of the facility's policies and procedures for responding to incidents. There must be proper documentation of the participation of inmates in these education sessions.

There are also special training and education requirements for staff that conduct investigations into reports of sexual abuse. In addition, every correctional agency must ensure that medical and mental healthcare practitioners who work regularly in its facilities have been trained in detecting, assessing, responding to, and reporting sexual abuse and sexual harassment. There must be proper documentation of participation in all such training sessions.[14]

Screening for Risk of Sexual Victimization and Abusiveness

Some inmates are at greater risk of being sexually abused (see chapter 4). Some inmates are more likely to sexually abuse other inmates. The provisions within this category of regulations focus on screening inmates in order to identify likely victims and likely abusers and on taking appropriate measures to keep likely victims away from likely abusers.

The key issues regarding screening are when it is to take place, how it is to be conducted, and how the information obtained from screening is to be used. Plainly, it would be best if screening information could be obtained as soon as an individual arrives at a facility, especially since many inmates suffer sexual abuse within the first day of their incarceration (see part I). But the national standards do not require immediate screening. The regulations for adult prisons and jails, community confinement facilities, and juvenile facilities require only that an intake screening take place within seventy-two hours of arrival. There must be further screening later, to reassess the risk that the inmate will be sexually abused or be sexually abusive, taking into account any relevant information that the facility has received since the intake screening. In adult prisons and jails and community confinement facilities, further screening must take place within thirty days of arrival at the facility. In juvenile facilities, further screening must take place periodically during the period of confinement.

The regulations for adult prisons and jails, community confinement facilities, and juvenile facilities require an "objective screening instrument" to be used for screening. The regulations do not define what is meant by an objective screening instrument, but in fact the term is widely used to mean a form questionnaire, usually developed on the basis of specialized knowledge, but requiring no special knowledge or skills on the part of the individual conducting the screening or the individual being screened. In adult prisons and jails and community confinement facilities, the screening must take account of factors relevant to vulnerability to sexual abuse, including the inmate's age and physical build and whether the inmate has a mental, physical, or developmental disability. It must also take account of factors relevant to being sexually abusive, including any prior history of being violent or sexually abusive.

The regulations provide that, in these facilities, the information obtained from screening is to be used for making appropriate decisions regarding each inmate's housing, work, education, and various program assignments. In addition, the regulations for adult prisons and jails and juvenile facilities focus on the issue of placement in segregated housing. In many of these facilities the only immediate way to protect an inmate from sexual abuse is to place him or her in segregated housing, with the detriments of isolation and loss of services and programs (see chapter 4). The regulations now provide that segregated housing should be used as a means of protection only as a last resort and that any decision to segregate an inmate for his or her protection must be properly documented and regularly reassessed.[15]

Reporting

This category of the regulations deals with the procedures for reporting and registering complaints of sexual abuse and sexual harassment. A particular concern, raised in comments to the Department of Justice by many current and former inmates, was the need for a means to report incidents privately and also to an entity independent of the correctional agency.

Accordingly, the regulations require the correctional agency to provide "multiple internal ways for inmates to privately report sexual abuse and sexual harassment, retaliation by other inmates or staff for reporting sexual abuse and sexual harassment, and staff neglect or violation of responsibilities that may have contributed to such incidents." They require that "[s]taff shall accept reports made verbally, in writing, anonymously, and from third parties and shall promptly document any verbal reports." They also require there to be "at least one way for inmates to report abuse or harassment to a public or private entity or office that is not part of the agency, and that is able to receive and immediately forward inmate reports of sexual abuse and sexual harassment to agency officials, allowing the inmate to remain anonymous upon request."[16]

This category also focuses on the internal grievance procedures of correctional agencies. Recall that some agencies have implemented convoluted and unfair grievance procedures with very severe filing deadlines, and inmates who fail to negotiate these grievance procedures can be barred from seeking judicial remedies under the provision of the PLRA regarding exhaustion of administrative remedies. A key provision in the regulations now prohibits any time limit on when an inmate may submit a grievance regarding an allegation of sexual abuse. It also requires that inmates be allowed the assistance of other inmates, staff members, family members, attorneys, and outside advocates in filing a grievance. In addition, the agency must reach its decision on the grievance in a timely fashion, as specified in the regulation.[17]

This category of the regulations also deals with the need for inmate victims of sexual abuse to have access to emotional support services from outside the incarceration facility. It requires correctional authorities to inform inmates of such support services and to permit reasonable telephone or mail communication with them with as much confidentiality as possible. In addition, it encourages correctional authorities to reach agreement with community service providers to provide support services. Note also that the correctional authority must establish a way for any third party to report sexual abuse or sexual harassment of an inmate and must make information on how to do so publicly available.[18]

Official Response Following an Inmate Report

This category of the regulations sets out appropriate procedures for correctional agencies to follow regarding incidents of sexual abuse or sexual harassment. A key provision is that facilities must develop a written institutional plan to coordinate actions taken in response to an incident. The plan must encompass the responsibilities of staff who first respond to an incident as well as those of medical and mental health practitioners, investigators, and senior corrections staff.

The detailed provisions include requirements that when an incident occurs or is suspected, staff must separate the alleged victim and abuser and take various steps to preserve evidence of sexual abuse. Staff must also properly report the incident.

The provisions also encompass appropriate procedures to follow regarding retaliation against inmates or staff for reporting an incident. Facilities must develop policies to protect inmates and staff against retaliation for reporting sexual abuse or sexual harassment or for cooperating with investigations. A particular provision is that, following a report of sexual abuse, the facility must monitor the conduct and treatment of the victim and of the staff or inmates who reported the abuse, to see if there are changes that suggest possible retaliation.[19]

Investigations

This category of the regulations deals with administrative and criminal investigations into allegations of sexual abuse and sexual harassment. It sets out appropriate procedures for agencies to follow regarding such matters as preservation of evidence, interviewing, and documentation.

A particular provision deals with the concern that administrative investigations reject too many allegations of sexual abuse or sexual harassment as not "substantiated." The provision now requires that an allegation must be deemed substantiated if it is supported by a preponderance of the evidence.[20]

Discipline

The regulations here require that staff and inmates who violate policies regarding sexual abuse and sexual harassment will be subject to disciplinary sanctions. A staff member who actually engages in sexual abuse can expect to be fired and reported to law enforcement.

A particular provision prohibits disciplining inmates who engage in "willing" sexual activity with staff. Another provision prohibits treating consensual sex between inmates as sexual abuse.[21]

Medical and Mental Care

The regulations in this category require correctional agencies to provide inmate victims of sexual abuse with unimpeded access to emergency and ongoing medical and mental health care. This must include information about and timely access to prophylaxis against sexually transmitted infections.

For women victims of sexual abuse by male staff or inmates, the medical services provided must include information about and timely access to emergency contraception, as well as pregnancy tests. When the sexual abuse causes pregnancy, the victim must "receive timely and comprehensive information about and timely access to all lawful pregnancy-related services."

The standard of care provided to inmates must be consistent with the community level of care. In a departure from the practice of many correctional agencies, the regulations require that all these services must be provided free of charge to inmates and must not be made contingent on naming the abuser or cooperating with any investigation.[22]

Data Collection and Review

The regulations in this category require correctional agencies to conduct a sexual abuse incident review at the conclusion of every sexual abuse investigation. The only exception is if the allegation is determined to be unfounded (see chapter 2). The review team must include upper-level management officials, with input from supervisors, investigators, and medical or mental health practitioners. It must consider whether the investigation indicates a need for changes in policy, practice, physical structures, staffing, or monitoring.

The review team makes its report and recommendations to the head of the facility and the PREA coordinator or compliance manager. The facility must either implement the review team's recommendations or document its reasons for not doing so.

In addition, each correctional agency must collect and aggregate its data on incidents of sexual abuse, use the data to identify problem areas, and take corrective action on an ongoing basis. Each agency must at least annually prepare a report of its findings and corrective actions, with comparisons with prior years and an assessment of progress in addressing sexual abuse. The aggregated sexual abuse data and the reports must be made readily available to the public, with personal and security-related information removed as appropriate.[23]

Auditing and Corrective Action

The regulations in this category address the crucial issue of external oversight of incarceration facilities. As the secretary of the California Department of Corrections and Rehabilitation, who was formerly inspector general of that institution, insisted in testimony before the NPREC, the problem of sexual abuse in incarceration "cannot be solved without some form of public oversight of our Nation's prisons and jails."[24]

Accordingly, the regulations require every incarceration facility (except any lockups that do not house detainees overnight) to be comprehensively audited for compliance with PREA standards at least every three years. The auditor must be certified by the Department of Justice and must not be part of, or under the authority of, the correctional agency whose facility is being audited.

The auditor must be free to enter and tour facilities, review documents, and interview staff and inmates, as the auditor deems appropriate. In addition, inmates must be permitted to communicate confidentially with the auditor.

If the audit finds that the facility does not meet PREA standards, the auditor and the correctional agency are to jointly develop a corrective action plan, and the auditor is to verify implementation of the plan. The auditor's final report must be made readily available to the public, with personal information removed as appropriate.[25]

FEDERAL, STATE, AND LOCAL COMPLIANCE

Federal Agencies

A number of federal agencies operate incarceration facilities. These include the Bureau of Prisons and the United States Marshals Service, which are agencies of the Department of Justice. But agencies of other federal government departments also operate incarceration facilities. In these facilities, as in other American incarceration facilities, sexual abuse is pervasive. In particular, it is well recognized that sexual abuse is pervasive in the facilities operated by and on behalf of the United States Immigration and Customs Enforcement, which is an agency of the Department of Homeland Security. There is also concern regarding high levels of sexual abuse in Native American tribal detention facilities operated by the Bureau of Indian Affairs, which is an agency of the Department of the Interior.[26]

PREA explicitly provides that the national standards are immediately binding in regard to facilities operated by or on behalf of the Bureau of Prisons. In addition, the Department of Justice has used its authority to decide that the national standards apply to its own agency, the United States Marshals Service.

After some public debate and discussion, the Department of Justice has now concluded that PREA applies to all incarceration facilities that are operated by or on behalf of any federal department. But this does not in itself result in effective implementation of the PREA national standards, because PREA does not include any provision dealing with how PREA requirements are to be implemented in federal incarceration facilities other than those of the Bureau of Prisons. In particular, there is no provision in PREA that makes the national standards binding on any agency of the Department of Homeland Security or the Department of the Interior.

In fact, the Department of Justice has conceded that the agencies of other federal departments have their own authorities to regulate conditions of incarceration and so are not bound by the national standards. The Department of Justice declares that it will work with other federal departments to develop regulations that will satisfy the requirements of PREA. Accordingly, U.S. President Barack Obama has directed all federal agencies that operate confinement facilities to work with the Department of Justice to achieve this goal.[27]

State and Local Agencies

The terms of PREA encompass every incarceration facility operated by or on behalf of a state or local government. But this does not in itself result in effective implementation of the PREA national standards in state or local incarceration facilities. The reason is simply that the PREA national standards are not mandatory for state and local governments. PREA does not impose any legal obligation whatsoever on state or local government to act in accordance with its declared principles or to comply with the national standards issued under its authority.

A state may face a financial penalty if the facilities that it operates or that are operated on its behalf fail to meet the PREA national standards. But the penalty is relatively slight. Under section 8 of PREA, the state may lose 5 percent of any federal grant funds for prison purposes that it would otherwise have received. The state will avoid even this loss if it gives an assurance that it will use the 5 percent of funds at issue for the purpose of enabling it to comply with the PREA national standards in the future.

This potential loss of funds does not apply to local government. PREA does not provide for any penalty at all on a local government if the facilities that it operates or that are operated on its behalf fail to meet the PREA national standards.[28]

In fact, the Department of Justice believes that state and local government correctional authorities will *not* undertake full nationwide implementation of the PREA national standards. Introducing its cost analysis of the PREA national standards, the RIA explains:

The cost estimates set forth in this section are the costs of full nationwide compliance with, and implementation of, the national standards in all covered facilities. . . . [H]owever, PREA does not require full nationwide compliance, nor does it enact a mechanism for the Department [of Justice] to direct or enforce such compliance. Fiscal realities faced by agencies throughout the country make it virtually certain that the total costs actually incurred will in the aggregate fall well short of the full nationwide compliance costs calculated in this RIA.

The costs actually incurred will depend on the specific choices that State, local, and private correction agencies make with regard to adoption of the standards, and correspondingly on the outlays that those agencies are willing and able to make in choosing to implement the standards in their facilities.[29]

THE COST ANALYSIS OF THE PREA NATIONAL STANDARDS

Chapter 9 explained the unified form that the Department of Justice has adopted for all of its cost assessments for implementing the PREA national standards. Recall that its approach is to estimate costs as if they were spread uniformly over a fifteen-year period, starting from 2012 and going out to 2026.

On this basis, the Booz Allen Hamilton analysis provided the cost estimates for state, local, and private incarceration facilities to comply with the final PREA national standards. The Department of Justice provided its own internal assessments for the Bureau of Prisons and the United States Marshals Service.

The Department of Justice assessment in the RIA is that the annualized cost of full nationwide compliance with the PREA national standards would be around $470 million. This is less than one-twelfth of the $6 billion annualized assessment for the NPREC-recommended national standards. Of the approximately $470 million cost, about $65 million would be required for prisons, $165 million for jails, $130 million for juvenile facilities, $95 million for lockups, and $13 million for community confinement facilities.[30]

The most costly part of the regulations is the prevention-planning category. Within this category, full nationwide compliance would entail annualized costs of around $110 million for the provisions requiring a PREA coordinator and compliance manager and $120 million for the provisions relating to staffing, supervision, and monitoring. The other notably costly categories are training, with an annualized cost of around $80 million, and screening, with an annualized cost of around $60 million. Thus, full nationwide compliance with the regulations for prevention planning, training, and screening would cost about $370 million annually, which is about 80 percent of the annualized cost of the PREA national standards as a whole.[31]

Regarding the overall cost, recall that section 8 of PREA stipulates that the PREA national standards must not "impose substantial additional costs compared to the costs presently expended by Federal, State, and local prison authorities." The total annual nationwide expenditure on correctional operations is nearly $80 billion. The $470 million cost assessment for the PREA national standards is about 0.6 percent of this total. Accordingly, the Department of Justice concludes "that the 'additional costs' imposed by the PREA standards are not 'substantial' within the meaning of the statute."[32]

The Department of Justice argues that this relatively modest cost level gives correctional authorities the best possible incentive to comply with the PREA national standards. In particular, it rejects some public comments that called for more stringent standards along the lines of the NPREC-recommended national standards: "[W]e are not persuaded that making the standards more stringent would make them more effective if increased stringency leads to increased costs. It may in fact have the opposite effect if agencies find the cost of compliance so prohibitive as to remove any incentive to adopt them."[33]

THE COST JUSTIFICATION ANALYSIS
OF THE PREA NATIONAL STANDARDS

Finally, the RIA considers whether the PREA national standards are justified by the benefits that they would bring if they were fully implemented nationwide. Plainly, these benefits would be the reduction in sexual abuse in incarceration resulting from implementing the regulations.

The approach of the RIA is to undertake a break-even analysis. The idea of this is to determine how much of a reduction in sexual abuse in incarceration would be needed for the monetary value of this reduction to break even with the costs of implementing the PREA national standards.

To ascribe a monetary value to a reduction in sexual abuse in incarceration, the RIA draws on its assessment of the quantifiable cost of this abuse (see chapter 5). Recall that the RIA in fact made a number of different assessments of the quantifiable cost of sexual abuse, by applying the WTA and WTP cost estimates separately to each of its three assessments of the prevalence of sexual abuse in incarceration (principal, adjusted, and lower-bound). In its break-even analysis, the RIA now applies each of those assessments of the quantifiable cost of sexual abuse separately in regard to sexual abuse in prisons, jails, juvenile facilities, lockups, and community confinement facilities.

The overall result of the break-even analysis, which the RIA presents in a number of tables, is that the PREA national standards would be fully justified if they reduced the prevalence of sexual abuse by only about 1.5 percent in adult facilities and only 3 percent in juvenile facilities. Note that this does not require a reduction each year from the previous year. It merely requires maintaining each year a reduction of no more than about 1.5 percent in adult facilities and 3 percent in juvenile facilities *from the present level*. That is, to fully justify implementing the PREA-recommended standards, all that is needed is this continuing percentage reduction from the present level of sexual abuse of inmates.[34]

In terms of numbers of victims of sexual abuse in incarceration, the RIA concludes that an annual reduction of around 2,300 (across all facility types) would be enough to break even with the cost of implementing the PREA national standards. Again, this does not require a reduction each year from the previous year. It merely requires maintaining each year a reduction of no more than around 2,300 victims *from the present level*. That is, to fully justify implementing the PREA-recommended standards, all that is needed is this continuing reduction from the present level of sexual abuse of inmates.

It remains, though, to consider whether fully implementing the PREA national standards would in fact achieve this level of reduction. The RIA declares: "We believe it reasonable to expect that when fully adopted and implemented, the standards will achieve at least this level of reduction in the prevalence of prison sexual abuse. When one considers the non-monetized benefits of avoiding prison rape, the break-even thresholds become much lower." In general, corrections agencies and advocacy groups have agreed that these Department of Justice predictions as to the effectiveness of the PREA national standards are reasonable, and indeed conservative.[35]

In fact, the RIA is willing to go further. It considers that it is "appropriate and conservative to assume that, if fully implemented, the [national] standards . . . will succeed in reducing the prevalence of prison rape by at least 4% per year" from current levels.[36]

Chapter 11

The Future of the American Institution of Prison Rape

As of 2012, PREA has been in force for ten years. Yet it is clear from the surveys, court cases, reports, and symbols of popular culture discussed in earlier chapters that all forms of sexual abuse continue to pervade the American system of incarceration. At the present day, prison rape is still an American institution.[1]

Although PREA professed as its leading purpose to "establish a zero-tolerance standard for the incidence of prison rape in prisons in the United States," a mere profession of zero tolerance is not enough to deal with an entrenched institution. In Hall's action for civil damages for sexual abuse by corrections officer Terrell, the federal trial court observed:

"You have the right to be safe from sexual assault/rape. You have the right to be safe from unwanted sexual advances." Thus are inmates of the Colorado Department of Corrections (CDOC) counseled under the agency's "Prison Rape Elimination Procedure," Administrative Regulation Number 100–40. Indeed, CDOC declares that it "has a zero-tolerance policy relating to sexual assault/rape and sexual misconduct. It is the policy of the DOC to fully investigate and aggressively prosecute those who are involved in such conduct."

For Amanda Hall, an inmate at Denver Women's Correctional Facility, the right to be safe from sexual assault and rape by one of her guards turned out to be worth no more than the paper upon which Regulation 100–40 was printed.

Similarly, the U.S. military establishment has for years professed zero tolerance of sexual abuse, but, despite this, sexual abuse remains scandalously prevalent in the armed forces.[2]

THE POTENTIAL EFFECT OF THE
PREA NATIONAL STANDARDS

A question for the future is whether the PREA national standards will lead to the demise of the American institution of prison rape. Certainly, it seems reasonable to conclude that if every incarceration facility nationwide fully complied with the national standards, there would be a substantial reduction in all forms of sexual abuse in incarceration. But it is not clear that the reduction would be substantial enough.

For example, it might be optimistic to expect a reduction of as much as 50 percent from the current level, yet even this might not be enough. Recall that the current most conservative estimate of the prevalence of sexual abuse in incarceration is that in a single year there are at least 149,200 victims, of whom at least 55,400 suffer violent or repeated rape (see chapter 2). If there were no more than a 50 percent reduction from this level, there would still be at least 74,600 victims, with at least 27,700 of them suffering violent or repeated rape, in a single year. With sexual abuse at this level it would still be appropriate to regard prison rape as an American institution.

Yet a 50 percent reduction is optimistic because, as chapters 9 and 10 explained, the national standards are a severe compromise between likely effectiveness and cost. The Department of Justice acknowledges that they are not the most effective standards that could be devised but was unwilling to promulgate more stringent standards, largely for reasons of cost. In fact, the Department of Justice goes no further than claiming that the national standards would, if fully implemented, succeed in reducing the prevalence of prison rape by at least 4 percent per year from current levels (see chapter 10). But while a reduction of 4 percent would mean a great deal to the thousands of individuals spared being victims of sexual abuse, it would not significantly weaken the American institution of prison rape.

A further fundamental problem regarding the national standards is that they will likely not be fully implemented nationwide. The only entities that are legally obliged to comply with the national standards are the federal Bureau of Prisons and the United States Marshals Service. The Department of Homeland Security and the Bureau of Indian Affairs, which also operate incarceration facilities pervaded by sexual abuse, are supposed to develop their own standards but have yet to do so. State and local incarceration systems are under no legal obligation to comply with the national standards. In fact, the Department of Justice explicitly declares that it does not expect full nationwide implementation of the national standards (see chapter 10).

We can, though, reasonably expect those state and local correctional authorities that are currently committed to eliminating sexual abuse in their incarceration facilities to maintain their commitment. We can also expect that a number of other correctional authorities may come to share that commitment. These correctional authorities will fully comply with the national standards, and some of them may well implement more stringent standards.

In addition, we can expect that a good number of correctional authorities will be concerned to a greater or lesser extent with the prevalence of sexual abuse in their incarceration facilities. Because compliance with the national standards is voluntary, the extent of their efforts to combat sexual abuse will depend on the costs they face in implementing the national standards. As the RIA observes, "the true impact of the [national standards] . . . will depend on the specific choices that State, local, and private correctional agencies make with regard to adoption of the standards, and correspondingly on the annual cash outlays that those agencies are willing and able to make in choosing to implement the standards in their facilities."[3]

Support is now available for correctional authorities that seek to comply, to a greater or lesser extent, with the national standards. The National Council on Crime and Delinquency, a prestigious public policy organization that focuses on criminal justice, and the Bureau of Justice Assistance, an agency of the Department of Justice, have cooperated in the newly established National PREA Resource Center. The purpose of this important organization is to provide assistance to correctional authorities to comply with the national standards. It also provides assistance to inmates and their families. To achieve its goals, it cooperates with a broad range of corrections, law enforcement, and victims' services organizations to provide training, technical support, and various resources available as needed.[4]

However, the motivation for cultural change must ultimately come from within correctional authorities themselves. A substantial number of state and local correctional authorities have been indifferent to pervasive sexual abuse in their facilities. Some have even intentionally employed sexual abuse to control inmates (see chapters 3 and 6). Many of these authorities are likely to stubbornly resist change.

Strong leadership with a commitment to cultural change at the most senior levels of correctional administration is needed to effectively combat sexual abuse. Some correctional authorities do already have fine leadership, but many do not. The culture of many correctional authorities is changing, but it is not clear how far the changes will progress (see chapter 3). Certainly, the national standards alone will not produce good leadership or generate the necessary cultural changes in correctional authorities and their staff.

It is also a substantial challenge to implement cultural change throughout all levels of corrections staff. Richard B. Hoffman, former executive director of the NPREC, explains: "Putting the new [national] standards into effect will require strong efforts to transmit the endorsement of anti-abuse policies by prison system leaders—state corrections commissioners, correctional association officers and unions—to the working-level correctional officers. . . . [C]hange at the operating level comes slowly. . . . [I]t takes persistent training and constant follow-up to produce measurable improvement in day-to-day behavior."[5]

THE POTENTIAL INFLUENCE
OF THE PROSECUTION SERVICES

Whatever the PREA national standards or any other regulations mandate, predatory corrections officers and inmates will go on sexually abusing vulnerable inmates as long as they have little reason to fear being held accountable. At the present time, very few sexual abusers of inmates are held accountable, so predatory corrections officers and inmates know that they enjoy virtual impunity. An important reason for this continuing impunity is the reluctance of many state and federal prosecutors to prosecute cases of sexual abuse in incarceration (see chapter 7).

Accordingly, a strong commitment on the part of prosecutors is essential to combating sexual abuse in the American incarceration system. This will require major cultural changes in many prosecution services. Prosecutors will need to fully recognize "incarcerated individuals as members of the community and as deserving of their services as any other victim of crime."[6] But many of them have not yet done so.

As part of their cultural changes, prosecutors will need to abandon their practice of threatening sexual abuse in incarceration to gain advantage over defendants. This is a shameful practice that has no place in a civilized society, but it has not yet been abandoned.

THE POTENTIAL INFLUENCE OF THE COURTS

Although state and local correctional agencies are not legally obliged to comply with the PREA national standards, the RIA suggests that "other consequences may flow from the issuance of national standards, which could provide incentives for voluntary compliance on the part of those agencies. For example, these standards may influence the standard of care that courts will apply in considering legal and constitutional claims brought against corrections agencies and their employees arising out of allegations of sexual abuse."[7]

In particular, the national standards could feasibly influence the application of the Eighth Amendment doctrine of "deliberate indifference" in the federal courts. Recall from chapter 8 that a corrections officer cannot be found liable in a lawsuit for sexual abuse of an inmate unless there was an excessive risk of harm to the inmate and the officer showed deliberate indifference to it. This means that the officer was subjectively aware of the risk and, despite this, failed to protect the inmate.

It has been notoriously difficult to establish that higher-ranking officers in the corrections hierarchy had the necessary subjective awareness. However, shortly after PREA was enacted, one writer suggested that "PREA will make knowledge about the threat of prison rape sufficiently widespread that awareness of the information generated by the Act may be imputed to reasonable officials."[8] There has been no evidence of this so far, but the promulgation of the PREA national standards might possibly change the situation.

To understand how this could happen, suppose that an inmate suffers sexual abuse in an incarceration facility that is not in compliance with the PREA national standards and brings a lawsuit. The inmate could reasonably argue that the correctional authorities through to the highest level in the hierarchy must have been subjectively aware of the national standards and of the fact that their facility was not in compliance with them.

However, the inmate would still face two difficulties in his lawsuit. One is that he would have to prove causation. That is, he would have to establish to the satisfaction of the court that the facility's failure to comply with the PREA national standards was the actual cause of the risk of harm to him. This could succeed, although in many cases it would be difficult (see chapter 8).

The other difficulty would be to persuade the court to take the national standards into account in determining what kind of behavior on the part of the correctional authorities constitutes deliberate indifference. So, for example, one commentator suggests that the national standards "could soon take the place of expert testimony as a means of establishing for juries that wardens disregarded their duty to supervise or train prison staff."[9] Again, this could succeed but might be difficult.

In fact, the Department of Justice has compounded this difficulty by acknowledging that correctional authorities are bound to take cost into account in deciding whether to comply with the national standards. It is hard to argue that correctional authorities are deliberately indifferent if they behave in a way that the Department of Justice has accepted as inevitable.

Another way in which the courts might act is to take the PREA national standards into account in determining whether to require a state to reform its incarceration system. In *Brown v Plata*, the Supreme Court recognizes that the systemic inadequacy of the medical and mental health care provided to California prison inmates violates the Eighth Amendment. Accordingly, the court upholds the decision of the lower federal courts requiring the state to reduce its prison population. The courts might well take noncompliance with the PREA national standards into account as a factor in determining that a state incarceration system fails to meet Eighth Amendment requirements regarding the protection of inmates from harm.[10] But they have not yet done so.

In general, the courts could surely recognize the PREA national standards as signifying that the time has come to focus their various resources on combating sexual abuse in the American incarceration system. "Now that both the legislative and executive branches of the federal government have placed emphasis on reducing prison rape, it seems reasonable to suggest that the judiciary will, in its own way, begin to do so as well."[11] But there is as yet no evidence of this.

THE POTENTIAL INFLUENCE OF THE GENERAL CULTURE

Sexual abuse will surely continue to pervade the American incarceration system as long as the general populace remains largely unconcerned. As Hoffman observes, "[t]oo many Americans regard the sexual abuse of prisoners as normal and tolerable . . . [as] is confirmed by the persistence of prison rape as a subject of humor—online, in film and on late-night TV talk shows."[12] So a question for the future is whether the general populace will recognize that prison rape is not a trivial matter, and certainly not a subject for humor or entertainment, but, rather, a source of shame to every one of us.

CONCLUSION

Prison rape has long been an American institution, but the crucial question is whether it will remain an American institution in the future. The promulgation of the PREA national standards is a substantial positive step and a ground for hope that sexual abuse in American incarceration will eventually be substantially reduced. But compliance with the national standards is largely voluntary, many correctional authorities are indifferent, prosecutors use the threat of sexual abuse in incarceration to gain advantage over defendants, the courts currently offer little protection against sexual abuse in incarceration, and the general society is not greatly concerned. It is possible to be hopeful, but there is only limited ground for optimism.

Over much of America it remains true today that, as a former chief justice of the Supreme Court observed forty years ago, "we exhibit an astonishing indifference to what happens to those who are sentenced."[13] In fact, too many Americans are also indifferent to what happens to those who are held by police, sheriffs, and other authorities without being sentenced and in many cases without even being charged with a criminal offense.

This culture must change throughout the correctional system, the judicial system, and the general society. Implementing this cultural change will require strong and enduring efforts and expenditures over a number of years and presents major challenges. But unless there is a continuing commitment to overcome the challenges, it remains all too possible that prison rape will shamefully survive as an American institution.

Notes

INTRODUCTION

1. See the discussion of USA v Cobb in chapter 6.

CHAPTER 1: RECOGNITION OF THE PREVALENCE OF SEXUAL ABUSE

1. States in which prisons and jails form an integrated system include Alaska, Connecticut, Delaware, Hawaii, Rhode Island, and Vermont. See Guerino, Harrison, and Sabol, *Prisoners in 2010,* 10–11.

2. For discussion of this in California following a Supreme Court order to reduce the prison population, see Singer, *Jury Duty,* ch. 13. In this book, references to the Supreme Court always mean the U.S. Supreme Court.

3. See Harrison and Beck, *Prison and Jail Inmates at Midyear 2004,* 7.

4. National Prison Rape Elimination Commission, *Report,* 163.

5. At midyear 2010, the estimated national populations were 1,605,127 for prisons and 748,728 for jails, giving a total of 2,353,855. See Guerino, Harrison, and Sabol, *Prisoners in 2010,* 1; Minton, *Jail Inmates at Midyear 2010,* 1. The estimate of the number of lockups is from United States Department of Justice, *Initial Regulatory Impact Analysis,* 14. For the community supervision estimates, see Glaze and Bonczar, *Probation and Parole in the United States, 2010,* 1.

6. See United States Department of Justice, *Regulatory Impact Assessment,* 28; ibid., 41 (footnote omitted). Text references to the Department of Justice always mean the United States (federal) Department of Justice.

7. Investigators of conditions of incarceration in America have reported on pervasive sexual abuse since the early nineteenth century. See Dumond, "The Impact of Prisoner Sexual Violence," 145, with references to original sources.

8. Prison Rape Elimination Act, § 2(12).

9. Kish v County of Milwaukee, 441 F2d at 903.

10. Ibid. at 902–3; ibid. at 904–5.

11. US v Bailey, 444 US at 421–22 (Blackmun and Brennan JJ, dissenting) (paragraph breaks suppressed).

12. Donaldson, Testimony at Massachusetts Legislative Hearing. For "bandit," "jocker," and "daddy" in male prison slang, see Sabo, Kupers, and London, *Prison Masculinities*, 118. Roughly speaking, a jocker is a general term for a dominant male inmate sexual abuser. A bandit is a jocker who sexually coerces. A daddy is an inmate who pairs off with another inmate whom he protects and controls.

13. Anderson v Redman, 429 F Supp. at 1117. For doubt regarding whether sexual activity between inmates can ever be truly consensual, see Dumond, "The Impact of Prisoner Sexual Violence," 163.

14. Donaldson, Testimony at Massachusetts Legislative Hearing (paragraph breaks suppressed).

15. Davis, "Sexual Assaults," 10.

16. Ibid., 9.

17. See ibid., 10–11, giving data from which the assessment in the text is derived.

18. Ibid., 15.

19. Buchanan, "Our Prisons, Ourselves," 18. For discussion, see ibid., 53–80.

20. Struckman-Johnson et al., "Sexual Coercion Reported by Men and Women in Prison," 67.

21. Ibid., 68.

22. See Human Rights Watch, *All Too Familiar*, 20–21.

23. Struckman-Johnson et al., "Sexual Coercion Reported by Men and Women in Prison," 74.

24. For the reluctance of inmates to report sexual abuse to corrections officers, see ibid., 75 ("Only one half said that they had told anyone about the incident [of being pressured or forced to have sexual contact], and only 29% had informed prison officials."). The quotation is from Beck and Hughes, *Sexual Violence Reported by Correctional Authorities, 2004*, 2.

25. Alberti v Heard, 600 F Supp. at 450; Grubbs v Bradley, 552 F Supp. at 1078; Pugh v Locke, 406 F Supp. at 325.

26. Comstock v McCrary, 273 F3d at 699 n. 2; Davis, "Sexual Assaults," 11; see Goldfarb, *Jails, the Ultimate Ghetto*, 325–26.

27. Withers v Levine, 615 F2d at 160; see National Prison Rape Elimination Commission, *Report*, 71.

28. See Gullatte v Potts, 654 F2d at 1009–10.

29. Struckman-Johnson et al., "Sexual Coercion Reported by Men and Women in Prison," 68.

30. Ibid., 71; for the results of prior studies, see ibid., 68; Struckman-Johnson and Struckman-Johnson, "Sexual Coercion Rates," 387. See also Struckman-Johnson and Struckman-Johnson, "Sexual Coercion Reported by Women in Three Midwestern Prisons."

31. Human Rights Watch, *No Escape,* 132 (brackets and bracketed text in original). The term "seg" is inmate slang for segregation or administrative segregation. The original spelling is retained in victim accounts throughout this book.

32. Ibid., 135.

33. Women Prisoners v District of Columbia, 877 F Supp. at 667; Human Rights Watch, *All Too Familiar,* 127 (paragraph break suppressed).

34. Human Rights Watch, *All Too Familiar,* 259–60 (internal quotation marks omitted, punctuation slightly altered). A follow-up report (Human Rights Watch, *Nowhere to Hide*) detailed extensive case histories of retaliation against women in Michigan prisons.

35. Women Prisoners v District of Columbia, 877 F Supp. at 666.

36. See Just Detention International, *A Brief History.* This organization will be referred to throughout as Just Detention International, even regarding its activities during the period when it was called Stop Prisoner Rape.

37. Just Detention International, *Comments Submitted to the Department of Justice,* 3; ibid., 6.

38. For this account of the case and quotations from it in the following paragraphs, see Lucas v White, 63 F Supp. 2d at 1050–55.

CHAPTER 2: ASSESSMENT OF THE PREVALENCE OF SEXUAL ABUSE

1. For examples of laws and policies, see United States Department of Justice, National Institute of Corrections, *Sexual Misconduct in Prisons* (2000). For concerns regarding effectiveness, see part II.

2. Ted Kennedy, D-Mass., and Jeff Sessions, R-Ala., introduced the bill in the Senate. Frank Wolf, R-Va., and Bobby Scott, D-Va., introduced it in the House of Representatives.

3. Prison Rape Elimination Act, § 2(2).

4. Ibid. § 4(1). Weisberg and Mills, "Violence Silence," undervalue this and other aspects of PREA.

5. Human Rights Watch, *All Too Familiar,* 128 n. 3.

6. For the variety of individuals held in jails, see chapter 1. The quotation is from Just Detention International, *Action Update,* October 2011, 2 (paragraph breaks suppressed).

7. National Prison Rape Elimination Commission, *Report,* 161 (internal quotation marks omitted).

8. Ibid., 163; ibid., 167–68, citing to original testimony sources (internal quotation marks omitted).

9. The BJS report is Beck and Johnson, *Sexual Victimization Reported by Former State Prisoners, 2008.* For the Department of Justice view, see United

States Department of Justice, *National Standards to Prevent, Detect, and Respond to Prison Rape: Final Rule,* 37113–14; see also chapter 10.

10. United States Department of Justice, *Regulatory Impact Assessment,* 35 (footnote omitted).

11. The BJS classifies its series and reports slightly differently. See Beck and Johnson, *Sexual Victimization Reported by Former State Prisoners, 2008,* 7.

12. This is in accordance with the PREA purpose to "standardize the definitions used for collecting data on the incidence of prison rape." Prison Rape Elimination Act, § 3(5).

13. In the first series of reports, the definitions encompass "contact of any person without his or her consent, or of a person who is unable to consent or refuse." Under this definition, a *nonconsensual sexual act* entails: "contact between the penis and the vagina or the penis and the anus including penetration, however slight; or contact between the mouth and the penis, vagina, or anus; or penetration of the anal or genital opening of another person by a hand, finger, or other object." An *abusive sexual contact* entails: "Intentional touching, either directly or through the clothing, of the genitalia, anus, groin, breast, inner thigh, or buttocks of any person." Starting from the 2005 report in the first series, the definition of abusive sexual contact was modified to "exclud[e] incidents in which the intent of the sexual contact is to harm or debilitate rather than sexually exploit." The definitions have undergone slight word changes in successive reports. Beck and Hughes, *Sexual Violence Reported by Correctional Authorities, 2004,* 3; Beck and Harrison, *Sexual Violence Reported by Correctional Authorities, 2005,* 3; Beck, Harrison, and Adams, *Sexual Violence Reported by Correctional Authorities, 2006,* 9; Guerino and Beck, *Sexual Victimization Reported by Adult Correctional Authorities, 2007–2008,* 2.

According to these definitions, nonconsensual manual sexual stimulation performed by an inmate on a male corrections officer or inmate would not constitute a nonconsensual sexual act. But the second series of BJS reports gives a definition of nonconsensual sexual acts that encompasses not only penetrative acts but also "hand jobs, and other sexual acts." Beck et al., *Sexual Victimization in Prisons and Jails Reported by Inmates, 2008–09,* 7. Since the BJS strives for uniform definitions, it is reasonable to presume that such acts are to be included in the definition of nonconsensual sexual acts for its first series of reports as well.

14. United States Department of Justice, *National Standards to Prevent, Detect, and Respond to Prison Rape: Notice of Proposed Rulemaking,* 6251. The national standards are discussed in part IV.

15. "Staff sexual misconduct includes any sexual behavior or act directed toward an inmate by staff, including romantic relationships. Such acts include: intentional touching of the genitalia, anus, groin, breast, inner thigh, or buttocks with the intent to abuse, arouse, or gratify sexual desire; or completed, attempted, threatened, or requested sexual acts; or occurrences of indecent exposure, invasion of privacy, or staff voyeurism for sexual gratification. Staff sexual harassment includes repeated statements or comments of a sexual nature to an inmate by staff. Such statements include: demeaning

references to an inmate's sex or derogatory comments about his or her body or clothing; or repeated profane or obscene language or gestures." Guerino and Beck, *Sexual Victimization Reported by Adult Correctional Authorities, 2007–2008*, 2.

16. Buchanan, "Our Prisons, Ourselves," 4 n. 10.

17. Human Rights Watch, *All Too Familiar*, 82.

18. For the survey procedure, see Guerino and Beck, *Sexual Victimization Reported by Adult Correctional Authorities, 2007–2008*, 1–2. For facilities that failed to respond, see ibid., 10–12. The survey questionnaires are available at United States Department of Justice, Bureau of Justice Statistics, *Survey of Sexual Violence: Questionnaires*.

19. See United States Department of Justice, *Regulatory Impact Assessment*, 20–22.

20. Beck and Hughes, *Sexual Violence Reported by Correctional Authorities, 2004*; Beck and Harrison, *Sexual Violence Reported by Correctional Authorities, 2005*; Beck, Harrison, and Adams, *Sexual Violence Reported by Correctional Authorities, 2006*; Guerino and Beck, *Sexual Victimization Reported by Adult Correctional Authorities, 2007–2008*; Beck, Adams, and Guerino, *Sexual Violence Reported by Juvenile Correctional Authorities, 2005–06*.

21. For the data, see Guerino and Beck, *Sexual Victimization Reported by Adult Correctional Authorities, 2007–2008*, 3. The report does not state the total inmate population that the survey covers, but this may be computed from the rates per 1,000 inmates given ibid., table 1. The population is 2,205,300 in 2005 and 2,340,880 in 2008. For the numbers of allegations of sexual abuse, see ibid., table 2. There were 2,386 allegations of staff sexual misconduct in 2005 and 2,538 in 2008. This yields the figure of 1.08 allegations of staff sexual misconduct per 1,000 inmates in 2005 and also in 2008. There were 2,160 allegations of inmate-on-inmate nonconsensual sexual acts in 2005 and 2,343 in 2008. This gives a rate per 1,000 inmates of 0.98 in 2005 and 1.00 in 2008. There were 1,084 allegations of staff sexual harassment in 2005 and 1,169 in 2008. This gives a rate per 1,000 inmates of 0.49 in 2005 and 0.50 in 2008. There were 611 allegations of inmate-on-inmate abusive sexual contacts in 2005 and 1,417 in 2008. This gives a rate per 1,000 inmates of 0.28 in 2005 and 0.61 in 2008.

22. Beck and Hughes, *Sexual Violence Reported by Correctional Authorities, 2004*, 2.

23. Ibid., 6.

24. Guerino and Beck, *Sexual Victimization Reported by Adult Correctional Authorities, 2007–2008*, 5, table 5. The figures for the percentage of allegations of sexual abuse that end up being substantiated are: 12 percent of allegations of inmate-on-inmate nonconsensual sexual acts, 19 percent of allegations of inmate-on-inmate abusive sexual contacts, 19 percent of allegations of staff sexual misconduct, and 5 percent of allegations of staff sexual harassment. Ibid.

25. Beck, Adams, and Guerino, *Sexual Violence Reported by Juvenile Correctional Authorities, 2005–06*, 3.

26. The reports are Beck and Harrison, *Sexual Victimization in State and Federal Prisons Reported by Inmates, 2007*; Beck and Harrison, *Sexual Victimization in Local Jails Reported by Inmates, 2007*; Beck et al., *Sexual Victimization in Prisons and Jails Reported by Inmates, 2008–09*; Beck, Harrison, and Guerino, *Sexual Victimization in Juvenile Facilities Reported by Youth, 2008–09*.

For the survey methods used, as described in the following paragraphs of text and in the following notes, see Beck et al., *Sexual Victimization in Prisons and Jails Reported by Inmates, 2008–09*, 27–32. The following text paragraphs include quotations from this material that are not specifically noted as such. The survey questionnaires are available at United States Department of Justice, Bureau of Justice Statistics, *National Inmate Survey: Questionnaires*.

27. See Hockenberry, Sickmund, and Sladky, *Juvenile Residential Facility Census, 2008*, 2, table; Sabol, Minton, and Harrison, *Prison and Jail Inmates at Midyear 2006*, 4 (number in prisons), 5, table 9 (number in jails); Beck et al., *Sexual Victimization in Prisons and Jails Reported by Inmates, 2008–09*, 6 ("survey was administered to . . . inmates ages 18 or older").

28. United States Department of Justice, Office of Justice Programs, Review Panel on Prison Rape, *Hearings*, 37 (testimony of Allen Beck). A small number of inmates are provided with the questionnaire on paper instead of on computer. Most of these are inmates in segregation or very violent inmates. In the 2008–2009 survey of adult prisons and jails, less than 1 percent of those participating in the survey used the paper questionnaire. See Beck et al., *Sexual Victimization in Prisons and Jails Reported by Inmates, 2008–09*, 1.

29. Beck et al., *Sexual Victimization in Prisons and Jails Reported by Inmates, 2008–09*, 6.

30. Ibid., 31. For a detailed account of the BJS measures to check consistency, see United States Department of Justice, Office of Justice Programs, Review Panel on Prison Rape, *Hearings*, 50–51 (testimony of Allen Beck).

31. The RIA discussion of the choice of data source is United States Department of Justice, *Regulatory Impact Assessment*, 16–20.

32. Ibid., 17–18 (internal citation omitted).

33. Ibid., 20 (paragraph break suppressed).

34. Ibid., 21. The RIA discussion of prevalence and incidence data is ibid., 20–22.

35. *At Risk*, 47 (testimony of Spruce, K.). Bryson Martel was also known as Kendell Spruce. For discussion of the National Prison Rape Elimination Commission, a body set up under PREA, see chapter 9.

36. United States Department of Justice, *Regulatory Impact Assessment*, 22.

37. For assigning monetary costs to various types of sexual abuse, see chapter 5. The RIA discussion of the classification of sexual abuse of adult inmates, including the definitions of the levels of sexual abuse explained next in the text, is United States Department of Justice, *Regulatory Impact Assessment*, 22–26.

38. United States Department of Justice, *Regulatory Impact Assessment*, 25.

39. Beck et al., *Sexual Victimization in Prisons and Jails Reported by Inmates, 2008–09*, 7; United States Department of Justice, *Initial Regulatory Impact Analysis*, 12.

40. Smith, "Rethinking Prison Sex," 201–6; ibid., 203.

41. United States Department of Justice, Office of Justice Programs, Review Panel on Prison Rape, *Hearings* 36 (testimony of Allen Beck). For support for this view, and also discussion of cases where "inmates have targeted staff for sexual relations to obtain control over the staff, to obtain contraband or unauthorized privileges, or to leverage the sexual relationship for a lighter sentence," see United States Department of Justice, Office of the Inspector General, *Deterring Staff Sexual Abuse of Federal Inmates*, 5.

42. United States Department of Justice, *Regulatory Impact Assessment*, 26–27, which explains the classification of sexual abuse of juveniles in juvenile facilities, as set out in the following paragraphs.

43. Beck et al., *Sexual Victimization in Prisons and Jails Reported by Inmates, 2008–09*, 31.

44. United States Department of Justice, *Initial Regulatory Impact Analysis*, 8–9.

45. The RIA discussion of prevalence and incidence data is United States Department of Justice, *Regulatory Impact Assessment*, 28–30.

46. The RIA discussion of the modifying factors for underreporting and false reporting, as explained in the following paragraphs, is ibid., 30–34, and that for juvenile inmates is ibid., 36.

47. For the percentages of allegations in various categories that are classified as unfounded, see ibid., 31, tables 2.1, 2.2. For the adjusted assessment, the RIA made no adjustment regarding inmates who reported an injury. Regarding inmates who reported no injury but who were classified as "high incidence," the RIA moved a percentage (corresponding to the relevant percentage of unfounded allegations) to the corresponding "low incidence" classification. A similar percentage of low incidence victims were then simply removed from the count of victims. Ibid., 33–34.

48. For the lower-bound assessment, a percentage (corresponding to the relevant percentage of unfounded allegations) of victims were simply removed from the count of victims. Ibid., 34.

49. All of the prevalence figures given here are drawn from ibid., 37, table 3.1 (adult facilities) and 38, table 3.2 (juvenile facilities).

CHAPTER 3: RECENT DEVELOPMENTS

1. Smith, Interview: Tom Cahill (paragraph break suppressed).

2. Zweig and Blackmore, *Strategies to Prevent Prison Rape by Changing the Correctional Culture*, 3.

3. Ibid., 2.

4. Kaiser, *A Letter on Rape in Prisons*; see Clark, "Why Does Popular Culture Treat Prison Rape as a Joke?"

5. Williams and Stannow, "Rape Is Not Part of the Penalty."

6. National Prison Rape Elimination Commission, *Report,* 2.

7. Just Detention International, *Action Update,* March 2011, 1–2.

8. For this form of investigation, see chapter 8.

9. United States Department of Justice, Civil Rights Division, Findings Letter to Marlin N. Gusman, 11.

10. Ibid.

11. Ibid., 7–8.

12. Ibid., 23–26.

13. For Cumming's testimony, see United States Department of Justice, Office of Justice Programs, Review Panel on Prison Rape, *Hearings,* 87–90 (testimony of Elizabeth Cumming). For discussion of problems with grievance systems in corrections facilities, see chapter 8.

14. Ibid., 58 (question from Reginald Wilkinson); ibid., 58–59 (testimony of Allen Beck).

15. Fleisher and Krienert, *The Myth of Prison Rape,* 1; ibid., 54–55 (paragraph breaks suppressed); ibid., 1. In the last quotation, the authors in fact contradict their own disclaimer: "Inmates' comments about a lack of worry and fear of rape because rape isn't a possibility cannot be interpreted as a proxy measure for rape's prevalence." Ibid., 56.

Fleisher and Krienert make only selective reference to earlier surveys, research, and reports. The numerous accounts of pervasive sexual abuse such as are given here in chapter 1, together with the harrowing accounts by victims of their suffering such as are given here in chapter 4, are ignored or dismissed by them as "a handful of panic-inducing writings about prison rape." Fleisher and Krienert, *The Myth of Prison Rape,* 17.

The book by Fleisher and Krienert derives from a 2006 report entitled *The Culture of Prison Sexual Violence,* prepared by the same authors under a grant from the National Institute of Justice, an agency within the Department of Justice. The Department of Justice has not published the report.

16. Fleisher and Krienert, *The Myth of Prison Rape,* 34.

17. Ibid., 1; United States Department of Justice, Office of Justice Programs, Review Panel on Prison Rape, *Hearings,* 34–35 (testimony of Allen Beck) (paragraph break suppressed).

CHAPTER 4: THE SUFFERING OF VICTIMS

1. Davis, "Sexual Assaults," 9; see, for example, Hall v Terrell, 2009 US Dist. LEXIS 48870 at *5 n. 2 ("While the Court is reluctant to repeat Terrell's coarse language, it does so to convey accurately the nature of his conduct towards Hall.").

2. See Smith and Batiuk, "Sexual Victimization and Inmate Social Interaction," 33; National Prison Rape Elimination Commission, *Report,* 70 (footnote omitted).

3. Donaldson, *Rape of Incarcerated Americans.*

4. National Prison Rape Elimination Commission, *Report*, 69 (footnotes omitted).

5. Ibid., 17.

6. See Human Rights Watch, *All Too Familiar*, 225–26; United States Department of Justice, Office of the Inspector General. *Deterring Staff Sexual Abuse of Federal Inmates*, 5.

7. National Prison Rape Elimination Commission, *Report*, 72 (footnote omitted).

8. Ibid., 73–74 (footnotes omitted).

9. See Donaldson, Testimony at Massachusetts Legislative Hearing; Man and Cronan, "Forecasting Sexual Abuse in Prison," 127–28.

10. National Prison Rape Elimination Commission, *Report*, 36 (footnotes omitted).

11. Davis, "Sexual Assaults," 9.

12. Human Rights Watch, *All Too Familiar*, 74.

13. Letter from A.H. to Human Rights Watch, August 30, 1996, in Human Rights Watch, *No Escape*, xv.

14. Stop Prisoner Rape [Just Detention International], *Stories from Inside*, 6 (paragraph break suppressed).

15. See Just Detention International, *Comments Submitted to the Department of Justice*, 3.

16. National Prison Rape Elimination Commission, *Report*, 93–94 (footnotes omitted), quoting from *The Cost of Victimization*, 3 (Testimony of Cunningham, G.).

17. Hall v Terrell, 2009 US Dist. LEXIS 48870 at *9.

18. Calderón-Ortiz v Laboy-Alvarado, 300 F3d at 63 (footnote omitted). The case was a federal civil rights action for damages against corrections institution personnel. The case does not state the age of plaintiff Jesús Manuel Calderón-Ortiz. However, both he and his parents brought the action, showing that he was a minor at the time.

19. See Lovisa Stannow, untitled column in Just Detention International, *Action Update*, October 2011, 1 (paragraph break suppressed).

20. Stemple, "HBO's *OZ* and the Fight against Prisoner Rape," 176.

21. Stop Prisoner Rape [Just Detention International], *Stories from Inside*, 11.

22. LaMarca v Turner, 995 F2d at 1533.

23. Stop Prisoner Rape [Just Detention International], *Stories from Inside*, 14 (paragraph break suppressed).

24. See Linden, "Care of the Adult Patient after Sexual Assault," 835–39.

25. Prison Rape Elimination Act, § 2(6).

26. For further discussion of the conditions revealed in the *Brown v Plata* litigation, see Singer, *Jury Duty*, ch. 13. For the situation in jails, see National Prison Rape Elimination Commission, *Report*, 131, with references to original sources.

27. Coleman v Schwarzenegger, 2009 WL 2430820 at sec. I, *1 (internal quotation marks omitted).

28. Brown v Plata, 131 S Ct. at 1928.

29. Coleman v Schwarzenegger, 2009 WL 2430820 at sec. I, *1 (internal quotation marks omitted); Plata v Schwarzenegger, 21 (internal citations omitted).)

30. The quotation is from Plata v Schwarzenegger, 8. For incidents, see ibid., 9–13.

31. National Prison Rape Elimination Commission, *Report*, 16; ibid., 131. The PREA national standards, discussed in chapter 10, include provisions requiring that inmate victims of sexual abuse be provided with medical care free of charge, but it is not yet clear how far these provisions will actually be implemented.

32. California, *Sexual Abuse in Detention Elimination Act*, sec. 2638.

33. Hall v Terrell, 2009 US Dist. LEXIS 48870 at *10–*11.

34. *At Risk*, 33 (testimony of Parsell, T.J.).

35. Just Detention International, *Comments Submitted to the Department of Justice*, 6; ibid., 7.

36. See Beck and Johnson, *Sexual Victimization Reported by Former State Prisoners, 2008*, 31, table 19.

37. Human Rights Watch, *No Escape*, 22.

38. LaMarca v Turner, 995 F2d at 1533 (internal quotation marks suppressed).

39. See Lovisa Stannow, untitled column in Just Detention International, *Action Update*, October 2011, 1 (paragraph break suppressed).

40. Just Detention International, *Comments Submitted to the Department of Justice*, 6.

41. Human Rights Watch, *No Escape*, 99–101.

42. Linden, "Care of the Adult Patient after Sexual Assault," 836.

43. Just Detention International, *Comments Submitted to the Department of Justice*, 63. For a similar view, see United States Department of Justice, Office of the Inspector General, Evaluation and Inspections Division, *The Department of Justice's Efforts to Prevent Staff Sexual Abuse of Federal Inmates*, iv, viii.

44. US v Lara, 905 F2d at 601 (internal quotation marks suppressed).

45. Ruiz v Johnson, 37 F Supp. 2d at 907; see Man and Cronan, "Forecasting Sexual Abuse in Prison," 146 n. 101.

46. Just Detention International, *Comments Submitted to the Department of Justice*, 6–7; see chapter 10.

47. See Beck and Johnson, *Sexual Victimization Reported by Former State Prisoners, 2008*, 31, table 19. The survey allowed multiple responses for this item. Ibid., 31. Accordingly, the figures cited in the text are not necessarily cumulative. For example, in some cases the authorities may have responded by confining the victim to his cell and then later placing him in protective housing.

48. The quotation is from Just Detention International, *Comments Submitted to the Department of Justice*, 4. For the limits to the protection that segregation could offer, see chapters 1 and 2.

49. Human Rights Watch, *No Escape,* 19.

50. For Donaldson, see Donaldson, Testimony at Massachusetts Legislative Hearing; Man and Cronan, "Forecasting Sexual Abuse in Prison," 127–28. For Martel, see "A Courageous Advocate for Justice," in Just Detention International, *Action Update,* October 2010, 2.

51. *The Cost of Victimization,* 67 (testimony of Shirley, M.)

52. National Prison Rape Elimination Commission, *Report,* 69.

53. Stop Prisoner Rape [Just Detention International], *Stories from Inside,* 11.

54. *At Risk,* 21 (testimony of Hernandez, H.).

55. The following discussion is drawn from National Prison Rape Elimination Commission, *Report,* 126–29, and includes direct quotations, not specifically noted as such, from the *Report* and original sources cited there. See also Linden, "Care of the Adult Patient after Sexual Assault," 838–39.

CHAPTER 5: THE COST TO SOCIETY AT LARGE

1. For prison releases, see Guerino, Harrison, and Sabol, *Prisoners in 2010,* 1. For jail releases, see Minton, *Jail Inmates at Midyear 2010,* 1–2 (12.9 million admitted, and inmate population declined, so at least as many were released). See also chapter 1.

2. See Hughes and Wilson, *Reentry Trends,* 1.

3. *The Cost of Victimization,* 80 (testimony of Cahill, T.).

4. Prison Rape Elimination Act, §§ 2(7), (8), (11).

5. For discussion, see United States Department of Justice, *Regulatory Impact Assessment,* 39–44.

6. Miller, Taylor, and Sheppard, *Costs of Sexual Violence in Minnesota.* The authors of this study provide further information on their sources and methods in Miller, Taylor, and Sheppard, *Costs of Sexual Violence in Minnesota: Detailed Methods Supplement.* The RIA (United States Department of Justice, *Regulatory Impact Assessment,* 43) also referred to, but did not use data from, an earlier study using the victim compensation model: United States Department of Justice, National Institute of Justice, *Victim Costs and Consequences.*

7. United States Department of Justice, *Regulatory Impact Assessment,* 50.

8. Ibid., 49.

9. This issue pervades the various articles in Greifinger, *Public Health behind Bars.*

10. United States Department of Justice, *Regulatory Impact Assessment,* 48.

11. Ibid., 45 (quotation emphasis in original).

12. Ibid., 49–50. The RIA states in its text (ibid., 50) that it uses 1.75 times the Miller estimate as its own estimate for juveniles in juvenile facilities. But in its computations the RIA actually uses a multiplier of 1.5, not 1.75. See ibid., 54, table 4.4, 58, table 4.6, and 59, table 4.7.

13. Ibid., 50 (quotation footnote omitted).

14. Ibid., 48 (footnote omitted); ibid., 48–49.

15. Ibid., 50–51.

16. For the adjustments, see ibid., 36. For the exclusion of juveniles held in adult facilities from all BJS surveys, see chapter 2.

17. United States Department of Justice, *Regulatory Impact Assessment*, 53.

18. Ibid., 52–53.

19. These assessments are ibid., 54, tables 4.3 and 4.4.

20. Ibid., 55 (adults), 58 (juveniles in juvenile facilities).

21. Ibid., 52–53.

22. Ibid., 57, table 4.5 (adults), 59, table 4.7 (juveniles in juvenile facilities). For juveniles in juvenile facilities, there is a small, unexplained difference between the sum given in the text (ibid., 59) and the sum given in the accompanying table (ibid., 59, table 4.7).

23. Ibid., 57–58.

24. Ibid., 58 (brackets and bracketed text in quotation in original).

25. Ibid., 59–62. The assessments for each level of sexual abuse are tabulated ibid., 63, tables 5.1 (adults), 5.2 (juveniles in juvenile facilities), and 5.3 (juveniles in adult prisons and jails).

26. Ibid., 40, 42; Cohen et al., "Willingness-to-Pay for Crime Control Programs," 93.

27. United States Department of Justice, *Regulatory Impact Assessment*, 40, quoting Cohen et al., "Willingness-to-Pay for Crime Control Programs," 93 n. 5; United States Department of Justice, *Regulatory Impact Assessment*, 41.

28. United States Department of Justice, *Regulatory Impact Assessment*, 41.

29. Ibid., 42.

30. Ibid., 43.

31. Ibid. The WTP estimate appears as a level 1 alternative in the RIA tabulation of assessments for the levels of sexual abuse, ibid., 63, table 5.1.

32. Ibid., 64, table 6.1. The amounts have been rounded.

33. Ibid., 65, table 6.6 (adults); 66, table 6.8 (juveniles). Note that the figures in table 6.6 incorporate an adjustment for juveniles held in adult facilities, see ibid., 52, 64 n. 96.

34. Ibid., 64, table 6.2.

35. Ibid., 64, table 6.3 (adults); 65, table 6.5 (juveniles). Note that the figures in table 6.3 incorporate an adjustment for juveniles held in adult facilities, see ibid., 52, 64 n. 96.

36. See Wood, *Survey of the Antiquities of the City of Oxford*, 269 (spelling changed from "gaol" to "jail").

37. Bacon, *The Works of Francis Bacon*, 646.

38. Lind, *An Essay on the Most Effectual Means of Preserving the Health of Seamen*, 3–6.

39. Howard, *The State of the Prisons in England and Wales*, 20.

40. See United States Department of Health and Human Services, Centers for Disease Control and Prevention, "Prevention and Control of Tuberculosis in Correctional and Detention Facilities," 2–4.

41. Lerner, "MRSA Bacteria Escape from Jails" (paragraph breaks and internal quotation marks suppressed).

42. See United States Department of Health and Human Services, Centers for Disease Control and Prevention, *Sexually Transmitted Disease Surveillance, 2010*, 83–84; Sexually Transmitted Disease Program, Los Angeles County Department of Health Services, *STD Prevalence Monitoring*, letter from Peter R. Kerndt on unnumbered first page.

43. For discussion, see, for example, Buck et al., "Hepatitis B Vaccination in Prison"; Davis and Pacchiana, "Health Profile of the State Prison Population and Returning Offenders."

44. National Commission on Correctional Health Care, *The Health Status of Soon-to-Be Released Inmates*, vol. 1, x.

At midyear 1997, the estimated national prison and jail population was 1,725,842. See Gilliard and Beck, *Prison and Jail Inmates at Midyear 1997*, 1. At midyear 2010, the estimated national populations were 1,605,127 for prisons and 748,728 for jails, giving a total of 2,353,855. See Guerino, Harrison, and Sabol, *Prisoners in 2010*, 1; Minton, *Jail Inmates at Midyear 2010*, 1.

45. See Freudenberg, "Community Health Services for Returning Jail and Prison Inmates," 374–78.

46. See, e.g., ibid., 380–81; United States Department of Health and Human Services, Centers for Disease Control and Prevention, "Tuberculosis Transmission in Multiple Correctional Facilities," 734; Rogers et al., "Incarceration, High-Risk Sexual Partnerships" and sources cited there.

47. Lerner, "MRSA Bacteria Escape from Jails."

48. This is a recurrent theme in the various articles in Greifinger, *Public Health behind Bars*.

49. Donaldson, Testimony at Massachusetts Legislative Hearing.

CHAPTER 6: THE MORAL COST TO AMERICAN SOCIETY

1. For discussion of the commitment in PREA and prospects regarding its fulfillment, see part IV. For the continuing pervasiveness of sexual abuse in the American system of incarceration, see part I. The quotation is from Appiah, "What Will Future Generations Condemn Us For?"

2. Palmer, " 'Hi, My Name Isn't Justice, Honey,' and Shame on Lockyer." Lockyer later expressed regret for what he called this "crude remark." Lockyer, letter to the editor.

3. Sabo, Kupers, and London, Introduction, in *Prison Masculinities*, 12; Pinar, *The Gender of Racial Politics and Violence in America*, 1065–66.

4. Parenti, "Rape as a Disciplinary Tactic" (paragraph breaks suppressed). For the involvement of Pondexter, see Stratton, "The Making of Bonecrusher."

5. Richardson v Penfold, 839 F2d at 394 (internal brackets removed).

6. Kaiser, "A Letter on Rape in Prisons." See also Stemple, "HBO's *OZ* and the Fight against Prisoner Rape," 168.

7. USA v Cobb, § 8.

8. Ibid., § 14; ibid., § 19.

9. See Crary, "Prison-Rape Quote Slows Extradition."

10. See Singer, *Jury Duty*, ch. 10.

11. The quotations are from Waldron, "Torture and Positive Law," 1738; ibid., 1728. For wide variation in the reported level of sexual abuse from one incarceration facility to another, see, for example, Beck and Harrison, *Sexual Victimization in State and Federal Prisons Reported by Inmates, 2007*, 2.

12. The first quotation is from Wolf, "Judicial Torture and the NatWest 3" (paragraph breaks suppressed). For similar observations on the pressure to plea-bargain, see Bazelon, *The Adversary Process*, 12676 col. 2. The second quotation is from Licker, letter to the editor.

13. The television series is Fontana, *OZ*. For detailed discussion of the depiction of pervasive prisoner rape in *OZ*, see Stemple, "HBO's *OZ* and the Fight against Prisoner Rape"; the quotation in the text is at 172. For a generally accurate listing of popular television programs referring to *OZ*, see "*Oz* (TV series)" under the heading "References in other media."

14. Schneider, *Big Stan*; Odenkirk, *Let's Go to Prison*.

15. The game is Sebelius, *Don't Drop the Soap*. The creator of the game is the son of Kathleen Sebelius, formerly governor of the state of Kansas and at the time of writing secretary of health and human services in the federal government, and of Keith Gary Sebelius, a federal magistrate judge. For the quotation in the text, see *Associated Press*, "Governor's Son Creates Prison-Themed Game," which also reports that the Sebelius parents "are very proud of their son John's creativity and talent" as demonstrated in the game.

16. Old Hippie's Gift Shop, "Your Asshole in Jail."

17. Burger, Address to the Bar of the City of New York, 17 (emphasis in original); US v Bailey, 444 US at 423 (Blackmun and Brennan JJ, dissenting).

18. Farmer v Brennan, 511 US at 833 (citations omitted, internal quotation marks and brackets indicating interpolations suppressed).

19. For levels of moral responsibility, see May, *Sharing Responsibility*, 114, 135. For discussion of moral responsibility for failure to act, see ibid., 27, 119–20. For the heightened responsibility of individuals in leadership roles with power to control or influence, see ibid., 115, 121.

20. For examples of failure to take sexual abuse in incarceration seriously enough to devote resources to combat it, see chapters 3, 7, and 8. The quotations are from May, *Sharing Responsibility*, 47, 49.

21. *Brainerd Dispatch*, "Why I Am Proud to Be an American."

22. For discussion of shame regarding the failings in relation to pride regarding the accomplishments of a society, see May, *Sharing Responsibility*, 153–55.

CHAPTER 7: STATE AND COMPARABLE FEDERAL LAWSUITS

1. For a full account of sentencing as discussed in the following paragraphs, with references to original sources, see Singer, *Jury Duty*, ch. 10.

2. US v Lara, 905 F2d at 605.

3. US v Gonzalez, 945 F2d at 526; ibid. at 527. In Koon v US, the Supreme Court upheld a downward departure in the sentence of a former police officer

on the ground that he would be vulnerable to abuse in incarceration, although it did not specify whether the abuse would likely be sexual.

4. US v Gonzalez, 945 F2d at 529; see Sigler, "Just Deserts," 573.

5. See Funk, "Short Sex Offender's Probation Upheld." Note that the judge was subsequently voted off the bench; see *North Platte Bulletin*, "Judge Who Gave Short Man Probation Ousted."

6. US v K, 160 F Supp. 2d at 423.

7. National Prison Rape Elimination Commission, *Report*, 121 (footnote omitted).

8. Ibid., 13; ibid., 120.

9. Atassi, "Prison Guard Gets Seven Years for Raping Inmate" (internal quotation marks suppressed in first quotation).

10. For the account in the following paragraphs, see State of Oregon website, www.oregon.gov; Zaitz, "Abuse of Women Inmates at Oregon's Coffee Creek Prison Goes On for Years"; Gustafson, "Halting Prison Sex Scandals Has Far-Reaching Effects."

11. For the BJS distinction, see chapter 2. The statute is Oregon, *Custodial Sexual Misconduct*.

12. See Zaitz, "Abuse of Women Inmates at Oregon's Coffee Creek Prison Goes On for Years"; Wilson, "Sex Scandal Rocks Oregon's 'Camp Cupcake' Women's Prison—Again."

13. See Zaitz, "Abuse of Women Inmates at Oregon's Coffee Creek Prison Goes On for Years."

14. See *CBS News*, "Ex-Sheriff Sentenced in Sex Abuse Scandal."

15. Hall v Terrell, 2009 US Dist. LEXIS 48870 at *3–*4 (court's internal references suppressed). For this kind of federal court action, see chapter 8.

16. For listings of current prosecutions and verdicts, see *End Silence*, under Adult Prisons and Jails: In the News.

17. National Prison Rape Elimination Commission, *Report*, 120 (footnote omitted, internal quotation marks suppressed).

18. See Idaho v Thompson; Bonner, "Guilty of Prison Rape"; Idaho Department of Corrections, press release.

19. For the effect of the prospect or actuality of lawsuits on corrections policies and behavior, see Schlanger, "Inmate Litigation," 1664–90. For discussion of who ultimately pays damages awards, see ibid., 1676 n. 391.

20. See Gustafson, "Halting Prison Sex Scandals Has Far-Reaching Effects"; Zaitz, "Abuse of Women Inmates at Oregon's Coffee Creek Prison Goes On for Years."

21. For the Burgess settlement, see Jackson, "Custer County Reaches $10 Million Settlement." For other recent settlements, see *End Silence*, under Adult Prisons and Jails: In the News.

22. United States Department of Justice, Civil Rights Division, Findings Letter to John Engler (for findings letters, see chapter 8); Human Rights Watch, *All Too Familiar*, 224.

23. See Neal v Department of Corrections (2009) at 2.

24. Neal v Department of Corrections (on rehearing), 592 NW2d at 373–76.

25. Neal v Department of Corrections (2005) at 8–10. The ELCRA amendment came into effect in March 2000. Ibid., 8.

26. Mason v Granholm, 2007 US Dist. LEXIS 4579 at *11–*13 (footnotes omitted, paragraph breaks suppressed).

27. See Neal v Department of Corrections (2009) at 8–9 (internal brackets removed).

28. See Seidel, "Jury Awarded $15.4 Million to Inmates."

29. See Neal v Department of Corrections (2009) at 2; Levy, "Mich. to Pay $100M for Inmate Abuse"; Seidel, "Jury Awarded $15.4 Million to Inmates"; Neal v Department of Corrections, Plan of Allocation of Settlement Proceeds, 2.

30. See Neal v Department of Corrections, Plan of Allocation of Settlement Proceeds, 3.

31. *Wayne Law,* "Wayne Law Alumna Deborah LaBelle Reflects" (indirect-speech interpolation omitted); Human Rights Watch, *Nowhere to Hide.*

CHAPTER 8: FEDERAL CONSTITUTIONAL LAWSUITS

1. See, for example, Gibbons and Katzenbach, *Confronting Confinement,* 84–85. In many of the states the judiciary lacks political independence, see Singer, *Jury Duty,* ch. 4.

2. Civil Action for Deprivation of Rights.

3. Although this chapter deals with constitutional violations, the case of Maine v Thiboutot holds that an action can also be brought under section 1983 for a violation of rights granted under a federal statute.

4. The emphasized text is quoted from Monroe v Pape, 365 US at 172.

5. Chavez v Poleate, 2010 US Dist. LEXIS 15643 at *2 (obvious typographical error of "we" for "he" corrected).

6. For inmates of facilities operated by the federal government, all that is available in place of a section 1983 lawsuit is a so-called Bivens action, under the holding in Bivens v Six Unknown Fed. Narcotics Agents.

7. The exhaustion requirement is Prison Litigation Reform Act, 42 USC § 1997e(a). The full title of the act is the Prison Litigation Reform Act of 1995, but it was enacted in 1996. For the effectiveness of the PLRA in reducing the number of section 1983 inmate lawsuits, see Schlanger, "Inmate Litigation," 1633–34. Schlanger notes that the states feared that, following enactment of the PLRA, lawsuits would be filed in state instead of federal courts and that to prevent this most states have enacted provisions similar to those of the PLRA. Ibid., 1635–36.

8. For discussion, including limited attempts by some federal courts to incorporate basic requirements of reasonableness into the term "available," see Schlanger, "Inmate Litigation," 1627–28; Ries, "Duty-to-Protect Claims by Inmates," 934–36; McComb, "Civil Rights of Prisoners," 51–55; Boston, *The Prison Litigation Reform Act,* ch. 4.

9. Bright, Statement regarding the Prison Abuse Remedies Act; Schlanger, "Inmate Litigation," 1650.

10. Gibbons and Katzenbach, *Confronting Confinement*, 87; National Prison Rape Elimination Commission, *Report*, 93 and 217, Standard RE–2.

Another PLRA provision that has given concern is a bar on actions "for mental or emotional injury suffered while in custody without a prior showing of physical injury." Prison Litigation Reform Act, 28 USC § 1346(b)(2), 42 USC § 1997e(e). At least one federal district court has held that rape does not in itself constitute physical injury. The court barred a claim alleging that prison officers forcibly sodomized prisoners because, in the court's words, "the plaintiffs do not make any claim of physical injury beyond the bare allegation of sexual assault . . . [and so] have failed to meet the physical injury requirement of the [PLRA]." Hancock v Payne, 2006 WL 21751 at *3. The report *Confronting Confinement* roundly criticizes this provision of the PLRA and calls upon Congress to eliminate it. Gibbons and Katzenbach, *Confronting Confinement*, 86. The NPREC report states "that victims of sexual abuse are losing vital avenues for relief because they cannot prove physical injury as defined in the PLRA" and also calls on Congress to amend this provision. National Prison Rape Elimination Commission, *Report*, 95.

11. American Bar Association, Criminal Justice Section, *Report to the House of Delegates,* 4 (paragraph break suppressed).

12. See chapter 7. As discussed shortly, states have immunity from § 1983 damages claims. In some cases, a state officer sued in his personal capacity has claimed that because the state will indemnify him, the lawsuit against him is in effect a lawsuit against the state and should therefore be dismissed. Federal courts have rejected this argument in cases where the state was not compelled to indemnify the officer but has merely exercised its discretion to do so: "A government may not manufacture immunity for its employees by agreeing to indemnify them." Spruytte v Walters, 753 F2d at 512 n. 6. But when state law requires the state to indemnify the officer the situation is not clear, see Reyes v Sazan, 168 F3d at 162–63.

Out of concern that the threat of personal liability might hamper officials in the performance of their public duties, courts have developed the doctrine of *qualified immunity*. This doctrine limits the ability of individuals to sue officials under section 1983 in their personal capacity, by permitting such a lawsuit only when the constitutional right that was allegedly violated is a "clearly established" right. The Supreme Court declares: "Qualified immunity balances two important interests—the need to hold public officials accountable when they exercise power irresponsibly and the need to shield officials from harassment, distraction, and liability when they perform their duties reasonably." Pearson v Callahan, 555 US at 231. The Supreme Court held in Butz v Economou that federal officials also have qualified immunity.

13. Chavez v Poleate, 2010 US Dist. LEXIS 15643 at *9–*13.

14. Parrish v Ball, 594 F3d at 996.

15. Ibid. at 1002.

16. The doctrine that a lawsuit against a person in his official capacity is equivalent to a lawsuit against the entity of which that person is an official goes

back at least as far as the 1828 Supreme Court case of Governor of Georgia v Madrazo. In the context of § 1983 lawsuits, the court has explained that official-capacity lawsuits "generally represent only another way of pleading an action against an entity of which an officer is an agent." Monell v Department of Social Services of the City of New York, 436 US at 690 n. 55.

17. Alden v Maine, 527 US at 728.

18. Fitzpatrick v Bitzer, 427 US at 456.

19. An official entity within a state also enjoys immunity from § 1983 lawsuits if it is sufficiently part of the state government to be regarded as an "arm of the state." The federal courts determine whether an entity is an arm of the state on the basis of five factors: "whether a money judgment would be satisfied out of state funds, whether the entity performs central governmental functions, whether the entity may sue or be sued, whether the entity has the power to take property in its own name or only the name of the state, and the corporate status of the entity." Mitchell v Los Angeles Community College District, 861 F2d at 201. Note that state law controls all these five factors that federal courts apply.

20. Will v Michigan Department of State Police, 491 US at 64–71. Note also that inmates of a federal facility cannot bring a lawsuit against the facility or any part of the federal government. A Bivens action can be brought against individual federal officers only. FDIC v Meyer, 510 US at 485.

21. Ex parte Young, 209 US at 159. This doctrine was confirmed in Will v Michigan Department of State Police, 491 US at 71 n. 10. It should apply similarly in bringing a lawsuit against federal officials.

22. Compensatory damages are available against a local government entity, but punitive damages are not available. The reason given is that punitive damages would place an undue burden on the taxpayers, who are the ultimately payers of damages awards against a local government entity or its officials in their official capacity. City of Newport v Fact Concerts, 453 US at 258–71.

23. Monell v Department of Social Services of the City of New York, 436 US at 690–91. More precisely, the court states here: "Local governing bodies . . . can be sued directly under § 1983 for monetary, declaratory, or injunctive relief where . . . the action that is alleged to be unconstitutional implements or executes a policy statement, ordinance, regulation, or decision officially adopted and promulgated by that body's officers. . . . [They also] may be sued for constitutional deprivations visited pursuant to governmental 'custom' even though such a custom has not received formal approval through the body's official decisionmaking channels." Liability is also appropriate for violations of constitutional rights stemming from a "usage" or "practice" of local government. The term "policy or custom" is a shorthand that the court itself uses for its full list of types of local government action for which liability is appropriate. Los Angeles County v Humphries, 131 S Ct. at 452.

24. City of Canton v Harris, 489 US at 390.

25. Parrish v Ball, 594 F3d at 997; ibid. at 1000.

26. The policy considerations that justify qualified immunity for corrections officers in government-operated facilities sued in their personal capacity do not apply to officers of private facilities, and accordingly they do not have qualified immunity. For discussion with case references, see Kritchevsky, "Civil Rights Liability of Private Entities."

The 2012 Supreme Court decision in Minneci v Pollard, coupled with its earlier decision in Correctional Services Corporation v Malesko, bars an inmate of a privately operated federal facility from bringing a federal lawsuit against the corporation or its officers. Rather, inmates must rely on the tort law of the state in which the facility is located.

27. Usually the Bill of Rights refers to the first ten amendments to the federal Constitution. But the Ninth and Tenth are irrelevant to the incorporation doctrine discussed here, so that in the context of incorporation it is common simply to refer to the first eight amendments as the Bill of Rights. The incorporation doctrine is based on the Supreme Court's interpretation of the Fourteenth Amendment to the Constitution, which denies the states the power to "deprive any person of life, liberty, or property, without due process of law." See Singer, *Jury Duty*, ch. 7. In Robinson v California, the court made the Eighth Amendment provision against cruel and unusual punishments applicable to the states.

28. Redman v County of San Diego, 942 F2d at 1449 (opinion), 1450 (dissent, agreeing on this issue).

29. Weems v US, 217 US at 357–58, 364–65, 381.

30. Deshaney v Winnebago County Social Services Department, 489 US at 200; Estelle v Gamble, 429 US at 103–4.

31. Farmer v Brennan, 511 US at 831. Farmer was incarcerated in a federal facility and brought a Bivens action, but the "deliberate indifference" standard applies in Bivens actions exactly as in § 1983 lawsuits.

32. Farmer v Brennan, 511 US at 832–33 (internal citations, quotation marks, brackets, and ellipses omitted).

33. Ibid. at 837.

34. Ibid. at 838.

35. Schlanger, "Inmate Litigation," 1606; ibid., 1607.

36. The following account of the case is from Palton v Jackson, 2009 US Dist. LEXIS 83176 at *2–*7, and from *Prison Legal News*, "Arkansas Federal Jury Awards $261,000 to Male Prisoner Raped by Male Guard."

37. See *ADC Advocate*, "Promotions."

38. For review and discussion of a range of cases, see Giller, "Patriarchy on Lockdown," 676–87; Ries, "Duty-to-Protect Claims by Inmates," 945–58. For an explanation of summary judgment in the trial process, see Singer, *Jury Duty*, ch. 1.

39. The Civil Rights of Institutionalized Persons Act was enacted in 1980 but substantially amended by the Prison Litigation Reform Act and further amended by the Patient Protection and Affordable Care Act of 2010. The discussion in the text is current, relating to the statute as amended. The statute applies whenever the attorney general has reasonable cause to believe that inmates

are being subjected "to egregious or flagrant conditions which deprive such persons of any rights, privileges, or immunities secured or protected by the Constitution or laws of the United States causing such persons to suffer grievous harm, and that such deprivation is pursuant to a pattern or practice of resistance to the full enjoyment of such rights, privileges, or immunities." Civil Rights of Institutionalized Persons Act, 42 USC § 1997a(a).

40. National Prison Rape Elimination Commission, *Report*, 96. It used to be possible for recalcitrant correctional authorities to hamper CRIPA investigations by refusing to allow federal officials access to their facilities. But section 10606(d)(2) of the Patient Protection and Affordable Care Act amends CRIPA to grant the Department of Justice appropriate powers.

41. For an example of an effective CRIPA investigation, see National Prison Rape Elimination Commission, *Report*, 96–97. The quotations are from Gibbons and Katzenbach, *Confronting Confinement*, 84; National Prison Rape Elimination Commission, *Report*, 97. The recent Department of Justice reports to Congress are United States Department of Justice, Office of Legislative Affairs, *Department of Justice Activities under the Civil Rights of Institutionalized Persons Act, Fiscal Year 2010*, and *Department of Justice Activities under the Civil Rights of Institutionalized Persons Act, Fiscal Year 2011*.

CHAPTER 9: THE FIRST TEN YEARS

1. The provisions discussed in this chapter are the correspondingly numbered sections of the Prison Rape Elimination Act. For the PREA estimate of the number of incidents of sexual abuse in incarceration, see chapter 2. For vulnerable categories of inmates, see chapter 4. For social costs of sexual abuse in incarceration in terms of spread of disease and increased violence, see chapter 5.

2. The statute establishing the National Institute of Corrections is 18 USC § 319.

3. Science, State, Justice, Commerce, and Related Agencies Appropriations Act, 2006, Title I; Revised Continuing Appropriations Resolution, 2007, Division B, Title I; Consolidated Appropriations Act, 2008, Division B, Title II. There was an appropriation of $13 million in 2003, before passage of PREA. Consolidated Appropriations Resolution, 2003, Division B, Title I. There was an appropriation of about $37 million in each of 2004 and 2005. Consolidated Appropriations Act, 2004, Division B, Title I; Consolidated Appropriations Act, 2005, Division B, Title I. See also Golden, "Looking Behind the Locked Door," 6.

4. The statute refers to this body as the National Prison Rape Reduction Commission, but it has been known as the National Prison Rape Elimination Commission.

5. Except where otherwise noted, the following account is drawn from National Prison Rape Elimination Commission, *Report*, 25–28, and includes direct quotations that are not specifically noted as such.

6. Kaiser and Stannow, "The Way to Stop Prison Rape."

7. The findings and discussion of them are in the executive summary in National Prison Rape Elimination Commission, *Report*, 3–24.

8. The recommended national standards and further recommendations are ibid., 215–38. The following discussion includes direct quotations from there that are not specifically noted as such. The proposed national standards are discussed later in this chapter, and the final national standards are discussed in chapter 10.

9. The various forms of searches are defined in the final national standards, discussed in chapter 10.

10. Reggie B. Walton, chairman, in National Prison Rape Elimination Commission, Press Conference Announcing the Release of the Commission's Report and Standards (web audio stream, transcribed by Michael Singer).

11. For this discussion, see United States Department of Justice, *National Standards to Prevent, Detect, and Respond to Prison Rape: Notice of Proposed Rulemaking*, 6249.

12. Booz Allen Hamilton, *Prison Rape Elimination Act (PREA): Cost Impact Analysis*.

13. For recognition of these problems with the Booz, Allen, Hamilton study, see United States Department of Justice, *Initial Regulatory Impact Analysis*, 34–35; United States Department of Justice, *Regulatory Impact Assessment*, 73–74, from which the quotation is at 74. For argument that the Booz Allen Hamilton study's reliance on corrections professionals likely produced exaggerated cost estimates, see Kaiser and Stannow, "The Way to Stop Prison Rape"; Just Detention International, *Comments Submitted to the Department of Justice*, 31.

14. See United States Department of Justice, *Initial Regulatory Impact Analysis*, 32–33.

15. United States Department of Justice, *Regulatory Impact Assessment*, 74–75. The Department of Justice uniformly uses a fairly standard 7 percent discount rate in the RIA to translate each cost that will be incurred in the future to present value. It then uses this same discount rate to translate the entire resulting present-value cost into fifteen years of equal annual payment installments.

16. Ibid., 168, table 16.1.

17. For the RIA assessments, see chapter 5. If the lower-bound estimate is adopted, then $6 billion is 22.3 percent of $26.9 billion. If the more realistic estimate is adopted, then $6 billion is 11.6 percent of $51.9 billion.

18. For the requirement of conducting a cost/benefit analysis, see United States Department of Justice, *Regulatory Impact Assessment*, 9. For the issue of the prospective benefit of the PREA national standards, see chapter 10.

19. The 2011 publications are United States Department of Justice, *National Standards to Prevent, Detect, and Respond to Prison Rape: Notice of Proposed Rulemaking*, and United States Department of Justice, *Initial Regulatory Impact Analysis*. For the public input, see United States Department of Justice,

Regulatory Impact Assessment, 13–14. Chapter 10 notes some of the specific questions that the Department of Justice posed.

CHAPTER 10: THE NATIONAL STANDARDS

1. The Department of Justice has decided that PREA does not extend to nonresidential community corrections. United States Department of Justice, *National Standards to Prevent, Detect, and Respond to Prison Rape: Final Rule*, 37113.

2. Prison Rape Elimination Act National Standards, § 115.11(b) (adult prisons and jails), § 115.111(b) (lockups), § 115.211(b) (community confinement facilities), § 115.311(b) (juvenile facilities).

3. Ibid., § 115.11(c) (adult prisons and jails), § 115.311(c) (juvenile facilities).

4. United States Department of Justice, *National Standards to Prevent, Detect, and Respond to Prison Rape: Notice of Proposed Rulemaking*, 6251–52; see United States Department of Justice, *National Standards to Prevent, Detect, and Respond to Prison Rape: Final Rule*, 37125; Prison Rape Elimination Act National Standards, § 115.13 (adult prisons and jails), § 115.113 (lockups), § 115.213 (community confinement facilities), § 115.313 (juvenile facilities).

5. United States Department of Justice, *National Standards to Prevent, Detect, and Respond to Prison Rape: Final Rule*, 37118–26; Prison Rape Elimination Act National Standards, § 115.13.

6. Prison Rape Elimination Act National Standards, § 115.113 (lockups), § 115.213 (community confinement facilities); United States Department of Justice, *National Standards to Prevent, Detect, and Respond to Prison Rape: Final Rule*, 37119.

7. Prison Rape Elimination Act National Standards, § 115.13 (adult prisons and jails), § 115.113 (lockups), § 115.213 (community confinement facilities).

8. Prison Rape Elimination Act National Standards, § 115.313 (juvenile facilities).

9. Prison Rape Elimination Act National Standards, § 115.14 (adult prisons and jails), § 115.114 (lockups); United States Department of Justice, *National Standards to Prevent, Detect, and Respond to Prison Rape: Final Rule*, 37129.

10. A visual body cavity search is "a search of the anal or genital opening." Prison Rape Elimination Act National Standards, § 115.15. A strip search is "a search that requires a person to remove or arrange some or all clothing so as to permit a visual inspection of the person's breasts, buttocks, or genitalia." Ibid., § 115.5. A pat-down search is "a running of the hands over the clothed body of an inmate, detainee, or resident by an employee to determine whether the individual possesses contraband." Ibid. References to "viewing" are concerned with viewing of "breasts, buttocks, or genitalia." United States Department of Justice, *National Standards to Prevent, Detect, and Respond to Prison Rape: Final Rule*, 37108.

11. United States Department of Justice, *National Standards to Prevent, Detect, and Respond to Prison Rape: Notice of Proposed Rulemaking*, 6253.

12. For the discussion of cross-gender searching and viewing, see *National Standards to Prevent, Detect, and Respond to Prison Rape: Final Rule*, 37130–36. The provisions are Prison Rape Elimination Act National Standards, § 115.15 (adult prisons and jails, permitting a 3–5 year delay in implementation), § 115.115 (lockups, not restricting cross-gender pat-down searches at all but not permitting any delay in implementation), § 115.215 (community confinement facilities, permitting a 3–5 year delay in implementation), § 115.315 (juvenile facilities, not permitting any delay in implementation). For discussion of sexual abuse by female staff of male inmates, see Buchanan, "Engendering Rape," 1638–39, 1672–81, and original sources cited there.

13. The provisions in the category of responsiveness planning are Prison Rape Elimination Act National Standards, § 115.21–22 (adult prisons and jails), § 115.121–22 (lockups), § 115.221–22 (community confinement facilities), § 115.321–22 (juvenile facilities).

14. The provisions are ibid., § 115.31–35 (adult prisons and jails), § 115.131–32, 134 (lockups; since these are short-term holding facilities, there is no provision for detainee education or for medical and mental health-care practitioner training and education), § 115.231–35 (community confinement facilities), § 115.331–35 (juvenile facilities).

15. The provisions are ibid., § 115.41–43 (adult prisons and jails), § 115.141 (lockups), § 115.241–42 (community confinement facilities), § 115.341–42 (juvenile facilities). The regulations for lockups are rudimentary, requiring only the most basic screening measures to mitigate the risk of sexual abuse of vulnerable detainees.

16. For the comments on the provision for inmate reporting, see United States Department of Justice, *National Standards to Prevent, Detect, and Respond to Prison Rape: Final Rule*, 37155–57. The provision is Prison Rape Elimination Act National Standards, § 115.51 (adult prisons and jails), § 115.151 (lockups), § 115.251 (community confinement facilities), § 115.351 (juvenile facilities). For adult prisons and jails and juvenile facilities, the correctional agency must actually *provide* at least one way for inmates to report to an external entity, but for lockups and community confinement facilities the correctional agency needs to only inform inmates of the way to do so.

17. For grievance procedures and the PLRA, see chapter 8. The provision is Prison Rape Elimination Act National Standards, § 115.52 (adult prisons and jails), § 115.252 (community confinement facilities), § 115.352 (juvenile facilities). There is no equivalent provision for lockups.

18. The provision on outside emotional support services is ibid., § 115.53 (adult prisons and jails), § 115.253 (community confinement facilities), § 115.353 (juvenile facilities). There is no equivalent provision for lockups. The provision on third-party reporting is ibid., § 115.54 (adult prisons and jails), § 115.154 (lockups), § 115.254 (community confinement facilities), § 115.354 (juvenile facilities).

19. The provisions on official response are ibid., § 115.61–68 (adult prisons and jails), § 115.161–67 (lockups), § 115.261–67 (community confinement facilities), § 115.361–68 (juvenile facilities).

20. For issues regarding allegations rejected as not "substantiated," see chapter 2. The provisions on investigations are Prison Rape Elimination Act National Standards, § 115.71–73 (adult prisons and jails), § 115.171–72 (lockups), § 115.271–73 (community confinement facilities), § 115.371–73 (juvenile facilities).

21. The provision on discipline is Prison Rape Elimination Act National Standards, § 115.76–78 (adult prisons and jails), § 115.176–78 (lockups), § 115.276–78 (community confinement facilities), § 115.376–78 (juvenile facilities).

For concerns regarding sexual activity between an inmate and a staff member as "willing," see chapter 2. For concerns regarding consensual sexual activity between inmates, see chapter 1. Under the particular provision, correctional agencies may prohibit sexual activity between inmates but may not treat the activity as sexual abuse if it is not coerced.

22. The provisions on medical and mental care are Prison Rape Elimination Act National Standards, § 115.81–83 (adult prisons and jails), § 115.182 (lockups), § 115.282–83 (community confinement facilities), § 115.381–83 (juvenile facilities). Since individuals are detained in lockups relatively briefly, lockups are not required to provide ongoing medical or mental health care. For current practices in correctional agencies, see chapter 4.

23. The provisions on data collection and review are Prison Rape Elimination Act National Standards, § 115.86–89 (adult prisons and jails), § 115.186–89 (lockups), § 115.286–89 (community confinement facilities), § 115.386–89 (juvenile facilities).

24. National Prison Rape Elimination Commission, *Report,* 89.

25. The provision requiring facilities to conduct audits is Prison Rape Elimination Act National Standards, § 115.93 (adult prisons and jails), § 115.193 (lockups), § 115.293 (community confinement facilities), § 115.393 (juvenile facilities). The audit standards provision is ibid., subpart E, § 115.401–5.

26. See National Prison Rape Elimination Commission, *Report,* 175–88 (immigration facilities), 26–27 (Native American tribal facilities).

27. This account is drawn from United States Department of Justice, *National Standards to Prevent, Detect, and Respond to Prison Rape: Final Rule,* 37107, 37112–13, and includes direct quotations that are not specifically noted as such. The directive to federal agencies is United States President, Memorandum.

28. Although state and local government correctional authorities are under no legal obligation to comply with the PREA national standards, they might possibly face adverse consequences if they do not. For example, the PREA national standards might influence the standard of "deliberate indifference" that the federal courts apply in lawsuits against correctional authorities. See chapter 8 for the deliberate indifference standard and chapter 11 for how the PREA national standards might influence the courts.

29. United States Department of Justice, *Regulatory Impact Assessment,* 70.

30. Ibid., 168, table 16.1.

31. Ibid., 6.

32. Ibid., 163.

33. Ibid., 168.

34. The break-even analysis is ibid., 157–63. The estimate for adult facilities given here in the text is from ibid., 158, table 15.2, which gives 1.54 percent as the break-even percentage for jails when applying the WTP cost estimate to the lower-bound prevalence assessment. All the other break-even percentages are far lower, so the overall percentage reduction needed to break even is in fact much less than 1.5 percent. The estimate for juvenile facilities given here in the text is from ibid., 159, table 15.2, where 2.83 percent is the highest break-even percentage.

35. Ibid., 157.

36. Ibid., 77.

CHAPTER 11: THE FUTURE OF THE AMERICAN INSTITUTION OF PRISON RAPE

1. Among numerous reports other than those previously discussed that regard prison rape as institutionalized in America are Amnesty International, *"Not Part of My Sentence"*; United States Department of Justice, National Institute of Corrections, *Sexual Misconduct in Prisons* (1996); United States General Accounting Office, *Women in Prison.*

2. The zero-tolerance provision is Prison Rape Elimination Act, § 3(1). The quotation is from Hall v Terrell, 2009 US Dist. LEXIS 48870 at *2–*3 (court's internal references suppressed). See also chapter 7. For the professed policy of zero tolerance of sexual abuse in the military, see United States Department of Defense, *Annual Report on Sexual Assault in the Military, Fiscal Year 2011,* 1. For the continuing prevalence of sexual abuse in the military, with data, see United States Department of Defense, *Annual Report on Sexual Assault in the Military, Fiscal Year 2011,* 28. For one of many news articles focusing on sexual abuse in the military as a continuing scandal, see Trudeau and Sutton, "When Rapists Wear Uniforms."

3. United States Department of Justice, *Regulatory Impact Assessment,* 6.

4. See National PREA Resource Center, website.

5. Hoffman, "Ending Prison Rape" (paragraph breaks suppressed).

6. National Prison Rape Elimination Commission, *Report,* 13.

7. United States Department of Justice, *Regulatory Impact Assessment,* 14.

8. Ries, "Duty-to-Protect Claims by Inmates," 980.

9. Ibid., 985.

10. For Brown v Plata, see chapter 4; Singer, *Jury Duty,* ch. 13.

11. Thompson, Nored, and Cheeseman Dial, "The Prison Rape Elimination Act," 433.

12. Hoffman, "Ending Prison Rape."

13. Burger, Address to the Bar of the City of New York, 19.

Bibliography

BOOKS, ARTICLES, REPORTS, ETC.

ADC Advocate, "Promotions." *Arkansas Department of Correction Employee Newsletter,* August 2010, 9. Accessed May 24, 2012. http://adc.arkansas. gov/resources/Documents/August_2010_ADC_Advocate.pdf.

Amnesty International, "Not Part of My Sentence": Violations of the Human Rights of Women in Custody. AMR 51/019/1999. 1999. Accessed February 9, 2012. http://www.amnesty.org/en/library/asset/AMR51/019/1999/ en/7588269a-e33d-11dd-808b-bfd8d459a3de/amr510191999en.pdf.

Appiah, Kwame Anthony. "What Will Future Generations Condemn Us For?" *Washington Post,* September 26, 2010. Accessed December 21, 2011. http://www.washingtonpost.com/wp-dyn/content/article/2010/09/24/ AR2010092404113.html.

Associated Press, "Governor's Son Creates Prison-Themed Game." January 27, 2008. Accessed June 30, 2012. http://www.msnbc.msn.com/id/ 22870462/.

Atassi, Leila. "Prison Guard Gets Seven Years for Raping Inmate." *Cleveland Plain Dealer,* October 3, 2008, updated September 2, 2010. Accessed May 14, 2012. http://blog.cleveland.com/metro/2008/10/prison_guard_ gets_seven_years.html.

At Risk: Sexual Abuse and Vulnerable Groups Behind Bars. San Francisco: National Prison Rape Elimination Commission Public Hearing, August 19, 2005.

Bacon, Francis. *The Works of Francis Bacon.* Edited by James Spedding, Robert Leslie Ellis, and Douglas Denon Heath. Vol. 2. London: Longman, 1857.

Bazelon, David. *The Adversary Process: Who Needs It?* 12th Annual James Madison Lecture, New York University School of Law, April 1971. Reprinted in U.S. Congressional Record, vol. 117, part 10, 12675–79 (Senate, April 29, 1971).

Beck, Allen J., and Candace Johnson. *Sexual Victimization Reported by Former State Prisoners, 2008.* United States Department of Justice, Bureau of Justice Statistics, 2012. Accessed May 18, 2012. http://bjs.ojp.usdoj.gov/content/pub/pdf/svrfsp08.pdf.

Beck, Allen J., Devon B. Adams, and Paul Guerino. *Sexual Violence Reported by Juvenile Correctional Authorities, 2005–06.* United States Department of Justice, Bureau of Justice Statistics, 2008. Accessed February 10, 2012. http://bjs.ojp.usdoj.gov/content/pub/pdf/svrjca0506.pdf.

Beck, Allen J., and Paige M. Harrison. *Sexual Victimization in Local Jails Reported by Inmates, 2007.* United States Department of Justice, Bureau of Justice Statistics, 2008. Accessed February 10, 2012. http://bjs.ojp.usdoj.gov/content/pub/pdf/svljri07.pdf.

Beck, Allen J., and Paige M. Harrison. *Sexual Victimization in State and Federal Prisons Reported by Inmates, 2007.* United States Department of Justice, Bureau of Justice Statistics, 2008. Accessed February 10, 2012. http://bjs.ojp.usdoj.gov/content/pub/pdf/svsfpri07.pdf.

Beck, Allen J., and Paige M. Harrison. *Sexual Violence Reported by Correctional Authorities, 2005.* United States Department of Justice, Bureau of Justice Statistics, 2006. Accessed February 10, 2012. http://bjs.ojp.usdoj.gov/content/pub/pdf/svrca05.pdf.

Beck, Allen J., Paige M. Harrison, and Devon B. Adams. *Sexual Violence Reported by Correctional Authorities, 2006.* United States Department of Justice, Bureau of Justice Statistics, 2007. Accessed February 10, 2012. http://bjs.ojp.usdoj.gov/content/pub/pdf/svrca06.pdf.

Beck, Allen J., Paige M. Harrison, Marcus Berzofsky, Rachel Caspar, and Christopher Krebs. *Sexual Victimization in Prisons and Jails Reported by Inmates, 2008–09.* United States Department of Justice, Bureau of Justice Statistics, 2010. Accessed February 10, 2012. http://bjs.ojp.usdoj.gov/content/pub/pdf/svpjri0809.pdf.

Beck, Allen J., Paige M. Harrison, and Paul Guerino. *Sexual Victimization in Juvenile Facilities Reported by Youth, 2008–09.* United States Department of Justice, Bureau of Justice Statistics, 2010. Accessed February 10, 2012. http://bjs.ojp.usdoj.gov/content/pub/pdf/svjfry09.pdf.

Beck, Allen J., and Timothy A. Hughes. *Sexual Violence Reported by Correctional Authorities, 2004.* United States Department of Justice, Bureau of Justice Statistics, 2005. Accessed February 10, 2012. http://bjs.ojp.usdoj.gov/content/pub/pdf/svrca04.pdf.

Bonner, Jesse L. "Guilty of Prison Rape, an Idaho Inmate Gets Life." Associated Press, December 22, 2009. Accessed May 15, 2012. http://www.kboi2.com/news/79925697.html.

Booz Allen Hamilton. *Prison Rape Elimination Act (PREA): Cost Impact Analysis.* June 18, 2010. Accessed April 23, 2012. http://www.ojp.usdoj.gov/programs/pdfs/preacostimpactanalysis.pdf.

Boston, John. *The Prison Litigation Reform Act*. New York: Legal Aid Society Prisoners' Rights Project, 2004. Accessed May 18, 2012. http://www.wnylc.net/pb/docs/plra2cir04.pdf.

Brainerd Dispatch (MN), "Why I Am Proud to Be an American." Accessed July 8, 2012. http://brainerddispatch.com/lifestyle/2011–02–15/'why-i-am-proud-be-american'.

Bright, Stephen B. Statement regarding the Prison Abuse Remedies Act before the Subcommittee on Crime, Terrorism and Homeland Security, Committee on the Judiciary, U.S. House of Representatives (April 22, 2008). Accessed August 1, 2012. http://judiciary.house.gov/hearings/pdf/Bright080422.pdf.

Buchanan, Kim Shayo. "Engendering Rape." *UCLA Law Review* 59 (2012): 1630–88.

Buchanan, Kim Shayo. "Our Prisons, Ourselves: Race, Gender and the Rule of Law." *Yale Law and Policy Review* 29 (2010): 1–82.

Buck, Jessica M., Kathleen M. Morrow, Andrew Margolis, Gloria Eldridge, James Sosman, Robin MacGowan, Diane Binson, Deborah Kacanek, Timothy P. Flanigan, and The Project START Study Group. "Hepatitis B Vaccination in Prison: The Perspectives of Formerly Incarcerated Men." *Journal of Correctional Health Care* 12 (2006): 12–23.

Burger, Warren E. Address to the Bar of the City of New York. *Record of the Association of the Bar of the City of New York* 25 (March 1970 Supp.): 14–24.

CBS News, "Ex-Sheriff Sentenced in Sex Abuse Scandal." March 24, 2009. Accessed May 15, 2012. http://www.cbsnews.com/2100–201_162–4889548.html.

Clark, Anna. "Why Does Popular Culture Treat Prison Rape as a Joke?" *AlterNet*, August 17, 2009. Accessed July 29, 2012. http://www.alternet.org/story/141594/why_does_popular_culture_treat_prison_rape_as_a_joke/.

Cohen, Mark A., Roland T. Rust, Sara Steen, and Simon T. Tidd. "Willingness-to-Pay for Crime Control Programs." *Criminology* 42 (2004): 89–109.

The Cost of Victimization: Why Our Nation Must Confront Prison Rape. Washington, DC: National Prison Rape Elimination Commission Public Hearing, June 14, 2005.

Crary, David. "Prison-Rape Quote Slows Extradition." *Seattle Times*, October 30, 1997. Accessed June 30, 2012. http://community.seattletimes.nwsource.com/archive/?date=19971030&slug=2569348.

Davis, Alan J. "Sexual Assaults in the Philadelphia Prison System and Sheriff's Vans." *Trans-action* 6 (1968): 8–16.

Davis, Lois M., and Sharon Pacchiana. "Health Profile of the State Prison Population and Returning Offenders: Public Health Challenges." *Journal of Correctional Health Care* 10 (2004): 303–31.

Donaldson, Stephen. *Rape of Incarcerated Americans: A Preliminary Statistical Look*. Stop Prisoner Rape [Just Detention International], July 1995. Accessed March 19, 2012. http://www.justdetention.org/en/docs/doc_01_stats.aspx.

Donaldson, Stephen. Testimony at Massachusetts Legislative Hearing, Joint Committee on Public Safety, May 23, 1994. Accessed March 21, 2012.

http://web.archive.org/web/20080227051954/http://www.spr.org/en/docs/doc_01_massachusetts.asp.

Dumond, Robert F. "The Impact of Prisoner Sexual Violence: Challenges of Implementing Public Law 108–79—The Prison Rape Elimination Act." *Journal of Legislation* 32 (2006): 142–64.

End Silence: The Project on Addressing Prison Rape. Washington College of Law. Accessed May 15, 2012. http://www.wcl.american.edu/endsilence/.

Fleisher, Mark S., and Jessie L. Krienert. *The Culture of Prison Sexual Violence.* National Criminal Justice Reference Service, 2006. Accessed February 29, 2012. https://www.ncjrs.gov/pdffiles1/nij/grants/216515.pdf.

Fleisher, Mark S., and Jessie L. Krienert. *The Myth of Prison Rape: Sexual Culture in American Prisons.* Lanham, MD: Rowman and Littlefield, 2009.

Fontana, Tom. *Oz.* TV series. New York: Home Box Office, 1997–2003. DVD.

Freudenberg, Nicholas. "Community Health Services for Returning Jail and Prison Inmates." *Journal of Correctional Health Care* 10 (2004): 369–97.

Funk, Josh. "Short Sex Offender's Probation Upheld." *Washington Post,* July 17, 2007. http://www.washingtonpost.com/wp-dyn/content/article/2007/07/17/AR2007071700850.html.

Gardner, John, and Stephen Shute. "The Wrongness of Rape." In *Oxford Essays in Jurisprudence.* Fourth Series, edited by Jeremy Horder. 193–217. Oxford: Oxford University Press, 1999.

Gibbons, John J., and Nicholas de B. Katzenbach. *Confronting Confinement.* Washington, DC: Commission on Safety and Abuse in America's Prisons; New York: Vera Institute of Justice, 2006.

Giller, Olga. "Patriarchy on Lockdown: Deliberate Indifference and Male Prison Rape." *Cardozo Women's Law Journal* 10 (2004): 659–89.

Gilliard, Darrell K., and Allen J. Beck. *Prison and Jail Inmates at Midyear 1997.* United States Department of Justice, Bureau of Justice Statistics, 1998. Accessed April 10, 2012. http://bjs.ojp.usdoj.gov/content/pub/pdf/pjim97.pdf.

Glaze, Lauren E., and Thomas P. Bonczar. *Probation and Parole in the United States, 2010.* United States Department of Justice, Bureau of Justice Statistics, 2011. Accessed March 28, 2012. http://bjs.ojp.usdoj.gov/content/pub/pdf/ppus10.pdf.

Golden, Deborah M. "Looking Behind the Locked Door: Prison Law Reform Proposals for the New Administration." *Harvard Law and Policy Review Online* 3 (November 13, 2008). Accessed July 29, 2012. http://www.hlpronline.com/Golden_HLPR_111308.pdf.

Goldfarb, Ronald L. *Jails, the Ultimate Ghetto.* Garden City, NY: Anchor Press/Doubleday, 1975.

Greifinger, Robert, ed. *Public Health behind Bars: From Prisons to Communities.* New York: Springer, 2010.

Guerino, Paul, and Allen J. Beck. *Sexual Victimization Reported by Adult Correctional Authorities, 2007–2008.* United States Department of Justice, Bureau of Justice Statistics, 2011. Accessed February 10, 2012. http://bjs.ojp.usdoj.gov/content/pub/pdf/svraca0708.pdf.

Guerino, Paul, Paige M. Harrison, and William J. Sabol. *Prisoners in 2010.* United States Department of Justice, Bureau of Justice Statistics, 2011. Accessed February 10, 2012. http://bjs.ojp.usdoj.gov/content/pub/pdf/p10.pdf.

Gustafson, Alan. "Halting Prison Sex Scandals Has Far-Reaching Effects." *Statesman Journal,* Salem, Oregon, December 4, 2005. Accessed May 14, 2012. http://pqasb.pqarchiver.com/statesmanjournal/access/1784678201. html?FMT=ABS&FMTS=ABS:FT&type=current&date=Dec+4%2C+20 05&author=&pub=Statesman+Journal&edition=&startpage=A.1&desc =Halting+prison+sex+scandals+has+far-reaching+effects.

Harrison, Paige M., and Allen J. Beck. *Prison and Jail Inmates at Midyear 2004.* United States Department of Justice, Bureau of Justice Statistics, 2005. Accessed February 10, 2012. http://www.bjs.gov/content/pub/pdf/pjim04.pdf.

Hockenberry, Sarah, Melissa Sickmund, and Anthony Sladky. *Juvenile Residential Facility Census, 2008: Selected Findings.* United States Department of Justice, Office of Justice Programs, Office of Juvenile Justice and Delinquency Prevention, 2011. Accessed February 25, 2012. https://www.ncjrs. gov/pdffiles1/ojjdp/231683.pdf.

Hoffman, Richard B. "Ending Prison Rape: The Next Steps." *Washington Post,* June 15, 2012, A-31.

Howard, John. *The State of the Prisons in England and Wales.* London, 1777.

Hughes, Timothy, and Doris James Wilson. *Reentry Trends in the United States.* Bureau of Justice Statistics, 2003. Accessed April 1, 2012. http://bjs.ojp. usdoj.gov/content/pub/pdf/reentry.pdf.

Human Rights Watch. *All Too Familiar: Sexual Abuse of Women in U.S. State Prisons.* New York: Human Rights Watch, 1996.

Human Rights Watch. *No Escape: Male Rape in U.S. Prisons.* New York: Human Rights Watch, 2001.

Human Rights Watch. *Nowhere to Hide: Retaliation against Women in Michigan State Prisons.* Human Rights Watch, 1998. Accessed February 7, 2012. http://www.unhcr.org/refworld/docid/3ae6a86718.html.

Idaho Department of Corrections. Press release, November 24, 2009. Accessed May 15, 2012. http://www.prisontalk.com/forums/archive/index. php/t-455930.html.

Jackson, Ron. "Custer County Reaches $10 Million Settlement in Female Inmate Abuse Lawsuit." *Tulsa World*, May 10, 2010. Accessed May 15, 2012. http://www.tulsaworld.com/news/article.aspx?subjectid=12& articleid=20100510_12_0_ARAPAH439300.

Just Detention International. *Action Update.* Various dates. Accessed August 2, 2012. http://www.justdetention.org/en/action_update.aspx.

Just Detention International. *A Brief History.* Accessed July 31, 2012. http:// www.justdetention.org/en/spr_history.aspx.

Just Detention International. *Comments Submitted to the Department of Justice Notice of Proposed Rulemaking on National Standards to Prevent, Detect, and Respond to Prison Rape.* Docket No. OAG-131; AG Order No. 3244–2011. April 4, 2011. Accessed May 2, 2012. http://www. justdetention.org/pdf/JDIPublicComments.pdf.

Kaiser, David. "A Letter on Rape in Prisons." *New York Review of Books* 54, no. 8 (May 10, 2007). Accessed March 2, 2012. http://www.nybooks.com/articles/20155.

Kaiser, David, and Lovisa Stannow. "The Way to Stop Prison Rape." *New York Review of Books* 57, no. 5 (March 25, 2010). Accessed April 23, 2012. http://www.nybooks.com/articles/23738.

Kritchevsky, Barbara. "Civil Rights Liability of Private Entities." *Cardozo Law Review* 26 (2004): 35–79.

Lerner, Louise. "MRSA Bacteria Escape from Jails to Cause Staph Infections among Local Children." *Chicago Maroon,* April 7, 2009. Accessed April 9, 2012. http://chicagomaroon.com/2009/4/7/under-the-microscope-mrsa-bacteria-breaks-out-of-jail-to-cause-staph-infections-among-local-children/.

Levy, Douglas L. "Mich. to Pay $100M for Inmate Abuse." *CorrectionsOne News,* July 27, 2009. Accessed May 17, 2012. http://www.correctionsone.com/jail-management/articles/1859953-Mich-to-pay-100M-for-inmate-abuse/.

Licker, Mark. Letter to the editor. *Financial Times* (UK), December 4, 2007. Accessed June 30, 2012. http://www.ft.com/cms/s/0/c80a7ff4-a20b-11dc-a13b-0000779fd2ac.html.

Lind, James. *An Essay on the Most Effectual Means of Preserving the Health of Seamen in the Royal Navy.* 2nd ed. London, 1762.

Linden, Judith A. "Care of the Adult Patient after Sexual Assault." *New England Journal of Medicine* 365 (2011): 834–41.

Lockyer, Bill. Letter to the editor. *Los Angeles Times,* June 20, 2001, B-12.

Man, Christopher D., and John P. Cronan. "Forecasting Sexual Abuse in Prison: The Prison Subculture of Masculinity as a Backdrop for 'Deliberate Indifference.'" *Journal of Criminal Law and Criminology* 92 (2001): 127–85.

May, Larry. *Sharing Responsibility.* Chicago: University of Chicago Press, 1992.

McComb, Devin. "Civil Rights of Prisoners: The Seventh Circuit and Exhaustion of Remedies under the Prison Litigation Reform Act." *Seventh Circuit Review* 1 (2006): 46–73.

Miller, Ted R., Dexter M. Taylor, and Monique A. Sheppard. *Costs of Sexual Violence in Minnesota.* Minnesota Department of Health, 2007. Accessed April 1, 2012. http://www.pire.org/documents/mn_brochure.pdf.

Miller, Ted R., Dexter M. Taylor, and Monique A. Sheppard. *Costs of Sexual Violence in Minnesota: Detailed Methods Supplement.* 2007. Accessed April 3, 2012. http://www.pire.org/documents/MNMethodsSupplement.pdf.

Minton, Todd D. *Jail Inmates at Midyear 2010—Statistical Tables.* United States Department of Justice, Bureau of Justice Statistics, 2011. Accessed April 1, 2012. http://bjs.ojp.usdoj.gov/content/pub/pdf/jim10st.pdf.

National Commission on Correctional Health Care. *The Health Status of Soon-to-Be Released Inmates: A Report to Congress.* 2 vols. 2002. Accessed April 5, 2012. http://www.ncchc.org/pubs/pubs_stbr.html.

National PREA Resource Center. Website. Accessed August 13, 2012. http://www.prearesourcecenter.org/.

National Prison Rape Elimination Commission. Press Conference Announcing the Release of the Commission's Report and Standards. Audio/video
stream, June 23, 2009. Accessed September 17, 2009. www.nprec.us
[page no longer available].

National Prison Rape Elimination Commission. *Report*. June 23, 2009. Accessed January 8, 2012. https://www.ncjrs.gov/pdffiles1/226680.pdf.

North Platte Bulletin (NE), "Judge Who Gave Short Man Probation Ousted."
November 6, 2008. Accessed July 8, 2012. http://www.northplattebullet
in.com/index.asp?show=news&action=readStory&storyID=15467&pag
eID=3#talkback.

Odenkirk, Bob. *Let's Go to Prison*. Movie. Los Angeles: Carsey-Werner Films
for Universal Pictures, 2006. DVD.

Old Hippie's Gift Shop. "Your Asshole in Jail." Accessed June 30, 2012. http://
www.cafepress.com/texasbigbird/1189348.

"*Oz* (TV series)." *Wikipedia*. Accessed June 30, 2012. http://en.wikipedia.org/
wiki/Oz_(TV_series).

Palmer, Tom G. " 'Hi, My Name Isn't Justice, Honey,' and Shame on Lockyer."
Los Angeles Times, June 6, 2001, B-11.

Parenti, Christian. "Rape as a Disciplinary Tactic." *Salon*, August 23, 1999.
Accessed June 26, 1999. http://www.salon.com/1999/08/23/prisons_3/.

Pinar, William F. *The Gender of Racial Politics and Violence in America: Lynch-
ing, Prison Rape, and the Crisis of Masculinity*. New York: Peter Lang,
2001.

Prison Legal News, "Arkansas Federal Jury Awards $261,000 to Male Prisoner
Raped by Male Guard." Vol. 21, no. 7, July 2010, 42. Accessed May 24, 2012.
https://www.prisonlegalnews.org/(S(m0xtlg5542tyyo45o34nsmms))/
includes/_public/_issues/pln_2010/07pln10.pdf.

Ries, David K. "Duty-to-Protect Claims by Inmates after the Prison Rape Elimination Act." *Brooklyn Journal of Law and Policy* 13 (2005): 915–90.

Robertson, James E. "A Clean Heart and an Empty Head: The Supreme Court
and Sexual Terrorism in Prison." *North Carolina Law Review* 81 (2003):
433–81.

Rogers, Susan M., Maria R. Khan, Sylvia Tan, Charles F. Turner, William C.
Miller, and Emily Erbelding. "Incarceration, High-Risk Sexual Partnerships and Sexually Transmitted Infections in an Urban Population." *Sexually Transmitted Infections* 88 (2012): 63–68.

Sabo, Don, Terry A. Kupers, and Willie London, eds. *Prison Masculinities*. Philadelphia: Temple University Press, 2001.

Sabol, William J., Todd D. Minton, and Paige M. Harrison. *Prison and Jail
Inmates at Midyear 2006*. United States Department of Justice, Bureau of
Justice Statistics Bulletin, 2008. Accessed February 25, 2012. http://bjs.
ojp.usdoj.gov/content/pub/pdf/pjim06.pdf.

Schlanger, Margot. "Inmate Litigation." *Harvard Law Review* 115 (2003):
1555–706.

Schneider, Rob. *Big Stan*. Movie. Los Angeles: Crystal Sky Pictures, 2007. DVD.

Sebelius, John. *Don't Drop the Soap.* Board game. Gillius, Inc. Accessed June 30, 2012. http://www.gilliusinc.com/dropsoap.html.

Seidel, Jeff. "Jury Awarded $15.4 Million to Inmates." *Detroit Free Press,* January 7, 2009. Accessed July 29, 2012. http://www.freep.com/article/20090107/NEWS06/901070395.

Sexually Transmitted Disease Program, Los Angeles County Department of Health Services. *STD Prevalence Monitoring among Self-Identified Men Who Have Sex with Men (MSM) Inmates in Los Angeles County Men's Central Jail.* Annual Report, 2005: 1–11. Accessed April 11, 2012. http://publichealth.lacounty.gov/std/docs/k11_report_2005.pdf.

Sigler, Mary. "By the Light of Virtue: Prison Rape and the Corruption of Character." *Iowa Law Review* 91 (2006): 561–607.

Sigler, Mary. "Just Deserts, Prison Rape, and the Pleasing Fiction of Guideline Sentencing." *Arizona State Law Journal* 38 (2006): 561–80.

Singer, Michael. *Jury Duty: Reclaiming Your Political Power and Taking Responsibility.* Westport, CT: Praeger, 2012.

Smith, Brenda V. "Rethinking Prison Sex: Self-Expression and Safety." *Columbia Journal of Gender and Law* 15 (2006): 185–234.

Smith, Norman E., and Mary Ellen Batiuk. "Sexual Victimization and Inmate Social Interaction." *Prison Journal* 69 (1989): 29–38.

Smith, Phillip. Interview: Tom Cahill, President of Stop Prisoner Rape [Just Detention International]. *Alternet.* Accessed April 6, 2012. http://www.alternet.org/module/printversion/10818.

Stemple, Lara. "HBO's OZ and the Fight against Prisoner Rape: Chronicles from the Front Line." In *Third Wave Feminism and Television: Jane Puts It in a Box,* edited by Merri Lisa Johnson, 166–88. London: Taurus, 2007.

Stop Prisoner Rape [Just Detention International]. *Stories from Inside: Prisoner Rape and the War on Drugs.* Stop Prisoner Rape, 2007. Accessed March 25, 2012. http://www.justdetention.org/pdf/StoriesFromInside032207.pdf.

Stratton, Richard. "The Making of Bonecrusher." *Esquire,* September 1, 1999. Accessed June 26, 2012. http://www.esquire.com/features/ESQ0999-SEP_BONECRUSHER.

Struckman-Johnson, Cindy, and David Struckman-Johnson. "Sexual Coercion Rates in Seven Midwestern Prison Facilities for Men." *Prison Journal* 80 (2000): 379–90.

Struckman-Johnson, Cindy, and David Struckman-Johnson. "Sexual Coercion Reported by Women in Three Midwestern Prisons." *Journal of Sex Research* 39 (2002): 217–27.

Struckman-Johnson, Cindy, David Struckman-Johnson, Lisa Rucker, Kurt Bumby, and Stephen Donaldson. "Sexual Coercion Reported by Men and Women in Prison." *Journal of Sex Research* 33 (1996): 67–76.

Thompson, R. Alan, Lisa S. Nored, and Kelly Cheeseman Dial. "The Prison Rape Elimination Act (PREA): An Evaluation of Policy Compliance with Illustrative Excerpts." *Criminal Justice Policy Review,* 19, no. 4 (2008): 414–37.

Trudeau, Garry, and Loree Sutton. "When Rapists Wear Uniforms." *Washington Post,* July 1, 2012, A19.

United States Department of Defense, *Annual Report on Sexual Assault in the Military, Fiscal Year 2011.* Accessed August 8, 2012. http://www.sapr.mil/media/pdf/reports/Department_of_Defense_Fiscal_Year_2011_Annual_Report_on_Sexual_Assault_in_the_Military.pdf.

United States Department of Health and Human Services, Centers for Disease Control and Prevention. "Prevention and Control of Tuberculosis in Correctional and Detention Facilities: Recommendations from CDC." *Morbidity and Mortality Weekly Report 55,* no. RR–9 (2006): 1–54. Accessed April 9, 2012. http://www.cdc.gov/mmwr/PDF/rr/rr5509.pdf.

United States Department of Health and Human Services, Centers for Disease Control and Prevention. *Sexually Transmitted Disease Surveillance, 2010.* 2011. Accessed April 7, 2012. http://www.cdc.gov/std/stats10/surv2010.pdf.

United States Department of Health and Human Services, Centers for Disease Control and Prevention. "Tuberculosis Transmission in Multiple Correctional Facilities—Kansas, 2002–2003." *Morbidity and Mortality Weekly Report 53,* no. 32 (2004): 734–38. Accessed April 10, 2012. http://www.cdc.gov/mmwr/PDF/wk/mm5332.pdf.

United States Department of Justice, Bureau of Justice Statistics. *National Inmate Survey: Questionnaires.* Accessed February 16, 2012. http://bjs.ojp.usdoj.gov/index.cfm?ty=dcdetail&iid=278.

United States Department of Justice, Bureau of Justice Statistics. *Survey of Sexual Violence: Questionnaires.* Accessed February 15, 2012. http://bjs.ojp.usdoj.gov/index.cfm?ty=dcdetail&iid=406.

United States Department of Justice, Civil Rights Division. Findings Letter to John Engler, Governor State of Michigan. March 27, 1995. Accessed May 27, 2012. http://www.clearinghouse.net/chDocs/public/PC-MI-0008-0003.pdf.

United States Department of Justice, Civil Rights Division. Findings Letter to Marlin N. Gusman, Orleans Parish Criminal Sheriff. September 11, 2009. Accessed March 3, 2012. http://www.justice.gov/crt/about/spl/documents/parish_findlet.pdf.

United States Department of Justice. *Initial Regulatory Impact Analysis for Notice of Proposed Rulemaking: Proposed National Standards to Prevent, Detect, and Respond to Prison Rape under the Prison Rape Elimination Act (PREA).* Docket No. OAG–131 RIN 1105–AB34. January 24, 2011. Accessed February 14, 2012. http://www.ojp.usdoj.gov/programs/pdfs/prea_nprm_iria.pdf.

United States Department of Justice. *National Standards to Prevent, Detect, and Respond to Prison Rape: Final Rule.* Code of Federal Regulations, title 28, part 115. Federal Register, vol. 77, 37106–232 (June 20, 2012).

United States Department of Justice. *National Standards to Prevent, Detect, and Respond to Prison Rape: Notice of Proposed Rulemaking.* Code of

Federal Regulations, title 28, part 115. Federal Register, vol. 76, 6248–302 (February 3, 2011).

United States Department of Justice, National Institute of Corrections. *Sexual Misconduct in Prisons: Law, Agency Response, and Prevention.* 1996. Accessed February 9, 2012. http://static.nicic.gov/Library/013508.pdf.

United States Department of Justice, National Institute of Corrections. *Sexual Misconduct in Prisons: Law, Remedies, and Incidence.* 2000. Accessed February 9, 2012. http://static.nicic.gov/Library/016112.pdf.

United States Department of Justice, National Institute of Justice. *Victim Costs and Consequences: A New Look.* 1996. Accessed April 1, 2012. https://www.ncjrs.gov/pdffiles/victcost.pdf.

United States Department of Justice, Office of Justice Programs, Review Panel on Prison Rape. *Hearings on Rape and Sexual Misconduct in U.S. Jails.* September 15, 2011. Transcript, amended copy. Accessed February 29, 2012. http://www.ojp.usdoj.gov/reviewpanel/pdfs_sept11/transcript_091511.pdf.

United States Department of Justice, Office of Legislative Affairs. *Department of Justice Activities under the Civil Rights of Institutionalized Persons Act, Fiscal Year 2010.* 2011. Accessed July 10, 2012. http://www.justice.gov/crt/about/spl/documents/split_cripa10.pdf.

United States Department of Justice, Office of Legislative Affairs. *Department of Justice Activities under the Civil Rights of Institutionalized Persons Act, Fiscal Year 2011.* 2012. Accessed July 10, 2012. http://www.justice.gov/crt/about/spl/documents/split_cripa11.pdf.

United States Department of Justice, Office of the Inspector General. *Deterring Staff Sexual Abuse of Federal Inmates.* 2005. Accessed May 16, 2012. http://www.justice.gov/oig/special/0504/final.pdf.

United States Department of Justice, Office of the Inspector General, Evaluation and Inspections Division. *The Department of Justice's Efforts to Prevent Staff Sexual Abuse of Federal Inmates.* Report Number I–2009–004. 2009. Accessed February 17, 2012. http://www.justice.gov/oig/reports/plus/e0904.pdf.

United States Department of Justice, *Regulatory Impact Assessment for PREA Final Rule.* May 2012. Accessed July 10, 2012. http://www.ojp.usdoj.gov/programs/pdfs/prea_ria.pdf.

United States General Accounting Office. *Women in Prison: Sexual Misconduct by Correctional Staff.* GAO/GGD-99–104. 1999. Accessed February 9, 2012. http://www.gao.gov/archive/1999/gg99104.pdf.

United States President. Memorandum. "Implementing the Prison Rape Elimination Act." Federal Register, vol. 77, 30873–74 (May 23, 2012).

Waldron, Jeremy. "Torture and Positive Law: Jurisprudence for the White House." *Columbia Law Review* 105 (2005): 1681–750.

Wayne Law. "Wayne Law Alumna Deborah LaBelle Reflects on a 13-Year Lawsuit, $100 Million Settlement." August 18, 2009. Accessed May 27, 2012. http://law.wayne.edu/news.php?id=3313.

Weisberg, Robert, and David Mills. "Violence Silence: Why No One Really Cares about Prison Rape." *Slate*, October 1, 2003. http://www.slate.com/id/2089095/.

Williams, Max, and Lovisa Stannow. "Rape Is Not Part of the Penalty." *Oregonian*, June 21, 2009, updated October 19, 2009. Accessed March 2, 2012. http://www.oregonlive.com/opinion/index.ssf/2009/06/rape_is_not_part_of_the_penalt.html

Wilson, Mark. "Sex Scandal Rocks Oregon's 'Camp Cupcake' Women's Prison—Again." Prison Legal News, n.d. Accessed May 14, 2012. https://www.prisonlegalnews.org/(S(iwo5eingbkugyr55z41wcz55))/displayArticle.aspx?articleid=24135&AspxAutoDetectCookieSupport=1.

Wolf, Martin. "Judicial Torture and the NatWest 3." *Financial Times*, November 30, 2007. Accessed June 30, 2012. http://www.ft.com/cms/s/0/2699c7c4–9ea0–11dc-b4e4–0000779fd2ac.html.

Wood, Anthony. *Survey of the Antiquities of the City of Oxford Composed in 1661–6, by Anthony Wood.* Edited by Andrew Clark. Vol. 1. Oxford: Oxford Historical Society, 1889.

Zaitz, Les. "Abuse of Women Inmates at Oregon's Coffee Creek Prison Goes On for Years." *Oregonian*, April 29, 2012, updated May 2, 2012. Accessed May 14, 2012. http://www.oregonlive.com/politics/index.ssf/2012/04/abuse_of_women_inmates_at_oreg.html.

Zweig, Janine M., and John Blackmore. *Strategies to Prevent Prison Rape by Changing the Correctional Culture.* Washington, DC: United States Department of Justice, Office of Justice Programs, National Institute of Justice, 2008.

STATUTES AND REGULATIONS: UNITED STATES—FEDERAL

Civil Action for Deprivation of Rights. Public Law 96–170, § 1 (Dec. 29, 1979); Public Law 104–317, title III, § 309(c) (Oct. 19, 1996), codified as amended at 42 USC § 1983 (2006).

Civil Rights of Institutionalized Persons Act. Public Law 96–247 (May 23, 1980), codified as amended at 42 USC § 1997.

Consolidated Appropriations Act, 2004. Public Law 108–199 (Jan. 23, 2004).

Consolidated Appropriations Act, 2005. Public Law 108–447 (Dec. 8, 2004).

Consolidated Appropriations Act, 2008. Public Law 110–161 (Dec. 26, 2007).

Consolidated Appropriations Resolution, 2003. Public Law 108–7 (Feb. 20, 2003).

Patient Protection and Affordable Care Act. Public Law 111–148 (Mar. 23, 2010).

Prison Litigation Reform Act of 1995. Public Law 104–134, §§ 801–810 (1996), codified as amended at 11 USC § 523; 18 USC §§ 983(h)(3), 3624(b), 3626; 28 USC §§ 1346(b), 1915,1915A, 1932; 42 USC §§ 1997.

Prison Rape Elimination Act National Standards. Code of Federal Regulations, title 28, part 115. Federal Register, vol. 77, 37197–232 (June 20, 2012).

Prison Rape Elimination Act of 2003 (PREA). Public Law 108–79, codified as amended at 42 USC §§ 15601–15609 (2006).
Revised Continuing Appropriations Resolution, 2007. Public Law 110–5 (Feb. 15, 2007).
Science, State, Justice, Commerce and Related Agencies Appropriations Act, 2006. Public Law 109–108 (Nov. 22, 2005).

STATUTES: UNITED STATES—STATES

California. *Sexual Abuse in Detention Elimination Act. Penal Code,* Part 3, title 1, c. 3, art. 3.
Oregon. *Custodial Sexual Misconduct.* ORS 163.408, 163.411, as amended.

JUDICIAL DECISIONS: CANADA

USA v Cobb, [2001] 1 SCR 587 (Supreme Court of Canada).

JUDICIAL DECISIONS: UNITED STATES—FEDERAL AND STATE

Alberti v Heard, 600 F Supp. 443 (SD Tex. 1984), *stay denied sub nom.* Alberti v Klevenhagen, 606 F Supp. 478 (SD Tex. 1985), *affirmed,* 790 F2d 1220 (5th Cir. 1986), *rehearing denied,* 799 F2d 992 (1986).
Alden v Maine, 527 US 706 (1999).
Anderson v Redman, 429 F Supp. 1105 (D Del. 1977).
Bivens v Six Unknown Fed. Narcotics Agents, 403 US 388 (1971).
Brown v Plata, 131 S Ct. 1910 (2011).
Butz v Economou, 438 US 478 (1978).
Calderón-Ortiz v Laboy-Alvarado, 300 F3d 60 (1st Cir. 2002).
Chavez v Poleate, 2010 US Dist. LEXIS 15643 (CD Utah Feb. 23, 2010).
City of Canton v Harris, 489 US 378 (1989).
City of Newport v Fact Concerts, 453 US 247 (1981).
Coleman v Schwarzenegger, 2009 WL 2430820 (ED Cal. Aug. 4, 2009), *stay denied,* 2009 WL 2851846 (ED Cal. Sept. 3, 2009), *stay denied,* 2009 WL 2915066 (US Supreme Ct. Sept. 11, 2009). See Brown v Plata.
Comstock v McCrary, 273 F3d 693 (6th Cir. 2001), *cert. denied,* 537 US 817 (2002).
Correctional Services Corporation v Malesko, 534 US 61 (2001).
Deshaney v Winnebago County Social Services Department, 489 US 189 (1989).
Estelle v Gamble, 429 US 97 (1976), *rehearing denied,* 429 US 1066 (1977).
Ex parte Young, 209 US 123 (1908).
Farmer v Brennan, 511 US 825 (1994).
FDIC v Meyer, 510 US 471 (1994).
Fitzpatrick v Bitzer, 427 US 445 (1976).
Governor of Georgia v Madrazo, 26 US 110 (1828).

Grubbs v Bradley, 552 F Supp. 1052 (MD Tenn. 1982).

Gullatte v Potts, 654 F2d 1007 (5th Cir. 1981).

Hall v Terrell, 2009 US Dist. LEXIS 48870 (D Colo. June 10, 2009).

Hancock v Payne, 2006 WL 21751 (SD Miss. Jan. 4, 2006).

Hans v Louisiana, 134 US 1 (1890).

Idaho v Thompson, Idaho Ct. App. (2011 Unpublished Opinion No. 601, Aug. 31, 2011). Accessed May 15, 2012. http://www.isc.idaho.gov/opinions/ Thompson%2037376.pdf.

Kish v County of Milwaukee, 441 F2d 901 (1971).

Koon v US, 518 US 81 (1996).

LaMarca v Turner, 995 F2d 1526 (11th Cir. 1993), *cert. denied,* 510 US 1164 (1994).

Los Angeles County v Humphries, 131 S Ct. 447 (2010).

Lucas v White, 63 F Supp. 2d 1046 (ND Cal. 1999).

Maine v Thiboutot, 448 US 1 (1980).

Mason v Granholm, 2007 US Dist. LEXIS 4579 (ED Mich. Jan. 23, 2007).

Minneci v Pollard, 132 S Ct. 617 (2012).

Mitchell v Los Angeles Community College District, 861 F2d 198 (9th Cir. 1988).

Monell v Department of Social Services of the City of New York, 436 US 658 (1978).

Monroe v Pape, 365 US 167 (1961).

Neal v Department of Corrections (on rehearing), 592 NW2d 370 (Mich. App. 1998).

Neal v Department of Corrections, Mich. App. (Washtenaw Circuit Court, Feb. 10, 2005) (unpublished). Accessed August 25, 2012. http://www.nealclassaction. com/2005.02–10_Neal_v_MDOC_Mich_Ct_App.pdf.

Neal v Department of Corrections, Mich. App. (Washtenaw Circuit Court, Jan. 27, 2009) (unpublished). Accessed August 25, 2012. http://www.clearinghouse. net/chDocs/public/PC-MI-0021–0002.pdf.

Neal v Department of Corrections, Plan of Allocation of Settlement Proceeds (Washtenaw Circuit Court, July 15, 2009). Accessed August 25, 2012. http://www.clearinghouse.net/chDocs/public/PC-MI-0021–0006.pdf.

Palton v Jackson, 2009 US Dist. LEXIS 83176 (ED Ark. Aug. 28, 2009).

Parrish v Ball, 594 F3d 993 (8th Cir. 2010).

Pearson v Callahan, 555 US 223 (2009).

Plata v Schwarzenegger. Findings of Fact and Conclusions of Law re Appointment of Receiver. No. C-01–1351 THE (ND Cal. Oct. 3, 2005). Accessed January 8, 2012. http://clearinghouse.wustl.edu/chDocs/public/PC-CA-0018–0007.pdf. See Coleman v Schwarzenegger and Brown v Plata.

Pugh v Locke, 406 F Supp. 318 (MD Ala. 1976), *sub nom.* Newman v Alabama, 559 F2d 283 (5th Cir. 1977), *rehearing en banc denied sub nom.* Pugh v Locke, 564 F2d 98 (5th Cir. 1977), *cert. granted in part, judgment reversed in part, and case remanded sub nom.* Alabama v Pugh, 438 US 781 (1978).

Redman v County of San Diego, 942 F2d 1435 (1991).

Reyes v Sazan, 168 F3d 158 (5th Cir. 1999).

Richardson v Penfold, 839 F2d 392 (7th Cir. 1988).

Robinson v California, 370 US 660 (1962).

Ruiz v Johnson, 37 F Supp. 2d 855 (SD Tex. 1999).

Spruytte v Walters, 753 F2d 498 (6th Cir. 1985), *cert denied,* 474 US 1054 (1986).

US v Bailey, 444 US 394 (1980).

US v Gonzales, 945 F2d 525 (1991).

US v K, 160 F Supp. 2d 421 (ED NY 2001).

US v Lara, 905 F2d 599 (1990).

Weems v US, 217 US 349 (1910).

Will v Michigan Department of State Police, 491 US 58 (1989).

Withers v Levine, 615 F2d 158 (4th Cir. 1980), *cert. denied,* 449 US 849 (1980).

Women Prisoners of the District of Columbia Department of Corrections v District of Columbia, 877 F Supp. 634 (D DC 1994), *vacated in part, modified in part,* 899 F Supp. 659 (D DC 1995), *vacated in part and remanded,* 93 F3d 910 (DC Cir. 1996).

Index

National Commission on Correctional Health Care, 73; Tuberculosis, 72; Typhus/Typhoid fever, 72
Doctrine of local government immunity, 108
Downward departure, 88

Elliott-Larsen Civil Rights Act (ELCRA), 95
Equal Employment Opportunity Act, 1972, 10
"Essentially nonexistent" grievance system, 39

Farmer v Brennan, 111–12
Federal appellate court decision, 2010 case, 104
Federal Civil Rights Act, 1964, 10
Federal constitutional lawsuits: abrogation doctrine, 106–7; Arkansas corrections system, 112–13; breaches of security, 112; color of law, 100; Commission on Safety and Abuse in America's Prisons, 102; *Confronting Confinement* (report), 102; constitutional rights of inmates, 109–13; CRIPA, 113–14; doctrine of local government immunity, 108; *Farmer v Brennan*, 111–12; federal appellate court decision in 2010 case, 104; *Hans v Louisiana*, 106; immunity against section 1983 lawsuits for monetary damages, 107; incorporation doctrine, 110; "in his personal (or individual) capacity," 102–3; lawsuits against local authorities and their officials, 107–9; lawsuits against officials in their official capacity, 105–6; lawsuits against officials in their personal capacity, 102–5; lawsuits against private corrections corporations and their officers, 109; lawsuits, section 1983, 99–101; *Palton v Jackson*, 112; "policy or

custom" doctrine, 108–9; PREA national standards, 102; Prison Litigation Reform Act (PLRA), 101; "punishment" under Eighth Amendment, 110–11; state sovereign immunity, 106–7; of title 42 of the United States Code, 99–100

Hans v Louisiana, 106
HIV/AIDS epidemic, 9–10
Homosexual abuse/assault, 5–6, 102
Housing of inmates, 38
Humiliations, 21

Incarceration facilities, 4
Incorporation doctrine, 110
Inmates, 3, 29–31; "abusive sexual contacts," 30; constitutional rights, *see* constitutional rights of inmates; high and low incidence, 31; level of coercion, 29–30; nonconsensual sexual acts, categories, 29–30; *per victim* classification, 29; prosecution of, 92; sexual abuse used for control of, 77–79; supervision of, 13, 38, 128; "willing" sex with staff, 30
Investigation, 8–9; black-on-white assaults, 9; CRIPA, 113; Davis Philadelphia, 7–9; Philadelphia system of incarceration, 7

Just Detention International (JDI), 14–15, 17, 36, 50
Juveniles, 31–32; other sexual acts, 32; serious sexual acts, 31; willing or consensual, 31–32

Long-term suffering of victims, 58–59; HIV and AIDS, 59; lasting effects, 58; physical injuries, 59; pregnancy, 59; psychological effects, 58; sexually transmitted diseases, 59
Lucas v White, 15–16

Society, moral cost to: abuse as entertainment, 81–82; abuse as threat
by prosecutors: negotiations between prosecutors and defendants,
80–81; abuse used for control of
inmates, 77–79; commitment to
combat sexual abuse, 83; pride to
be American, 83–84; public statements revealing, 80; responsibility,
82
Staffing levels, 38
"Staff sexual harassment," 21, 23
"Staff sexual misconduct," 21, 23, 31
State and comparable federal lawsuits: civil lawsuits in state courts,
93–97; prosecuting perpetrators,
89–93; sympathetic trial judge,
87–89;
State sovereign immunity, 106–7; abrogation doctrine, 106–7; *Hans v
Louisiana*, 106; immunity against
section 1983 lawsuits for monetary
damages, 107
Struckman-Johnson studies, 9–12;
code of silence, 11; HIV/AIDS epidemic, 9–10; male corrections officers, problem with, 10–11; survey
forms, 12
Substantive constitutional rights of
inmates, 109–13; Arkansas corrections system, 112–13; breaches of
security, 112; *Farmer v Brennan*,
111–12; incorporation doctrine,
110; *Palton v Jackson*, 112;
"punishment" under Eighth
Amendment, 110–11
Suffering of victims: *Brown v Plata*,
51–52; consequence of failure to
investigate, 56; with developmental
disabilities, 47; emotional vulnerability, 46; HIV and AIDS, 59; inadequate medical treatment, 51–54;
isolation, 57; lasting effects, 58;
level of care by federal court,
53; long-term suffering, 58–59;

male-to-female transgender, 47;
narrations of rape victims, 47–51;
physical injuries, 59; pregnancy,
59; pressure for not to complain,
55; protection and punishment,
56–57; psychological damage, 56,
58; 2009 report of the NPREC, 46;
SADEA, 53; "segregated housing,"
56; sexually transmitted diseases,
59; survivor accounts of sexual
abuse, 47–51; victims, explanation, 45–47
Survey forms, 12, 22
Survey of Sexual Violence (SSV), 22,
28
Survivor accounts of sexual abuse,
47–51; narrations of rape victims,
47–51
Sympathetic trial judge, 87–89;
downward departure, 87; Pretrial
Services, 89; sentencing guidelines,
87; *US v Gonzalez*, 88; *US v Lara*,
88

TV portrayal, 81

Underreporting of sexual abuse, 14
Uniform definitions, 20
United States Immigration and Cus-
toms Enforcement, 136
Urban Institute and Association of
State Correctional Administrators,
35
US v Gonzalez, 88
US v Lara, 88

Victim compensation model. *See*
Willingness-to-accept (WTA)
model (ex post model), assessment
Victims, explanation, 45–47; with
developmental disabilities, 47;
emotional vulnerability, 46; male-
to-female transgender, 47; 2009
report of NPREC, 46. *See also* Suffering of victims

About the Author

MICHAEL SINGER, MA, PhD, JD, is professor at the Dickson Poon School of Law of King's College London, England. He was previously law professor at the University of Pennsylvania and George Washington University and is a member of the State Bar of California. His many previous publications include *Jury Duty: Reclaiming Your Political Power and Taking Responsibility*, *The Law of Evidence* (with Jack H. Friedenthal), and *The Legacy of Positivism*. He holds a juris doctor degree from Stanford University, bachelor's and master's degrees in mathematics from Cambridge University, and a doctorate from London University.